Syria: The Desert & The Sown

Gertrude Lowthian Bell

GERTRUDE LOWTHIAN BELL

SYRIA

THE DESERT & THE SOWN

WITH MANY ILLUSTRATIONS AND A MAP

NEW EDITION

LONDON
WILLIAM HEINEMANN LTD

First printed, January 1907
Second Impression, March 1907
New and Cheaper Edition, October 1908
Second Impression, February 1919
Third Impression, June 1928

To A. C. L.

WHO KNOWS THE HEART
OF THE EAST

قَالَ تَأَبَّطَ شَرًّا

يَرَى الوَحْشَةَ الأُنْسَ الأَنِيسَ وَيَهْتَدِي * بِحَيْثُ اهْتَدَتْ أُمُّ النُّجُومِ الشَّوَابِكِ

He deems the Wild the sweetest of friends, and travels on
  Where travels above him the Mother of all the clustered stars.

TA'ABATA SHARRAN.

PREFACE

THOSE who venture to add a new volume to the vast literature of travel, unless they be men of learning or politicians, must be prepared with an excuse. My excuse is ready, as specious and I hope as plausible as such things should be. I desired to write not so much a book of travel as an account of the people whom I met or who accompanied me on my way, and to show what the world is like in which they live and how it appears to them. And since it was better that they should, as far as possible, tell their own tale, I have strung their words upon the thread of the road, relating as I heard them the stories with which shepherd and man-at-arms beguiled the hours of the march, the talk that passed from lip to lip round the camp-fire, in the black tent of the Arab and the guest-chamber of the Druze, as well as the more cautious utterances of Turkish and Syrian officials. Their statecraft consists of guesses, often shrewd enough, at the results that may spring from the clash of unknown forces, of which the strength and the aim are but dimly apprehended; their wisdom is that of men whose channels of information and standards for comparison are different from ours, and who bring a different set of preconceptions to bear upon the problems laid before them. The Oriental is like a very old child. He is unacquainted with many branches of knowledge which we have come to regard as of elementary necessity; frequently, but not always, his mind is little preoccupied with the need of acquiring them, and he concerns himself scarcely at all with what we call practical utility. He is not practical in our acceptation of the word, any more than a child is practical, and his utility is not ours. On the other hand, his action is guided by traditions of conduct and morality that go back to the beginnings of civilisation, traditions unmodified as yet by any important change in the manner of life to which they apply and out of which they arose. These things apart, he is as we are; human nature does not undergo a complete change east of Suez, nor is it impossible to be on terms of friendship and sympathy with the dwellers in those regions. In some respects it is even easier than in Europe. You will find in the East habits of intercourse less fettered by artificial chains, and a wider tolerance born of greater diversity. Society is divided by caste and sect and tribe into an infinite number of groups, each one of which is following a law of its own, and however fantastic, to our thinking, that law may be, to the Oriental it is an ample and a satisfactory explanation of all peculiarities. A man may go about in public veiled up to the eyes, or clad if he please only in a girdle: he will excite no remark. Why should he? Like every one else he is merely obeying his own law. So too the European may pass up and down the wildest places, encountering little curiosity and of criticism even less. The news he brings will be heard with interest, his opinions will be listened to with attention, but he will not be thought odd or mad, nor even mistaken, because his practices and the ways of his thought are at variance with those of the people among whom he finds himself. "'Ādat-hu:" it is his custom. And for this reason he will be the wiser if he does not seek to ingratiate himself with Orientals by trying to ape their habits, unless he is so skilful that he can pass as one of themselves. Let him treat the law of others respectfully, but he himself will meet with a far greater respect if he adheres strictly to his own. For a woman this rule is of the first importance, since a woman can never disguise herself effectually. That she should be known to come of a great and honoured stock, whose customs are inviolable, is her best claim to consideration.

None of the country through which I went is ground virgin to the traveller, though parts of it have been visited but seldom, and described only in works that are costly and often difficult to obtain. Of such places I have given a brief account, and as many photographs as seemed to be of value. I have also noted in the northern cities of Syria those vestiges of antiquity that catch the eye of a casual observer. There is still much exploration to be done in Syria and on the edge of the desert, and there are many difficult problems yet to be solved. The work has been well begun by de Vogüé, Wetzstein, Brünnow, Sachau, Dussaud, Puchstein and his colleagues, the members of the Princeton Expedition and others. To their books I refer those who would learn how immeasurably rich is the land in architectural monuments and in the epigraphic records of a far-reaching history.

My journey did not end at Alexandretta as this account ends. In Asia Minor I was, however, concerned mainly with archæology; the results of what work I did there have been published in a series of papers in the "Revue Archéologique," where, through the kindness of the editor, Monsieur Salomon Reinach, they have found a more suitable place than the pages of such a book as this could have offered them.

I do not know either the people or the language of Asia Minor well enough to come into anything like a close touch with the country, but I am prepared, even on a meagre acquaintance, to lay tokens of esteem at the feet of the Turkish peasant. He is gifted with many virtues, with the virtue of hospitality beyond all others.

I have been at some pains to relate the actual political conditions of unimportant persons. They do not appear so unimportant to one who is in their midst, and for my part I have always been grateful to those who have provided me with a clue to their relations with one another. But I am not concerned to justify or condemn the government of the Turk. I have lived long enough in Syria to realise that his rule is far from being the ideal of administration, and seen enough of the turbulent elements which he keeps more or less in order to know that his post is a difficult one. I do not believe that any government would give universal satisfaction; indeed, there are few which attain that desired end even in more united countries. Being English, I am persuaded that we are the people who could best have taken Syria in hand with the prospect of a success greater than that which might be attained by a moderately reasonable Sultan.

We have long recognised that the task will not fall to us We have unfortunately done more than this. Throughout the dominions of Turkey we have allowed a very great reputation to weaken and decline; reluctant to accept the responsibility of official interference, we have yet permitted the irresponsible protests, vehemently expressed, of a sentimentality that I make bold to qualify as ignorant, and our dealings with the Turk have thus presented an air of vacillation which he may be pardoned for considering perfidious and for regarding with animosity. These feelings, combined with the deep-seated dread of a great Asiatic Empire which is also mistress of Egypt and of the sea, have, I think, led the Porte to seize the first opportunity for open resistance to British demands, whether out of simple miscalculation of the spirit that would be aroused, or with the hope of foreign backing, it is immaterial to decide. The result is equally deplorable, and if I have gauged the matter at all correctly, the root of it lies in the disappearance of English influence at Constantinople. The position of authority that we occupied has been taken by another, yet it is and must be of far deeper importance to us than to any other that we should be able to guide when necessary the tortuous politics of Yildiz Kiosk. The greatest of all Mohammedan powers cannot afford to let her relations with the Khalif of Islām be regulated with so little consistency or firmness, and if the Sultan's obstinacy in the Tābah quarrel can prove to us how far the reins have slipped from our hands, it will have served its turn. Seated as we are upon the Mediterranean and having at our command, as I believe, a considerable amount of goodwill within the Turkish empire and the memories of an ancient friendship, it should not be impossible to recapture the place we have lost.

But these are matters outside the scope of the present book, and my *apologia* had best end where every Oriental writer would have begun: "In the name of God, the Merciful, the Compassionate!"

MOUNT GRACE PRIORY.

ILLUSTRATIONS

THE MOSQUE OF 'UMAR, JERUSALEM

CHAPTER I

To those bred under an elaborate social order few such moments of exhilaration can come as that which stands at the threshold of wild travel. The gates of the enclosed garden are thrown open, the chain at the entrance of the sanctuary is lowered, with a wary glance to right and left you step forth, and, behold! the immeasurable world. The world of adventure and of enterprise, dark with hurrying storms, glittering in raw sunlight, an unanswered question and an unanswerable doubt hidden in the fold of every hill. Into it you must go alone, separated from the troops of friends that walk the rose alleys, stripped of the purple and fine linen that impede the fighting arm, roofless, defenceless, without possessions. The voice of the wind shall be heard instead of the persuasive voices of counsellors, the touch of the rain and the prick of the frost shall be spurs sharper than praise or blame, and necessity shall speak with an authority unknown to that borrowed wisdom which men obey or discard at will. So you leave the sheltered close, and, like the man in the fairy story, you feel the bands break that were riveted about your heart as you enter the path that stretches across the rounded shoulder of the earth.

It was a stormy morning, the 5th of February. The west wind swept up from the Mediterranean, hurried across the plain where the Canaanites waged war with the stubborn hill dwellers of Judæa, and leapt the barrier of mountains to which the kings of Assyria and of Egypt had laid vain siege. It shouted the news of rain to Jerusalem and raced onwards

THE CHURCH OF THE HOLY SEPULCHRE, JERUSALEM

down the barren eastern slopes, cleared the deep bed of Jordan with a bound, and vanished across the hills of Moab into the desert. And all the hounds of the storm followed behind, a yelping pack, coursing eastward and rejoicing as they went.

No one with life in his body could stay in on such a day, but for me there was little question of choice. In the grey winter dawn the mules had gone forward carrying all my worldly goods—two tents, a canteen, and a month's provision of such slender luxuries as the austerest traveller can ill spare, two small mule trunks, filled mainly with photographic materials, a few books and a goodly sheaf of maps. The mules and the three muleteers I had brought with me from Beyrout, and liked well enough to take on into the further journey. The men were all from the Lebanon. A father and son, Christians both, came from a village above Beyrout: the father an old and toothless individual who mumbled, as he rode astride the mule trunks, blessings and pious ejaculations mingled with protestations of devotion to his most clement employer, but saw no need to make other contribution to the welfare of the party—Ibrahīm was the name of this ancient; the son, Ḥabīb, a young man of twenty-two or twenty-three, dark, upright and broad-shouldered, with a profile that a Greek might have envied and a bold glance under black brows. The third was a Druze, a big shambling man, incurably lazy, a rogue in his modest way, though he could always disarm my just indignation in the matter of stolen sugar or missing piastres with an appealing, lustrous eye that looked forth unblinking like the eye of a dog. He was greedy and rather stupid, defects that must be difficult to avoid on a diet of dry bread, rice and rancid butter; but when I took him into the midst of his blood enemies he slouched about his work and tramped after his mule and his donkey with the same air of passive detachment that he showed in the streets of Beyrout. His name was Muḥammad. The last member of the caravan was the cook. Mikhāil, a native of Jerusalem and a Christian whose religion did not sit heavy on his soul. He had travelled with Mr. Mark Sykes, and received from him the following character: "He doesn't know much about cooking, unless he has learnt since he was with me, but he never seems to care twopence whether he lives or whether he is killed." When I repeated these words to Mikhāil he relapsed into fits of suppressed

A STREET IN JERUSALEM

laughter, and I engaged him on the spot. It was an insufficient reason, and as good as many another. He served me well according to his lights; but he was a touchy, fiery little man, always ready to meet a possible offence half way, with an imagination to the limits of which I never attained during three months' acquaintance, and unfortunately he had learned other things besides cooking during the years that had elapsed since he and Mr. Sykes had been shipwrecked together on Lake Van. It was typical of him that he never troubled to tell me the story of that adventure, though once when I alluded to it he nodded his head and remarked: "We were as near death as a beggar to poverty, but your Excellency knows a man can die but once," whereas he bombarded my ears with tales of tourists who had declared they could not and would not travel in Syria unsustained by his culinary arts. The 'arak bottle was his fatal drawback; and after trying all prophylactic methods, from blandishment to the hunting-crop, I parted with him abruptly on the Cilician coast, not without regrets other than a natural longing for his tough ragôuts and cold pancakes.

ST. STEPHEN'S GATE, JERUSALEM

I had a great desire to ride alone down the desolate road to Jericho, as I had done before when my face was turned towards the desert, but Mikhāil was of opinion that it would be inconsistent with my dignity, and I knew that even his chattering companionship could not rob that road of solitude. At nine we were in the saddle, riding soberly round the walls of Jerusalem, down into the valley of Gethsemane, past the

A MAHOMMADAN PROCESSION PASSING THE GARDEN OF OLIVES

garden of the Agony and up on to the Mount of Olives. Here I paused to recapture the impression, which no familiarity can blunt, of the walled city on the hill, grey in a grey and stony landscape under the heavy sky, but illumined by the hope and the unquenchable longing of generations of pilgrims. Human aspiration, the blind reaching out of the fettered spirit towards a goal where all desire shall be satisfied and the soul

RUSSIAN PILGRIMS

find peace, these things surround the city like a halo, half glorious, half pitiful, shining with tears and blurred by many a disillusion. The west wind turned my horse and set him galloping over the brow of the hill and down the road that winds through the Wilderness of Judæa.

At the foot of the first descent there is a spring, 'Ain esh Shems, the Arabs call it, the Fountain of the Sun, but the Christian pilgrims have named it the Apostles' Well. In the winter you will seldom pass there without seeing some Russian peasants resting on their laborious way up from Jordan. Ten thousand of them pour yearly into the Holy Land, old men and women, for the most part, who have pinched and saved all their life long to lay together the £30 or so which will carry them to Jerusalem. From the furthest ends of the

Russian empire they come on foot to the Black Sea, where they take ship as deck passengers on board a dirty little Russian boat. I have travelled with 300 of them from Smyrna to Jaffa, myself the only passenger lodged in a cabin. It was mid-winter, stormy and cold for those who sleep on deck, even if they be clothed in sheepskin coats and wadded top-boots. My shipmates had brought their own provisions with them for economy's sake—a hunch of bread, a few olives, a raw onion, of such was their daily meal. Morning and evening they gathered in prayer before an icon hanging on the cook's galley, and the sound of their litanies went to Heaven mingled with the throb of the screw and the splash of the spray. The pilgrims reach Jerusalem before Christmas and stay till after Easter that they may light their tapers at the sacred fire that breaks out from the Sepulchre on the morning of the Resurrection. They wander on foot through all the holy places, lodging in big hostels built for them by the Russian Government. Many die from exposure and fatigue and the unaccustomed climate; but to die in Palestine is the best of favours that the Divine hand can bestow, for their bones rest softly in the Promised Land and their souls fly straight to Paradise. You will meet these most unsophisticated travellers on every high road, trudging patiently under the hot sun or through the winter rains, clothed always in the furs of their own country, and bearing in their hands a staff cut from the reed beds of Jordan. They add a sharp note of pathos to a landscape that touches so many of the themes of mournful poetry. I heard in Jerusalem a story which is a better illustration of their temper than pages of description. It was of a man who had been a housebreaker and had been caught in the act and sent to Siberia, where he did many years of penal servitude. But when his time was up he came home to his old mother with a changed heart, and they two set out together for the Holy Land that he might make expiation for his sins. Now at the season when the pilgrims are in Jerusalem, the riff-raff of Syria congregates there to cheat their simplicity and pester them for alms, and one of these vagabonds came and begged of the Russian penitent at a time when he had nothing to give. The Syrian, enraged at his refusal, struck the other to the earth and injured him so severely that he was in hospital for three months.

PILGRIMS RECEIVING BAPTISM IN JORDAN

When he recovered his consul came to him and said, "We have got the man who nearly killed you; before you leave you must give evidence against him." But the pilgrim answered, "No, let him go. I too am a criminal."

Beyond the fountain the road was empty, and though I knew it well I was struck again by the incredible desolation of it. No l'fe, no flowers, the bare stalks of last year's thistles, the bare hills and the stony road. And yet the Wilderness of Judæa has been nurse to the fiery spirit of man. Out of it strode grim prophets, menacing with doom a world of which they had neither part nor understanding; the valleys are full of the caves that held them, nay, some are peopled to this day by a race of starved and gaunt ascetics, clinging to a tradition of piety that common sense has found it hard to discredit. Before noon we reached the khān half way to Jericho, the place where legend has it that the Good Samaritan met the man fallen by the roadside, and I went in to lunch beyond reach of the boisterous wind. Three Germans of the commercial traveller class were writing on picture-postcards in the room of the inn, and bargaining with the khānji for imitation Bedouin knives. I sat and listened to their vulgar futile talk—it was the last I was to hear of European tongues for several weeks, but I found no cause to regret the civilisation I was leaving. The road dips east of the khān, and crosses a dry water-course which has been the scene of many tragedies. Under the banks the Bedouin used to lie in wait to rob and murder the pilgrims as they passed. Fifteen years ago the Jericho road was as lawless a track as is the country now that lies beyond Jordan: security has travelled a few miles eastward during the past decade. At length we came to the top of the last hill and saw the Jordan valley and the Dead Sea, backed by the misty steeps of Moab, the frontier of the desert. Jericho lay at our feet, an unromantic village of ramshackle hotels and huts wherein live the only Arabs the tourist ever comes to know, a base-born stock, half bred with negro slaves. I left my horse with the muleteers whom we had caught up on the slope—"Please God you prosper!" "Praise be to God! If your Excellency is well we are content"—and ran down the hill into the village. But Jericho was not enough for that first splendid day of the road. I desired eagerly to leave the tourists behind, and the hotels and the picture-postcards. Two hours more and we should reach Jordan bank, and at the head of the wooden bridge that leads from Occident to Orient we might camp in a sheltered place under mud hillocks and among thickets of reed and tamarisk. A halt to buy corn for the horses and the mules and we were off again across the narrow belt of cultivated land that lies round Jericho, and out on to the Ghōr, the Jordan valley.

The Jericho road is bare enough, but the valley of Jordan has an aspect of inhumanity that is almost evil. If the prophets of the Old Testament had fulminated their anathemas

MONASTERY OF KURUNTUL ABOVE JERICHO

against it as they did against Babylon or Tyre, no better proof of their prescience would exist; but they were silent, and the imagination must travel back to flaming visions of Gomorrah and of Sodom, dim legends of iniquity that haunted our own childhood as they haunted the childhood of the Semitic races. A heavy stifling atmosphere weighed upon this lowest level of the earth's surface; the wind was racing across the hill tops above us in the regions where men breathed the natural air, but the valley was stagnant and lifeless like a deep sea bottom. We brushed through low thickets of prickly sidr trees, the Spina Christi of which the branches are said to have been twisted into the Crown of Thorns. They are of two kinds these sidr bushes, the Arabs call them zaḳūm and dōm. From the zaḳūm they extract a medicinal oil, the dōm bears a small fruit like a crab apple that ripens to a reddish brown not uninviting in appearance. It is a very Dead Sea Fruit, pleasant to look upon and leaving on the lips a taste of sandy bitterness. The sidrs dwindled and vanished, and before us lay a sheet of hard mud on which no green thing grows. It is of a yellow colour, blotched with a venomous grey-white salt: almost unconsciously the eye appreciates its enmity to life. As we rode here a swirl of heavy rain swooped down upon us from the upper world. The muleteers looked grave, and even Mikhāil's face began to lengthen, for in front of us were the Slime Pits of Genesis, and no horse or mule can pass over them except they be dry. The rain lasted a very few minutes, but it was enough. The hard mud of the plain had assumed the consistency of butter, the horses' feet were shod in it up to the fetlocks, and my dog Kurt whined as he dragged his paws out of the yellow glue. So we came to the Slime Pits, the strangest feature of all that uncanny land. A quarter of a mile to the west of Jordan—the belt is much narrower to the east of the stream—the smooth plain resolves itself suddenly into a series of steep mud banks intersected by narrow gullies. The banks are not high, thirty or forty feet at the most, but the crests of them are so sharp and the sides so precipitous that the traveller must find his way across and round them with the utmost care. The shower had made these slopes as slippery as glass, even on foot it was almost impossible to keep upright. My horse fell as I was leading him; fortunately it was on a little ridge between mound and mound, and by the most astonishing gymnastics he managed to recover himself. I breathed a short thanksgiving when I saw my caravan emerge from the Slime Pits: we might, if the rain had lasted, have been imprisoned

CROSSING THE GHŌR

there for several hours, since if a horseman falls to the bottom of one of the sticky hollows he must wait there till it dries.

Along the river bank there was life. The ground was carpeted with young grass and yellow daisies, the rusty liveries of the tamarisk bushes showed some faint signs of Spring. I cantered on to the great bridge with its trellised

THE BRIDGE OVER JORDAN

sides and roof of beams—the most inspiring piece of architecture in the world, since it is the Gate of the Desert. There was the open place as I remembered it, covered with short turf, sheltered by the high mud banks, and, Heaven be praised! empty. We had had cause for anxiety on this head. The Turkish Government was at that time sending all the troops that could be levied to quell the insurrection in Yemen. The regiments of southern Syria were marched down to the bridge, and so on to 'Ammān, where they were entrained and sent along the Mecca railway to what was then the terminus, Ma'ān near Petra. From Ma'ān they had a horrible march across a sandy waste to the head of the Gulf of 'Aḳabah. Many hundreds of men and many thousands of camels perished before they reached the gulf, for the wells upon that road are three only (so said the Arabs), and one lies about two miles off the track, undiscoverable to those who are not familiar with the country.

We pitched tents, picketed the horses, and lighted a huge bonfire of tamarisk and willow. The night was grey and still; there was rain on the hills, but none with us—a few inches represents the annual fall in the valley of Jordan. We were not quite alone. The Turkish Government levies a small toll on all who pass backwards and forwards across the bridge, and keeps an agent there for that purpose. He lives in a wattle hut by the gate of the bridge, and one or two ragged Arabs of the Ghōr share his solitude. Among these was a grey-haired negro, who gathered wood for our fire, and on the strength of his services spent the night with us. He was a cheery soul, was Mabūḳ. He danced with pleasure, round the camp fire, untroubled by the consideration that he was one of the most preposterously misshapen of human beings. He told us tales of the soldiery, how they came down in rags, their boots dropping from their feet though it was but the first day's march, half starved too, poor wretches. A Ṭābūr (900 men) had passed through that morning, another was expected to-morrow—we had just missed them. "Māsha-'llah!" said Mikhāil, "your Excellency is fortunate. First you escape from the mud hills and then from the Redīfs." "Praise be to God!" murmured Mabūḳ, and from that day my star was recognised as a lucky one. From Mabūḳ we heard the first gossip of the desert. His talk was for ever of Ibn er Rashīd, the young chief of the Shammār, whose powerful uncle Muḥammad left him so uneasy a legacy of dominion in central Arabia. For two years I had heard no news of Nejd—what of Ibn Sā'oud, the ruler of Riāḍ and Ibn er Rashīd's rival? How went the war between them? Mabūḳ had heard many rumours; men did say that Ibn er Rashīd was in great straits, perhaps the Redīfs were bound for Nejd and not for Yemen, who knew? and had we heard that a sheikh of the Ṣukhūr had been murdered by the 'Ajārmeh, and as soon as the tribe came back from the eastern pasturages. . . . So the tale ran on through the familiar stages of

THE MONASTERY OF MAR SABA, WILDERNESS OF JUDÆA

blood feud and camel lifting, the gossip of the desert—I could have wept for joy at listening to it again. There was a Babel of Arabic tongues round my camp fire that evening, for Mikhāil spoke the vulgar cockney of Jerusalem, a language bereft of dignity, and Ḥabīb a dialect of the Lebanon at immense speed, and Muḥammad had the Beyrouti drawl with its slow expressionless swing, while from the negro's lips fell something approaching to the virile and splendid speech of the Bedouin. The men themselves were struck by the variations of accent, and once they turned to me and asked which was right. I could only reply, "God knows! for He is omniscient," and the answer received a laughing acceptance, though I confess I proffered it with some misgiving.

The dawn broke windless and grey. An hour and a half from the moment I was awakened till the mules were ready to start was the appointed rule, but sometimes we were off ten minutes earlier, and sometimes, alas! later. I spent the time in conversing with the guardian of the bridge, a native of Jerusalem. To my sympathetic ears did he confide his sorrows, the mean tricks that the Ottoman government was accustomed to play on him, and the hideous burden of existence during the summer heats. And then the remuneration! a mere nothing! His gains were larger, however, than he thought fit to name, for I subsequently discovered that he had charged me three piastres instead of two for each of my seven animals. It is easy to be on excellent terms with Orientals, and if their friendship has a price it is usually a small one. We crossed the Rubicon at three piastres a head and took the northern road which leads to Salt. The middle road goes to Ḥeshbān, where lives the great Sheikh of all the Arabs of the Belḳa, Sulṭān ibn 'Ali iḍ Ḍiāb ul 'Adwān, a proper rogue, and the southern to Mādeba in Moab. The eastern side of the Ghōr is much more fertile than the western. Enough water flows from the beautiful hills of Ajlūn to turn the plain into a garden, but the supply is not stored, and the Arabs of the 'Adwān tribes content themselves with the sowing of a little corn. The time of flowers was not yet. At the end of March the eastern Ghōr is a carpet of varied and lovely bloom, which lasts but a month in the fierce heat of the valley, indeed a month sees the plants through bud and bloom and ripened seed. A ragged Arab showed us the path. He had gone down to join the Redīfs, having been bought as a substitute at the price of fifty napoleons by a well-to-do inhabitant of Salt. When he reached the bridge he found he was too late, his regiment having passed through two days before. He was sorry, he would have liked to march forth to the war (moreover, I imagine the fifty liras would have to be refunded), but his daughter would be glad, for she had wept to see him go. He stopped to extricate one of his leather slippers from the mud.

THE WALL OF LAMENTATION, JERUSALEM

"Next year," quoth he, catching me up again, "please God I shall go to America."

I stared in amazement at the half-naked figure, the shoes dropping from the bare feet, the torn cloak slipping from the shoulders, the desert head-dress of kerchief and camel's hair rope.

"Can you speak any English?" I asked.

"No," he replied calmly, "but I shall have saved the price of the journey, and, by God! here there is no advancement."

I inquired what he would do when he reached the States.

"Buy and sell," he replied; "and when I have saved 200 liras I shall return."

The same story can be heard all over Syria. Hundreds go

out every year, finding wherever they land some of their compatriots to give them a helping hand. They hawk the streets with cheap wares, sleep under bridges, live on fare that no freeborn citizen would look at, and when they have saved 200 liras, more or less, they return, rich men in the estimation of their village. East of Jordan the exodus is not so great, yet once in the mountains of the Ḥaurān I stopped to ask my way of a Druze, and he answered me in the purest Yankee. I drew rein while he told me his tale, and at the end of it I asked him if he were going back. He looked round at the stone hovels of the village, knee deep in mud and melting snow: "You bet!" he replied, and as I turned away he threw a cheerful "So long!" after me.

JEWS OF BOKHARA

When we had ridden two hours we entered the hills by a winding valley which my friend called Wād el Ḥassanīyyeh, after the tribe of that name. It was full of anemones and white broom (rattam the Arabs call it), cyclamen, starch hyacinths, and wild almond trees. For plants without a use, however lovely they may be, there is no name in Arabic; they are all ḥashīsh, grass; whereas the smallest vegetable that can be of service is known and distinguished in their speech. The path—it was a mere bridle track—rose gradually. Just before we entered the mist that covered the top of the hill we saw the Dead Sea below us to the south, lying under the grey sky like a great sheet of clouded glass. We reached Salt at four o'clock in real mountain weather, a wet and driving mist. Moreover, the ground near the village was a swamp, owing to the rain that, passing over us the night before, had fallen here. I hesitated to camp unless I could find no drier lodging. The first thing was to seek out the house of Ḥabīb Effendi Fāris, whom I had come to Salt to see, though I did not know him. My claim upon him (for I relied entirely upon his help for the prosecution of my journey) was in this wise: he was married to the daughter of a native preacher in Ḥaifa, a worthy old man and a close friend of mine. Urfa on the Euphrates was the *Stammplatz* of the family, but Abu Namrūd had lived long at Salt and he knew the desert. The greater part of the hours during which he was supposed to teach me grammar were spent in listening to tales of the Arabs and of his son, Namrūd, who worked with Ḥabīb Fāris, and whose name was known to every Arab of the Belḳa.

"If ever you wish to enter there," said Abu Namrūd, "go to Namrūd." And to Namrūd accordingly I had come.

A very short inquiry revealed the dwelling of Ḥabīb Fāris. I was received warmly, Ḥabīb was out, Namrūd away (was my luck forsaking me?), but would I not come in and rest? The house was small and the children many: while I debated whether the soaked ground outside would not prove a better bed, there appeared a magnificent old man in full Arab dress, who took my horse by the bridle, declared that he and no other should lodge me, and so led me away. I left my horse at the khān, climbed a long and muddy stair, and entered a stone paved courtyard. Yūsef Effendi hurried forward and threw open the door of his guest-chamber. The floor and the divan were covered with thick carpets, the windows glazed (though many of the panes were broken), a European cheffonier stood against the wall: this was more than good enough. In a moment I was established, drinking Yūsef's coffee, and eating my own cake.

Yūsef Effendi Sukkar (upon him be peace!) is a Christian and one of the richest of the inhabitants of Salt. He is a laconic man, but as a host he has not his equal. He prepared me an excellent supper, and when I had eaten, the remains were set before Mikhāil. Having satisfied my physical needs he could not or would not do anything to allay my mental anxieties as to the further course. Fortunately at this moment Ḥabīb Fāris arrived, and his sister-in-law, Paulina, an old acquaintance, and several other worthies, all hastening to "honour themselves" at the prospect of an evening's talk. ("God forbid! the honour is mine!") We settled down to coffee, the bitter black coffee of the Arabs, which is better than any nectar. The cup is handed with a "Deign to accept," you pass it back empty, murmuring "May you live!" As you sip some one ejaculates, "A double health," and you reply, "Upon your heart!" When the cups had gone round once or twice and all necessary phrases of politeness had been exchanged I entered upon the business of the evening. How was I to reach the Druze mountains? the Government would probably refuse me permission, at 'Ammān there was a military post on the entrance of the desert road; at Boṣrā they knew me, I had slipped through their fingers five years before, a trick that would be difficult to play a second time from the same place. Ḥabīb Fāris considered, and finally we hammered out a plan between us. He would send me to-morrow to Ṭneib, his corn land on the edge of the desert; there I should find Namrūd who would despatch word to one of the big tribes, and with an escort from them I could ride up in safety to the hills. Yūsef's two small sons sat listening open-eyed, and at the end of the talk one of them brought me a scrap of an advertisement with the map of America upon it. Thereat I showed them my maps, and told them how big the world was and how fine a place, till at ten the party broke up

ABYSSINIAN PRIESTS

and Yūsef began spreading quilts for my bed. Then and not till then did I see my hostess. She was a woman of exceptional beauty, tall and pale, her face a full oval, her great eyes like stars. She wore Arab dress, a narrow dark blue robe that caught round her bare ankles as she walked, a dark blue cotton veil bound about her forehead with a red handkerchief and falling down her back almost to the ground. Her chin and neck were tattooed in delicate patterns with indigo, after the manner of the Bedouin women. She brought me water, which she poured over my hands, moved about the room silently, a dark and stately figure, and having finished her ministrations she disappeared as silently as she had come, and I saw her no more. "She came in and saluted me," said the poet, he who lay in durance at Mecca, "then she rose and took her leave, and when she departed my soul went out after her." No one sees Yūsef's wife. Christian though he be, he keeps her more strictly cloistered than any Moslem woman; and perhaps after all he is right.

The rain beat against the windows, and I lay down on the quilts with Mikhāil's exclamation in my ears: "Māsha-'llah! your Excellency is fortunate."

CHAPTER II

THE village of Salt is a prosperous community of over 10,000 souls, the half of them Christian. It lies in a rich country famous for grapes and apricots, its gardens are mentioned with praise as far back as the fourteenth century by the Arab geographer Abu'l Fida. There is a ruined castle, of what date I know not, on the hill above the clustered house roofs. The tradition among the inhabitants is that the town is very ancient; indeed, the Christians declare that in Salt was one of the first of the congregations of their faith, and there is even a legend that Christ was His own evangelist here. Although the apricot trees shewed nothing as yet but bare boughs the valley had an air of smiling wealth as I rode through it with Ḥabīb Fāris, who had mounted his mare to set me on my way. He had his share in the apricot orchards and the vineyards, and smiled agreeably, honest man, as I commended them. Who would not have smiled on such a morning? The sun shone, the earth glittered with frost, and the air had a sparkling transparency which comes only on a bright winter day after rain. But it was not merely a general sense of goodwill that had inspired my words; the Christians of Salt and of Mādeba are an intelligent and an industrious race, worthy to be praised. During the five years since I had visited this district they had pushed forward the limit of cultivation two hours' ride to the east, and proved the value of the land so conclusively that when the Ḥajj railway was opened through it the Sultan laid hands on a great tract stretching as far south as Ma'ān, intending to convert it into a chiflik, a royal farm. It will yield riches to him and to his tenants, for if he be an indifferent ruler, he is a good landlord.

Half an hour from Salt, Ḥabīb left me, committing me

to the care of his hind, Yūsef, a stalwart man, who strode by my side with his wooden club (Gunwā, the Arabs call it) over his shoulder. We journeyed through wide valleys, treeless, uninhabited, and almost uncultivated, round the head of the Belḳa plain, and past the opening of the Wādy Sīr, down which a man may ride through oak woods all the way to the Ghōr. There would be trees on the hills too if the charcoal burners would let them grow—we passed by many dwarf thickets of oak and thorn—but I would have nothing changed in the delicious land east of Jordan. A generation or two hence it will be deep in corn and scattered over with villages, the waters of the Wādy Sīr will turn mill-wheels, and perhaps there will even be roads: praise be to God! I shall not be there to see. In my time the uplands will still continue to be that delectable region of which Omar Khayyām sings: "The strip of herbage strown that just divides the desert from the sown"; they will still be empty save for a stray shepherd standing over his flock with a long-barrelled rifle; and when I meet the rare horseman who rides over those hills and ask him whence he comes, he will still answer: "May the world be wide to you! from the Arabs."

AN ARAB OF THE 'ADWĀN GUARDING CROPS

That was where we were going, to the Arabs. In the desert there are no Bedouin, the tent dwellers are all *'Arab* (with a fine roll of the initial guttural), just as there are no tents but houses—"houses of hair" they say sometimes if a qualification be needed, but usually just "houses" with a supreme disregard for any other significance to the word save that of a black goat's hair roof. You may be *'Arab* after a fashion even if you live between walls. The men of Salt are classed among the tribes of the Belḳa, with the Abādeh and the

Da'ja and the Ḥassaniyyeh and several more that form the great troup of the 'Adwān. Two powerful rulers dispute the mastership here of the Syrian desert, the Beni Ṣakhr and the 'Anazeh. There is a traditional friendship, barred by regrettable incidents, between the Ṣukhūr and the Belḳa, perhaps that was why I heard in these parts that the 'Anazeh were

AN ENCAMPMENT NEAR THE DEAD SEA

the more numerous but the less distinguished for courage of the two factions. I have a bowing acquaintance with one of the sons of Talāl ul Fāiz, the head of all the Beni Ṣakhr. I had met him five years before in these very plains, a month later in the season, by which time his tribe moves Jordan-wards out of the warm eastern pasturages. I was riding, escorted by a Circassian zaptieh, from Mādeba to Mshitta—it was before the Germans had sliced the carved façade from that wonderful building. The plain was covered with the flocks and the black tents of the Ṣukhūr, and as we rode through them three horsemen paced out to intercept us, black-browed, armed to the teeth, menacing of aspect. They threw us the salute from afar, but when they saw the soldier they turned and rode slowly back. The Circassian laughed. "That was Sheikh Fāiz," he said, "the son of Talāl. Like sheep, wāllah! like sheep are they when they meet one of us." I do not know the 'Anazeh, for their usual

THE THEATRE, 'AMMĀN

seat in winter is nearer the Euphrates, but with all deference to the Ṣukhūr I fancy that their rivals are the true aristocracy of the desert. Their ruling house, the Beni Sha'alān, bear the proudest name, and their mares are the best in all Arabia, so that even the Shammār, Ibn er Rashīd's people, seek after them to improve their own breed.

From the broken uplands that stand over the Ghōr, we entered ground with a shallow roll in it and many small ruined sites dotted over it. There was one at the head of the Wādy Sīr, and a quarter of an hour before we reached it we had seen a considerable mass of foundations and a big tank, which the Arabs call Birket Umm el 'Amūd (the tank of the Mother of the Pillar). Yūsef said its name was due to a column which used to stand in the middle of it, surrounded by the water; an Arab shot at it and broke it, and its fragments lie at the bottom of the tank. The mound or tell, to give it its native name, of Amēreh is covered with ruins, and further on at Yadūdeh there are rock-hewn tombs and sarcophagi lying at the edge of the tank. All the frontier of the desert is strewn with similar vestiges of a populous past, villages of the fifth and sixth centuries when Mādeba was a rich and flourishing Christian city, though some are certainly earlier still, perhaps pre-Roman. Yadūdeh of the tombs was inhabited by a Christian from Salt, the greatest corn-grower in these parts, who lived in a roughly built farm-house on the top of the tell; he too is one of the energetic new-comers who are engaged in spreading the skirts of cultivation. Here we left the rolling country and passed out into the edges of a limitless plain, green with scanty herbage, broken by a rounded tell or the back of a low ridge—and then the plain once more, restful to the eye yet never monotonous, steeped in the magic of the winter sunset, softly curving hollows to hold the mist, softly swelling slopes to hold the light, and over it all the dome of the sky which vaults the desert as it vaults the sea. The first hillock was that of Ṭneib. We got in, after a nine hours' march, at 5.30, just as the sun sank, and pitched tents on the southern slope. The mound was thick with ruins, low walls of rough-hewn stones laid without mortar, rock-cut cisterns, some no doubt originally intended not for water but for corn, for which purpose they are used at present, and an open tank filled up with earth. Namrūd had ridden over to visit a neighbouring cultivator, but one of his men set forth to tell him of my arrival and he returned at ten o'clock under the frosty starlight, with many protestations of pleasure and assurances that my wishes were easy of execution. So I went to sleep wrapped in the cold silence of the desert, and woke next day to a glittering world of sunshine and fair prospects.

The first thing to be done was to send out to the Arabs. After consultation, the Da'ja, a tribe of the Belḳa, were decided to be the nearest at hand and the most likely to prove of use, and a messenger was despatched to their tents. We spent the morning examining the mound and looking through a mass of copper coins that had turned up under Namrūd's ploughshare—Roman all of them, one showing dimly the features of Constantine, some earlier, but none of the later Byzantine period, nor any of the time of the Crusaders,

A GATEWAY, 'AMMĀN

as far as the evidence of coinage goes, Ṭneib has been deserted since the date of the Arab invasion. Namrūd had discovered the necropolis, but there was nothing to be found in the tombs, which had probably been rifled centuries before. They were rock-cut and of a cistern-like character. A double arch of the solid rock with space between for a narrow entrance on the surface of the ground, a few jutting excrescences on the side walls, footholds to those who must descend, loculi running like shelves round the chambers, one row on top of another, such was their appearance. Towards the bottom of the mound on the south side there were foundations of a building which looked as though it might have been a church. But these were poor results for a day's exploration, and in the golden afternoon we rode out two hours to the north into a wide valley set between low banks. There were ruins strewn at intervals round the edge of it, and to the east some broken walls standing up in the middle of the valley—Namrūd called the spot, Ḳuṣeir es Saḥl, the Little Castle of the Plain. Our objective was a group of buildings at the western end, Khureibet es Sūḳ. First we came to a small edifice (41 feet by 39 feet 8 inches, the greatest length being from east to west) half buried in the ground. Two sarcophagi outside pointed to its having been a mausoleum. The western wall was pierced by an arched doorway, the arch being decorated with a flat moulding. Above the level of the arch the walls narrowed by the extent of a small set-back, and two courses higher a moulded cornice ran round the building. A couple of hundred yards west of the Ḳaṣr or castle (the Arabs christen most ruins either castle or convent) there is a ruined temple. It had evidently been turned at some period to other uses than those for which it was intended, for there were ruined walls round the two rows of seven columns and inexplicable cross walls towards the western end of the colonnades. There appeared to have been a double court beyond, and still further west lay a complex of ruined foundations. The gateway was to the east, the jambs of it decorated with delicate carving, a fillet, a palmetto, another plain fillet, a torus worked with a vine scroll, a bead and reel, an egg and dart and a second palmetto on the cyma. The whole resembled very closely the work at Palmyra—it could scarcely rival the stone lace-work of Mshitta, and besides it had a soberer feeling, more closely akin to classical models, than is to be found there. To the north of the temple on top of a bit of rising ground, there was another ruin which proved to be a second mausoleum. It was an oblong rectangle of masonry, built of large stones carefully laid without mortar. At the south-east corner a stair led into a kind of ante-chamber, level with the surface of the ground at the east side owing to the slope of the hill. There were column bases on the outer side of this ante-chamber, the vestiges probably of a small colonnade which had adorned the east façade. Six sarcophagi were placed lengthways, two along each of the remaining walls, north,

THE TEMPLE, KHUREIBET ES SŪḲ

south and west. Below the base of the columns on either side of the stair ran a moulding, consisting of a bold torus between two fillets, and the same appeared on the inner side of the sarcophagi. The face of the buttress wall on the south side rose in two in-sets, otherwise the whole building was quite plain, though some of the fragments scattered round upon the grass were carved with a flowing vine pattern. This mausoleum recalls the pyramid tomb which is common

MAUSOLEUM, KHUREIBET ES SŪK

in northern Syria; I do not remember any other example of it so far south. It may have resembled the beautiful monument with a colonnaded front which is one of the glories of the southern Dāna, and the fragments of vine-scroll were perhaps part of the entablature.

When I returned to my tents a little before sunset, I learnt that the boy we had despatched in the morning had lingered by the way and, alarmed by the lateness of the hour, had returned without fulfilling his mission. This was sufficiently annoying, but it was nothing compared with the behaviour of the weather next day. I woke to find the great plain blotted out by mist and rain. All day the south wind drove against us, and the storm beat upon our canvas walls. In the evening Namrūd brought news that his cave had been invaded by guests. There were a few tents of the Ṣukhūr a mile or two away from us (the main body of the tribe was still far to the east, where the winter climate is less rigorous), and the day's rain had been too much for the male inhabitants. They had mounted their mares and ridden in to Ṭneib, leaving their women and children to shift for themselves during the night. An hour's society presented attractions after the long wet day, and I joined the company.

Namrūd's cave runs far into the ground, so far that it must penetrate to the very centre of the hill of Ṭneib. The first large chamber is obviously natural, except for the low sleeping places and mangers for cattle that have been quarried out round the walls. A narrow passage carved in the rock leads into a smaller room, and there are yet others behind which I took on trust, the hot stuffy air and the innumerable swarms of flies discouraging me from further exploration. That evening the cave presented a scene primitive and wild enough to satisfy the most adventurous spirit. The Arabs, some ten or a dozen men clothed in red leather boots and striped cloaks soaked with rain, were sitting in the centre round a fire of scrub, in the ashes of which stood the three coffee-pots essential to desert sociability. Behind them a woman cooked rice over a brighter fire that cast a flickering light into the recesses of the cave, and showed Namrūd's cattle munching chopped straw from the rock-hewn mangers. A place comparatively free from mud was cleared for me in the circle, a cup of coffee prepared, and the talk went forward while a man might smoke an Arab pipe five times. It was chiefly of the iniquities of the government. The arm of the law, or rather the mailed fist of misrule, is a constant menace upon the edges of the desert. This year it had been quickened to baleful activity by the necessities of war. Camels and mares had been commandeered wholesale along the borders without hope of compensation in money or in kind. The Arabs had gathered together such live stock as was left to them and sent them away five or six days to the east, where the soldiery dared not penetrate, and Namrūd had followed their example, keeping only such cattle as he needed for the plough. One after another of my fellow guests took up the tale: the guttural strong speech rumbled round the cave. By God and Muhammad the

Prophet of God we called down such curses upon the Circassian cavalry as should make those powerful horsemen reel in their saddles. From time to time a draped head, with black elf locks matted round the cheeks under the striped kerchief, bent forward towards the glow of the ashes to pick up a hot ember for the pipe bowl, a hand was stretched out to the coffee cups, or the cooking fire flashed up under a pile of thorn, the sudden light making the flies buzz and the cows move uneasily. Namrūd was not best pleased to see his hardly gathered store of fire-wood melt away and his coffee-beans disappear by handfuls into the mortar. ("Wāllah! they eat little when they feed themselves, but when they are guests much, they and their horses; and the corn is low at this late season.") But the word "guest" is sacred from Jordan to Euphrates and Namrūd knew well that he owed a great part of his position and of his security to a hospitality which was extended to all comers, no matter how inopportune. I added my quota to the conviviality of the party by distributing a box of cigarettes, and before I left a friendly feeling had been established between me and the men of the Beni Ṣakhr.

ARABS OF THE BELKA

The following day was little more promising than that which had preceded it. The muleteers were most unwilling to leave the shelter of the caves and expose their animals to such rain in the open desert, and reluctantly I agreed to postpone the journey, and sent them into Mādeba, three hours away, to buy oats for the horses, cautioning them not to mention from whom they came. It cleared a little in the afternoon, and I rode across the plain southwards to Ḳasṭal, a fortified Roman camp standing on a mound.

This type of camp was not uncommon on the eastern frontiers of the Empire, and was imitated by the Ghassānids when they established themselves in the Syrian desert, if indeed Mshitta was, as has been surmised, but a more exquisite example of the same kind of building. Ḳasṭal has a strong enclosing wall broken by a single gate to the east and by round bastions at the angles and along the sides. Within, there is a series of parallel vaulted chambers leaving an open court in the centre—the plan with slight variations of Ḳal'at el Beiḍa in the Ṣafa and of the modern caravanserai.* To the north there is a separate building, probably the Prætorium, the house of the commander of the fortress. It consists of an immense vaulted chamber, with a walled court in front of it, and a round tower at the south-west corner. The tower has a winding stair inside it and a band of decoration about the exterior, rinceaux above and fluted triglyphs below, with narrow blank metopes between them. The masonry is unusually good, the walls of great thickness; with such defences stretching to his furthest borders, the citizen of Rome might sleep secure o' nights.

When I passed by Ḳasṭal, five years before, it was uninhabited and the land round it uncultivated, but a few families of fellaḥīn had established themselves now under the broken vaults and the young corn was springing in the levels below the walls, circumstances which should no doubt warm the heart of the lover of humanity, but which will send a cold chill through the breast of the archæologist. There is no obliterator like the plough-share, and no destroyer like the peasant who seeks cut stones to build his hovel. I noted another sign of encroaching civilisation in the shape of two half-starved soldiers, the guard of the nearest halting-place on the Ḥajj railroad, which is called *Zīza* after the ruins

* Admirable plans and photographs of the fort have been published by Brünnow and Domaszewski in vol. ii. of their great work, "Die Provincia Arabia" This volume was not out at the time I visited Ḳasṭal.

a few miles to the west of it. The object of their visit was the lean hen which one of them held in his hand. He had reft it from its leaner companions in the fortress court—on what terms it were better not to inquire, for hungry men know no law. I was not particularly eager to have my presence on these frontiers notified to the authorities in 'Ammān, and I left rather hastily and rode eastward to Zīza.

The rains had filled the desert watercourses, they do not

A RUINED CHURCH, MADEBA

often flow so deep or so swiftly as the one we had to cross that afternoon. It had filled, too, to the brim the great Roman tank of Zīza, so that the Ṣukhūr would find water there all through the ensuing summer. The ruins are far more extensive than those at Ḳasṭal; there must have been a great city here, for the foundations of houses cover a wide area. Probably Ḳasṭal was the fortified camp guarding this city, and the two together shared the name of Zīza, which is mentioned in the Notitia: "Equites Dalmatici Illyriciana Zīza." There is a Saracenic Ḳal'ah, a fort, which was repaired by Sheikh Ṣoktan of the Ṣukhūr, and had been furnished by him, said Namrūd, with a splendour unknown to the desert; but it has now fallen to the Sultan, since it stands in the territory selected by him for his chiflik, and fallen also into ruin. The mounds behind are strewn with foundations, among them those of a mosque, the miḥrāb of which was still visible to the south. Zīza was occupied by a garrison of Egyptians in Ibrahīm Pasha's time, and it was his soldiers who completed the destruction of the ancient buildings. Before they came many edifices, including several Christian churches, were still standing in an almost perfect state of preservation, so the Arabs reported. We made our way homewards along the edge of the railway embankment, and as we went we talked of the possible advantages that the land might reap from that same line. Namrūd was doubtful on this subject. He looked askance at the officials and the soldiery, indeed he had more cause to fear official raiders, whose rapacity could not be disarmed by hospitality, than the Arabs, who were under too many obligations to him to do him much harm.

THE ḲAL'AH AT ZĪZA

He had sent up a few truck-loads of corn to Damascus the year before; yes, it was an easier form of transport than his camels, and quicker, if the goods arrived at all; but generally the corn sacks were so much lighter when they reached the city than when Namrūd packed them into the trucks that the profit vanished. This would improve perhaps in time—at the time when lamps and cushions and all the fittings of the desert railway except the bare seats were allowed to remain in the place for which they were made and bought. We spoke, too, of superstition and of fears that clutch the heart at night. There are certain places, said he, where the Arabs would never venture after dark—haunted wells to which thirsty men dared not approach, ruins where the weary would not seek shelter, hollows that were bad camping grounds for the solitary. What did they fear? Jinn; who could tell what men feared? He himself had startled an Arab almost out of his wits by jumping naked at him from a lonely pool in the half light of the dawn. The man ran back to his tents, and swore that he had seen a jinni, and that the flocks should not go down to water where it abode, till Namrūd came in and laughed at him and told his own tale.

We did not go straight back to my tents. I had been invited out to dine that evening by Sheikh Nahār of the Beni Ṣakhr, he who had spent the previous night in Namrūd's cave; and after consultation it had been decided that the invitation was one which a person of my exalted dignity would not be compromised by accepting.

A CHRISTIAN ENCAMPMENT

"But in general," added Namrūd, "you should go nowhere but to a great sheikh's tent, or you will fall into the hands of those who invite you only for the sake of the present you will give. Nahār—well, he is an honest man, though he be Meskīn,"—a word that covers all forms of mild contempt, from that which is extended to honest poverty, through imbecility to the first stages of feeble vice.

The Meskīn received me with the dignity of a prince, and motioned me to the place of honour on the ragged carpet between the square hole in the ground that serves as hearth and the partition that separates the women's quarters from the men's. We had tethered our horses to the long tent ropes that give such wonderful solidity to the frail dwelling, and our eyes wandered out from where we sat over the eastward sweep of the landscape—swell and fall, fall and swell, as though the desert breathed quietly under the gathering night.

The lee side of an Arab tent is always open to the air; if the wind shifts the women take down the tent wall and set it up against another quarter, and in a moment your house has changed its outlook and faces gaily to the most favourable prospect. It is so small and so light and yet so strongly anchored that the storms can do little to it; the coarse meshes of the goat's hair cloth swell and close together in the wet so that it needs continuous rain carried on a high wind before a cold stream leaks into the dwelling-place.

The coffee beans were roasted and crushed, the coffee-pots were simmering in the ashes, when there came three out of the East and halted at the open tent. They were thick-set, broad-shouldered men, with features of marked irregularity and projecting teeth, and they were cold and wet with rain. Room was made for them in the circle round the hearth, and they stretched out their fingers to the blaze, while the talk went on uninterrupted, for they were only three men of the Sherarāt, come down to buy corn in Moab, and the Sherarāt, though they are one of the largest and the most powerful of the tribes and the most famous breeders of camels, are of bad blood, and no Arab of the Belḳa would intermarry with them. They have no fixed haunts, not even in the time of the summer drought, but roam the inner desert scarcely caring if they go without water for days together. The conversation round Nahār's fire was of my journey. A negro of the Ṣukhūr, a powerful man with an intelligent face, was very anxious to come with me as guide to the Druze mountains, but he admitted that as soon as he reached the territory of those valiant hillmen he would have to turn and flee—there is always feud between the Druzes and the Beni Ṣakhr. The negro slaves of the Ṣukhūr are well used by their masters, who know their worth, and they have a position of their own in the desert, a glory reflected from the great tribe they serve. I was half inclined to accept the present offer in spite of the possible drawback of having the negro dead upon my hands at the first Druze village, when the current of my thoughts was interrupted by the arrival of yet another guest. He was a tall young man, with a handsome delicate face, a complexion that was almost fair, and long curls that were almost brown. As he approached, Nahār and the other sheikhs of the Ṣukhūr rose to meet him, and before he entered the tent, each in turn kissed him upon both cheeks. Namrūd rose also, and cried to him as he drew near :

"Good ? please God ! Who is with you ?"

The young man raised his hand and replied :

"God !"

He was alone.

FLOCKS OF THE ṢUKHŪR

Without seeming to notice the rest of the company, his eye embraced the three sheikhs of the Sherarāt eating mutton and curds in the entrance, and the strange woman by the fire, as with murmured salutations he passed into the back of the tent, refusing Nahār's offer of food. He was Ḳablān, of the ruling house of the Da'ja, cousin to the reigning sheikh, and, as I subsequently found, he had heard that Namrūd needed a guide for a foreigner—news travels apace in the desert—and had come to take me to his uncle's tents. We had not sat for more than five minutes after his arrival when Nahār whispered something to Namrūd, who turned to me and suggested that since we had dined we might go and take Ḳablān with us. I was surprised that the evening's gossip should be cut so short, but I knew better than to make any objection, and as we cantered home across Namrūd's ploughland and up the hill of Ṭneib, I heard the reason. There was blood between the Da'ja and the Sherarāt. At the first glance Gablān had recognised the lineage of his fellow guests, and had therefore retired silently into the depths of the tent. He would not dip his hand in the same mutton dish with them. Nahār knew, as who did not? the difficuly of the situation, but he could not tell how the men of the Sherarāt would take it, and, for fear of accidents, he had hurried us away. But by next morning the atmosphere had cleared (metaphorically, not literally), and a day of streaming rain kept the blood enemies sitting amicably round Namrūd's coffee-pots in the cave.

The third day's rain was as much as human patience could endure. I had forgotten by this time what it was like not to feel damp, to have warm feet and dry bed clothes. Gablān spent an hour with me in the morning, finding out what I wished of him. I explained that if he could take me through the desert where I should see no military post and leave me at the foot of the hills, I should desire no more. Gablān considered a moment.

"Oh lady," said he, "do you think you will be brought into conflict with the soldiery? for if so, I will take my rifle."

I replied that I did not contemplate declaring open war with all the Sultan's chivalry, and that with a little care I fancied that such a contingency might be avoided; but Gablān was of opinion that strategy went further when winged with a bullet, and decided that he would take his rifle with him all the same.

In the afternoon, having nothing better to do, I watched the Sherarāt buying corn from Namrūd. But for my incongruous presence and the lapse of a few thousand years, they might have been the sons of Jacob come down into Egypt to bicker over the weight of the sacks with their brother Joseph. The corn was kept in a deep dry hole cut in the rock, and was drawn out like so much water in golden bucketsful. It had been stored with chaff for its better protection, and the first business was to sift it at the well-head, a labour that could not be executed without much and angry discussion. Not even the camels were silent, but joined in the argument with groans and bubblings, as the Arabs loaded them with the full sacks. The Sheikhs of the Ṣukhūr and the Sherarāt sat round on stones in the drizzling mist, and sometimes they muttered, "God! God!" and sometimes they exclaimed, "He is merciful and compassionate!" Not infrequently the sifted corn was poured back among the unsifted, and a dialogue of this sort ensued:

Namrūd: "Upon thee! upon thee! oh boy! may thy dwelling be destroyed! may thy days come to harm!"

Beni Ṣakhr: "By the face of the Prophet of God! may He be exalted!"

Sherarāt (in suppressed chorus): "God! and Muḥammad the Prophet of God, upon Him be peace!"

A party in bare legs and a sheepskin: "Cold, cold! Wāllah! rain and cold!"

Namrūd: "Silence, oh brother! descend into the well and draw corn. It is warm there."

Beni Sakhr: "Praise be to God the Almighty!"

Chorus of Camels: "B-b-b-b-dd-G-r-r-o-o-a-a."

A ROMAN MILESTONE

Camel Drivers: "Be still, accursed ones! may you slip in the mud! may the wrath of God fall on you!"

Ṣukhur (in unison): "God! God! by the light of His Face!"

At dusk I went into the servants' tent and found Namrūd whispering tales of murder over the fire on which my dinner was a-cooking.

"In the days when I was a boy," said he (and they were not far behind us), "you could not cross the Ghōr in peace. But I had a mare who walked—wāllah! how she walked! Between sunrise and sunset she walked me from Mezerīb to Salt, and never broke her pace. And besides I was well known to all the Ghawārny (natives of the Ghōr). And one night in summer I had to go to Jerusalem—force upon me! I must ride. The waters of Jordan were low, and I crossed at the ford, for there was no bridge then. And as I reached the further bank I heard shouts and the snap of bullets. And I hid in the tamarisk bushes more than an hour till the moon was low, and then I rode forth softly. And at the entrance of the mud hills the mare started from the path, and I looked down and saw the body of a man, naked and covered with knife wounds. And he was quite dead. And as I gazed they sprang out on me from the mud hills, ten horsemen and I was but one. And I backed against the thicket and fired twice with my pistol, but they surrounded me and threw me from the mare and bound me, and setting me again upon the mare they led me away. And when they came to the halting place they fell to discussing whether they should kill me, and one said: 'Wāllah! let us make an end.' And he came near and looked into my face, and it was dawn. And he said: 'It is Namrūd!' for he knew me, and I had succoured him. And they unbound me and let me go, and I rode up to Jerusalem."

The muleteers and I listened with breathless interest as one story succeeded another.

"There are good customs and bad among the Arabs," said Namrūd, "but the good are many. Now when they wish to bring a blood feud to an end, the two enemies come together in the tent of him who was offended. And the lord of the tent bares his sword and turns to the south and draws a circle on the floor, calling upon God. Then he takes a shred of the cloth of the tent and a handful of ashes from the hearth and throws them in the circle, and seven times he strikes the line with his naked sword. And the offender leaps into the circle, and one of the relatives of his enemy cries aloud: 'I take the murder that he did upon me!' Then there is peace. Oh lady! the women have much power in the tribe, and the maidens are well looked on. For if a maiden says: 'I would have such an one for my husband,' he must marry her lest she should be put to shame. And if he has already four wives let him divorce one, and marry in her place the maiden who has chosen him. Such is the custom among the Arabs."

He turned to my Druze muleteer and continued :

"Oh Muḥammad ! have a care. The tents of the Ṣukhūr are near, and there is never any peace between the Beni Ṣakhr and the Druzes. And if they knew you, they would certainly kill you—not only would they kill you, but they would burn you alive, and the lady could not shield you, nor could I."

This was a grim light upon the character of my friend Nahār, who had exchanged with me hospitality against a kerchief, and the little group round the fire was somewhat taken back. But Mikhāil was equal to the occasion.

"Let not your Excellency think it," said he, deftly dishing up some stewed vegetables ; "he shall be a Christian till we reach the Jebel Druze, and his name is not Muḥammad but Ṭarīf, for that is a name the Christians use."

So we converted and baptized the astonished Muḥammad before the cutlets could be taken out of the frying-pan.

CHAPTER III

THE morning of Sunday, the 12th of February, was still stormy, but I resolved to go. The days spent at Tneib had not been wasted. An opportunity of watching hour by hour the life of one of these outlying farms comes seldom, but my thoughts had travelled forward, and I longed to follow the path they had taken. I caught them up, so it seemed to me, when Gablān, Namrūd and I heard the hoofs of our mares ring on the metals of the Ḥajj railway and set our faces towards the open desert. We rode east by north, leaving Mshitta a little to the south, and though no one who knew it in its loveliness could have borne to revisit those ravished walls, it must be not forgotten that there is something to be said for the act of vandalism that stripped them. If there had been good prospect that the ruin should stand as it had stood for over a thousand years, uninjured save by the winter rains, it ought to have been allowed to remain intact in the rolling country to which it gave so strange an impress of delicate and fantastic beauty; but the railway has come near, the plains will fill up, and neither Syrian fellāḥ nor Turkish soldier can be induced to spare walls that can be turned to practical uses. Therefore let those who saw it when it yet stood unimpaired, cherish its memory with gratitude, and without too deep a regret.

Namrūd and Gablān chatted without a pause. Late in the previous night two soldiers had presented themselves at the door of the cave, and having gained admittance they had told a strange tale. They had formed part, so they affirmed, of the troops that the Sultan had despatched from Baghdad to help Ibn er Rashīd against Ibn Sa'oud. They related how the latter had driven them back step by step to the very gates of Ḥāil, Ibn er Rashīd's capital, and how as the two armies lay facing one anothher Ibn Sa'oud with a few followers

MSHITTA

had ridden up to his enemy's tent and laid his hand upon the tent pole so that the prince of the Shammār had no choice but to let him enter. And then and there they had come to an agreement, Ibn er Rashīd relinquishing all his territory to within a mile or two of Ḥāil, but retaining that city and the

MSHITTA, THE FAÇADE

lands to the north of it, including Jōf, and recognising Ibn Sa'oud's sovereignty over Riāḍ and its extended fief. The two soldiers had made the best of their way westward across the desert, for they said most of their companions in arms were slain and the rest had fled. This was by far the most authentic news that I was to receive from Nejd, and I have reason to believe that it was substantially correct.* I questioned many of the Arabs as to Ibn er Rashīd's character :

* Since the events above recorded, Ibn Sa'oud has, I believe, come to terms with the Sultan after a vain appeal to a stronger ally, and Ibn er Rashīd is reported to be struggling to turn out the Turkish garrisons which were appointed nominally to aid him. Quite recently there has been a rumour that Ibn er Rashīd is dead.

the answer was almost invariably the same. "Shātir jiddan," they would say; "he is very shrewd," but after a moment they would add, "majnūn" ("but mad"). A reckless man and a hot-headed, so I read him, with a restless intelligence and little judgment, not strong enough, and perhaps not cruel enough, to enforce his authority over the unruly tribes whom his uncle, Muḥammad, held in a leash of fear (the history of the war has been one long series of betrayals on the part of his

MSHITTA, THE INNER HALLS

own allies), and too proud, if the desert judges him rightly, to accept the terms of the existing peace. He is persuaded that the English government armed Ibn Sa'oud against him, his reason being that it was the Sheikh of Kweit, believed to be our ally, who furnished that homeless exile with the means of re-establishing himself in the country his ancestors had ruled, hoping thereby to weaken the influence of the Sultan on the borders of Kweit. The beginning of the trouble was possibly the friendship with the Sultan into which Ibn er Rashīd saw fit to enter, a friendship blazoned to the world by the appearance of Shammāri mares in Constantinople and Circassian girls in Ḥāil; but as for the end, there is no end to war in the desert, and any grievance will serve the turn of an impetuous young sheikh.

Though we were riding through plains which were quite deserted and to the casual observer almost featureless, we seldom travelled for more than a mile without reaching a spot that had a name. In listening to Arab talk you are struck by this abundant nomenclature. If you ask where a certain sheikh has pitched his tents you will at once be given an exact answer. The map is blank, and when you reach the encampment the landscape is blank also. A rise in the ground, a big stone, a vestige of ruin, not to speak of every possible hollow in which there may be water either in winter or in

ARABS OF THE BELḲA

summer, these are marks sufficiently distinguishing to the nomad eye. Ride with an Arab and you shall realise why the pre-Mohammadan poems are so full of names, and also how vain a labour it would be to attempt to assign a definite spot to the greater number of them, for the same name recurs hundreds of times. We presently came to a little mound which Ġablān called Thelelet el Ḥirsheh and then to another rather smaller called Theleleh, and here Ġablān drew rein and pointed to a couple of fire-blackened stones upon the ground.

"That," said he, "was my hearth. Here I camped five years ago. Yonder was my father's tent, and the son of my uncle pitched his below the slope."

I might have been riding with Imr ul Ḳais, or with any of the great singers of the Age of Ignorance, whose odes take swinging flight lifted on just such a theme, the changeless theme of the evanescence of desert existence.

The clouds broke in rain upon us, and we left Theleleh and paced on east—an Arab when he travels seldom goes quicker than a walk—while Namrūd, according to his habit, beguiled the way with story telling.

"Oh lady," said he, "I will tell you a tale well known among the Arabs, without doubt Ġablān has heard it. There was a man—he is dead now, but his sons still live—who had a blood feud, and in the night his enemy fell upon him with many horsemen, and they drove away his flocks and his camels and his mares and seized his tents and all that he had. And he who had been a rich man and much honoured was reduced to the extreme of necessity. So he wandered forth till he came to the tents of a tribe that was neither the friend nor the foe of his people, and he went to the sheikh's tent and laid his hand on the tent pole and said: 'Oh sheikh! I am your guest'" ('Ana dakhīlak,' the phrase of one who seeks for hospitality and protection)." And the sheikh rose and led him in and seated him by the hearth, and treated him with kindness. And he gave him sheep and a few camels and cloth for a tent, and the man went away and prospered so that in ten years he was again as rich as before. Now after ten years it happened that misfortune fell upon the sheikh who had been his host, and he in turn lost all that he possessed. And the sheikh said: 'I will go to the tents of so-and-so, who is now rich, and he will treat me as I treated him.' Now when he reached the tents the man was away, but his son was within. And the sheikh laid his hand on the tent pole, and said, 'Ana dakhīlak,' and the man's son answered: 'I do not know you, but since you claim our protection come in and my mother will make you coffee.' So the sheikh came in, and the woman called him to her hearth and made him coffee, and it is an indignity among the Arabs that the coffee should be made by the women. And while he was sitting by the women's hearth, the lord of the tent returned, and his son went out and told him that the sheikh had come. And he said: 'We will keep him for the night since he is our guest, and at dawn we will send him away lest we should draw his feud upon ourselves.' And they put the sheikh in a corner of the tent and gave him only bread and coffee, and next day they bade him go. And they sent an escort of two horsemen with him for a day's journey, as is the usage among the Arabs with one who has sought their protection and goes in fear of his life, and then they left him to starve or to fall among his enemies. But such ingratitude is rare, praise be to God! and therefore the tale is not forgotten."

FELLĀḤ UL 'ISA AD DA'JA

We were now nearing some slopes that might almost be dignified with the name of hills. They formed a great semicircle that stretched away to the south and in the hollow of their arm Fellāḥ ul 'Isa had pitched his tents. The Da'ja, when I was with them, occupied all the plain below the amphitheatre of the Jebel el 'Alya and also the country to the north-west between the hills and the river Zerka Mujēmir, the young sheikh, was camped to the north, his two uncles, Fellāḥ ul 'Isa and Ḥamūd, the father of Ḳablān, together in the plain to the south. I did not happen to see Ḥamūd; he had ridden away to visit some of his herds. Ḳablān put his horse to a canter and went on ahead to announce our arrival. As we rode up to the big sheikh's tent a white-haired man came out to welcome us. This was my host, Fellāḥ ul 'Isa, a sheikh renowned throughout the Belḳa for his wisdom and possessed of an authority beyond that which an old man of a ruling house exercises over his own tribe. Six months before he had been an honoured guest among the Druzes, who are not used to receiving Arab sheikhs on terms of friendship, and for this reason Namrūd had selected him as the best of counsellors in the matter of my journey. We were obliged to sit in his tent till coffee had been made, which ceremony occupied a full hour. It was conducted in a dignified silence, broken only by the sound of the pestle crushing the beans in the mortar, a music dear to desert ears and not easy of accomplished execution. By the time coffee drinking was over the sun had come out and with Gablān and Namrūd I rode up the hills north of the camp to inspect some ruins reported by the Arabs.

The Jebel el 'Alya proved to be a rolling upland that extended for many miles, sloping gradually away to the north and north-east. The general trend of the range is from west to south-east; it rises abruptly out of the plains and carries upon its crest a series of ruins out of which I saw two. They seem to have been a line of forts guarding a frontier that, in the absence of inscriptions, may be conjectured to have been Ghassānid. The first of the ruined sites lay immediately above Fellāḥ ul 'Isa's camp—I surmise it to have been the Kaṣr el Ahla (a name unknown to the Da'ja) marked on the Palestine Exploration map close to the Ḥajj road. If this be so, it lies four or five miles further east than the map makers have placed it, and its name should be written Ḳaṣr el 'Alya. It was a small tell, ringed round with the foundations of walls that enclosed an indistinguishable mass of ruins. We rode forward some three or four miles to the east, and at the head of a shallow valley on the northern side of the Jebel el 'Alya we found a large tank, about 120 feet by 150 feet, carefully built of dressed stones and half full of earth. Above it, nearer the top of the hill, there was a group of ruins called by the Arabs El Muwaggar.* It must have been a military post, for there seemed to be few remains of small dwellings such as would point to the existence of a town. To the east lay a building that the Arabs maintain to have been a stable. It was planned like a church, in three parallel chambers, the nave being divided from the aisles by arcades of which six arches on either side were standing, round arches

* El Muwaḳḳar it is written, but the Bedouin change the hard k into a hard g. The site has been described in "Die Provincia Arabia," vol ii.

resting on piers of masonry. On the inner sides of these piers were holes through which to fasten tethering ropes, and possibly horses may at some period have been stabled between the arches. The three chambers were roofed with barrel vaults, and wall and vault alike were built of small stones set in brittle, crumbling mortar. A few hundred yards to the

A CAPITAL AT MUWAGGAR

north west there was a big open cistern, empty of water, with plastered sides and a flight of steps at one corner. The largest ruin was still further to the north-west, almost at the summit of the hill; it is called by the Arabs the Kasr, and was probably a fortress or barracks. The main entrance was to the east, and since the ground sloped away here, the *façade* was supported on a substructure of eight vaults, above which were traces of three, or perhaps four, doorways that could only have been approached by flights of steps. Moulded piers had stood on either side of the doorways--a few were still in their places—and the *façade* had been enriched with columns and a cornice, of which the fragments were strewn over the ground below together with capitals of various designs, all of them drawn from a Corinthian prototype, though many were widely dissimilar from the parent pattern. Some of the mouldings showed very simple *rinceaux,* a trefoil set in the alternate curves of a flowing stalk, others were torus-shaped and covered with the scales of the palm trunk pattern. The width of the *façade* was forty paces; behind it was an ante-chamber separated by a cross wall from a square enclosure. Whether there had been rooms round the inside of this enclosure I could not determine; it was heaped up with ruins and overgrown with turf. On either side of the eight parallel vaults there was another vaulted chamber forming ten in all; but the two supplementary vaults did not appear to have supported a superstructure of any kind, the massive side walls of the ante-chamber resting on the outer walls of the eight central vaults. The masonry was of squared stones with rubble between, set in mortar.

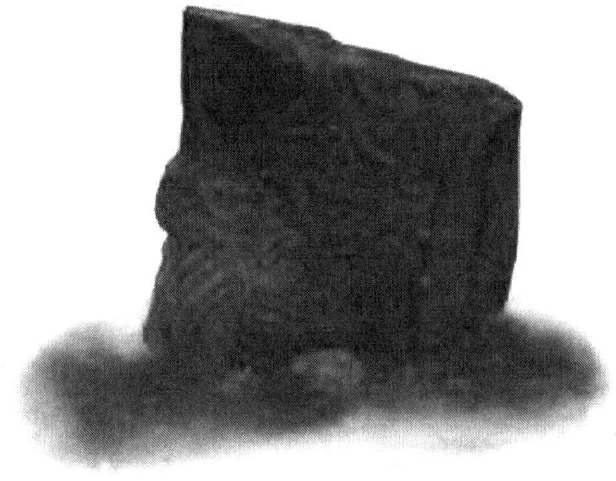

A CAPITAL AT MUWAḌḌAR

We rode back straight down the hill and so along the plain at its foot, passing another ruined site as we went, Najēreh was its name. Such heaped up mounds of cut stones the Arabs call "rujm"; it would be curious to know how far east they are to be found, how far the desert was inhabited by a permanent population. A day's journey from 'Alya, said Ḳablān, there is another fort called Kharāneh, and a third not far from it, Umm er Resās, and more besides, some of them with pictures, and all easy to visit in the winter when the western pasturages are comparatively empty.* As we rode he taught me to read the desert, to mark the hollow squares of big stones laid for the beds of Arab boys, and the semi-circular nests in the earth that the mother camels scoop out for their young. He taught me also the names of the plants that dotted the ground, and I found that though the flora of the desert is scanty in quantity, it is of many varieties, and that almost every kind has been put to some useful end by the Arabs. With the leaf of the utrufān they scent their butter, from the prickly kursa'aneh they make an excellent salad, on the dry sticks of the billān the camels feed, and the sheep on those of the shīḥ, the ashes of the gāli are used in soap boiling. The *rôle* of teacher amused Ġablān, and as we passed from one prickly blue-grey tuft to another equally blue-grey and prickly, he would say: "Oh lady, what is this?" and smile cheerfully if the answer came right.

A CAPITAL AT MUWAĠĠAR

I was to dine that night in Fellāḥ ul 'Isa's tent, and when the last bar of red light still lay across the west Ġablān came to fetch me. The little encampment was already alive with all the combination of noises that animates the desert after dark, the grunting and groaning of camels, the bleating of sheep and goats and the uninterrupted barking of dogs. There was no light in the sheikh's tent save that of the fire; my host sitting opposite me was sometimes hidden in a column of pungent smoke and sometimes illumined by a leaping flame. When a person of consideration comes as guest, a sheep must be killed in honour of the occasion, and accordingly we eat with our fingers a bountiful meal of mutton

* Several of these ruins were visited by Musil, but his book is not yet published.

and curds and flaps of bread. But even on feast nights the Arab eats astonishingly little, much less than a European woman with a good appetite, and when there is no guest in camp, bread and a bowl of camel's milk is all they need. It is true they spend most of the day asleep or gossiping in the sun, yet I have seen the 'Agēl making a four months' march on no more generous fare. Though they can go on such short commons, the Bedouin must seldom be without the sensation of hunger; they are always lean and thin, and any sickness that falls upon the tribe carries off a large proportion of its numbers. My servants feasted too, and since we had left Muḥammad, or rather Ṭarīf the Christian, to guard the tents in our absence, a wooden bowl was piled with food and sent out into the night "for the guest who has remained behind."

Fellāḥ ul 'Isa and Namrūd fell into an interesting discussion over the coffee, one that threw much light on the position of the tribes of the Belḳa. They are hard pressed by encroaching civilisation. Their summer quarters are gradually being filled up with fellaḥīn, and still worse, their summer watering places are now occupied by Circassian colonists settled by the Sultan in eastern Syria when the Russians turned them out of house and home in the Caucasus. The Circassians are a disagreeable people, morose and quarrelsome, but industrious and enterprising beyond measure, and in their daily contests with the Arabs they invariably come off victors. Recently they have made the drawing of water from the Zerka, on which the Bedouin are dependent during the summer, a *casus belli*, and it is becoming more and more impossible to go down to 'Ammān, the Circassian headquarters, for the few necessities of Arab life, such as coffee and sugar and tobacco. Namrūd was of opinion that the Belḳa tribes should have asked the Government to appoint a Ḳāimaḳām over their district to protect their interests; but Fellāḥ ul 'Isa hesitated to call in King Stork, fearing the military service he might impose, the enforced registration of cattle and other hateful practices. The truth is that the days of the Belḳa Arabs are numbered. To judge by the ruins, it will be possible, as it was possible in past centuries, to establish a fixed population all over their territory, and they will have to choose between themselves building villages and cultivating the ground or retreating to the east where water is almost unobtainable in the summer, and the heat far greater than they care to face.

Namrūd turned from these vexed questions to extol the English rule in Egypt. He had never been there, but he had heard tales from one of his cousins who was a clerk in Alexandria; he knew that the fellaḥīn had grown rich and that the desert was as peaceful as were the cities.

MILKING SHEEP

"Blood feud has ceased," said he, "and raiding; for when a man steals another's camels, look you what happens. The owner of the camels comes to the nearest konak and lays his complaint, and a zaptieh rides out alone through the desert till he reaches the robber's tent. Then he throws the salaam and enters. What does the lord of the tent do? he makes coffee and tries to treat the zaptieh as a guest. But when the soldier has drunk the coffee he places money by the hearth, saying, 'Take this piastre,' and so he pays for all he eats and drinks and accepts nothing. And in the morning he departs, leaving orders that in so many days the camels must be at the konak. Then the robber, being afraid, gathers together the camels and sends them in, and one, may be, is missing, so that the number is short. And the judge says to the lord of the camels, 'Are all the beasts here?' and he replies, 'There is one missing.' And he says, 'What is its value?' and he answers, 'Eight liras.' Then the judge says to the other, 'Pay him eight liras.' Wāllah! he pays."

Fellāḥ ul 'Isa expressed no direct approval of the advantages of this system, but he listened with interest while I explained the principles of the Fellaḥīn Bank, as far as I understood them, and at the end he asked whether Lord Cromer could not be induced to extend his rule to Syria, an invitation that I would not undertake to accept in his name. Five years before, in the Ḥaurān mountains, a similar question had been put to me, and the answering of it had taxed my diplomacy. The Druze sheikhs of Ḳanawāt had assembled in my tent under shadow of night, and after much cautious beating about the bush and many assurances from me that no one was listening, they had asked whether if the Turks again broke their treaties with the Mountain, the Druzes might take refuge with Lord Cromer in Egypt, and whether I would not charge myself with a message to him. I replied with the air of one weighing the proposition in all its aspects that the Druzes were people of the hill country, and that Egypt was a plain, and would therefore scarcely suit them. The Sheikh el Balad looked at the Sheikh ed Dīn, and the horrible vision of a land without mountain fastnesses in which to take refuge, or mountain paths easy to defend, must have opened before their eyes, for they replied that the matter required much thought, and I heard no more of it. Nevertheless the moral is obvious: all over Syria and even in the desert, whenever a man is ground down by injustice or mastered by his own incompetence, he wishes that he were under the rule that has given wealth to Egypt, and our occupation of that country, which did so much at first to alienate from us the sympathies of Mohammedans, has proved the finest advertisement of English methods of government.*

* The present unrest in Egypt may seem to throw a doubt upon the truth of these observations, but I do not believe this to be the case. The Egyptians have forgotten the miseries from which our administration rescued them, the Syrians and the people of the desert are still labouring under them, and in their eyes the position of their neighbours is one of unalloyed and enviable ease. But when once the wolf is driven from the door, the restraints imposed by an immutable law eat into the temper of a restless, unstable population accustomed to reckon with misrule and to profit by the frequent laxity and the occasional opportunities of undeserved advancement which characterise it. Justice is a capital thing when it guards your legal rights,

As I sat listening to the talk round me and looking out into the starlit night, my mind went back to the train of thought that had been the groundwork of the whole day, the theme that Ḡablān had started when he stopped and pointed out the traces of his former encampment, and I said :

ḠABLĀN IBN ḤAMŪD AD DA'JA

"In the ages before the Prophet your fathers spoke as you do and in the same language, but we who do not know your ways have lost the meaning of the words they used. Now tell me what is so-and-so, and so-and-so ?"

The men round the fire bent forward, and when a flame jumped up I saw their dark faces as they listened, and answered :

"By God ! did they say *that* before the Prophet ?"

"Māsha'llah ! we use that word still. It is the mark on the ground where the tent was pitched."

Thus encouraged I quoted the couplet of Imr ul Ḳais which Ḡablān's utterance had suggested.

"Stay ! let us weep the memory of the Beloved and her resting-place in the cleft of the shifting sands 'twixt ēd Dujēl and Ḥaumal."

Ḡablān, by the tent pole, lifted his head and exclaimed : "Māsha'llah ! that is 'Antara."

All poetry is ascribed to 'Antara by the unlettered Arab ; he knows no other name in literature.

I answered : "No ; 'Antara spoke otherwise. He said : 'Have the poets aforetime left ought to be added by me ?

but most damnable when you wish to usurp the rights of others. Fellāḥ ul 'Isa and his kind would not be slow to discover its defects.

or dost thou remember her house when thou lookest on the place?' And Lebīd spoke best of all when he said: 'And what is man but a tent and the folk thereof? one day they depart and the place is left desolate.'"

Ġablān made a gesture of assent.

"By God!" said he, "the plain is covered with places wherein I rested."

He had struck the note. I looked out beyond him into the night and saw the desert with his eyes, no longer empty but set thicker with human associations than any city. Every line of it took on significance, every stone was like the ghost of a hearth in which the warmth of Arab life was hardly cold, though the fire might have been extinguished this hundred years. It was a city of shadowy outlines visible one under the other, fleeting and changing, combining into new shapes elements that are as old as Time, the new indistinguishable from the old and the old from the new.

There is no name for it. The Arabs do not speak of desert or wilderness as we do. Why should they? To them it is neither desert nor wilderness, but a land of which they know every feature, a mother country whose smallest product has a use sufficient for their needs. They know, or at least they knew in the days when their thoughts shaped themselves in deathless verse, how to rejoice in the great spaces and how to honour the rush of the storm. In many a couplet they extolled the beauty of the watered spots; they sang of the fly that hummed there, as a man made glad with wine croons melodies for his sole ears to hear, and of the pools of rain that shone like silver pieces, or gleamed dark as the warrior's mail when the wind ruffled them. They had watched, as they crossed the barren watercourses, the laggard wonders of the night, when the stars seemed chained to the sky as though the dawn would never come. Imr ul Ḳais had seen the Pleiades caught like jewels in the net of a girdle, and with the wolf that howled in the dark he had claimed fellowship: "Thou and I are of one kindred, and, lo, the furrow that thou ploughest and that I plough shall yield one harvest." But by night or by day there was no overmastering terror, no meaningless fear and no enemy that could not be vanquished.

They did not cry for help, those poets of the Ignorance, either to man or God; but when danger fell upon them they remembered the maker of their sword, the lineage of their horse and the prowess of their tribe, and their own right hand was enough to carry them through. And then they gloried as men should glory whose blood flows hot in their veins, and gave no thanks where none were due.

This is the temper of verse as splendid of its kind as any that has fallen from the lips of men. Every string of Arab experience is touched in turn, and the deepest chords of feeling are resonant. There are no finer lines than those in which Lebīd sums up his appreciation of existence, a poem where each one of the fourteen couplets is instinct with a grave and tragic dignity beyond all praise. He looks sorrow in the face, old age and death, and ends with a solemn admission of the limitations of human wisdom: "By thy life! the casters of pebbles and the watchers of the flight of birds, how know they what God is doing?" The voice of warning is never the voice of dismay. It recurs often enough, but it does not check the wild daring of the singer. "Death is no chooser!" cries Tārafa, "the miser or the free-handed, Death has his rope round the swift flying heel of him!" But he adds: "What dost thou fear? To-day is thy life." And as fearlessly Zuhair sets forth his experience: "To-day I know and yesterday and the days that were, but for to-morrow mine eyes are sightless. For I have seen Doom let out in the dark like a blind camel; those it struck died and those it missed lived to grow old." The breath of inspiration touched all alike, old and young, men and women, and among the most exquisite remnants of the desert heritage is a dirge sung

ON THE ḤAJJ ROAD

by a sister for her dead brother, which is no less valuable as a
historical document than it is admirable in sentiment. An
Naḍr Ibn el Hārith was taken prisoner by Muḥammad at
Uthail, after the battle of Bedr, and by his order put to death,
and through the verses of Ḳutaila you catch the revolt of
feeling with which the Prophet's pretensions were greeted by
those of his contemporaries who would not submit to them,
coupled with the necessary respect due to a man whose race
was as good as their own. " Oh camel rider ! " she cries,

" Oh camel rider !   Uthail, methinks, if thou speedest well,
    shall lie before thee when breaks the fifth Dawn o'er thy road.
Take thou a word to a dead man there—and a greeting, sure,
    but meet it is that the riders bring from friends afar—
From me to him, yea and tears unstanched, in a flood they flow
    when he plies the well rope, and others choke me that stay
      behind.
Raise clear thy voice that an Naḍr may hear if thou call on him—
    can a dead man hear ?   Can he answer any that shouts his name ?
Day long the swords of his father's sons on his body played—
    Ah God ! the bonds of a brother's blood that were severed there !
Helpless, a-weary, to death they led him, with fight foredone ;
    short steps he takes with his fettered feet and his arms are bound.
Oh Muhammad ! sprung from a mother thou of a noble house,
    and thy father too was of goodly stock when the kin is told.
Had it cost thee dear to have granted grace that day to him ?
    yea, a man may pardon though anger burn in his bosom sore.
And the nearest he in the ties of kinship of all to thee,
    and the fittest he, if thou loosedst any to be set free.
Ah, hadst thou taken a ransom, sure with the best of all
    that my hand possessed I had paid thee, spending my utmost
      store."

And on yet stronger wing the wild free spirit of the desert
rose in his breast who lay in ward at Mecca, and he sang of
love and death with a voice that will not be silenced :

" My longing climbs up the steep with the riders of El Yemen,
    by their side, while my body lies in Mecca a prisoner.
I marvelled as she came darkling to me and entered free,
    while the prison door before me was bolted and surely barred.
She drew near and greeted me, then she rose and bade farewell,
    and when she turned my life well-nigh went forth with her.
Nay, think not that I am bowed with fear away from you,
    or that I tremble before death that stands so nigh.
Or that my soul quakes at all before your threatening,
    or that my spirit is broken by walking in these chains.

But a longing has smitten my heart born of love for thee,
as it was in the days aforetime when that I was free."*

The agony of the captive, the imagined vision of the heart's desire which no prison bars could exclude, then the fine protest lest his foes should dream that his spirit faltered, and the strong man's fearless memory of the passion that had shaken his life and left his soul still ready to vanquish death —there are few such epitomes of noble emotion. Born and bred on the soil of the desert, the singers of the Age of Ignorance have left behind them a record of their race that richer and wiser nations will find hard to equal.

* I have borrowed Sir Charles Lyall's beautiful and most scholarly translation of this and the preceding poem.

CHAPTER IV

THERE is an Arabic proverb which says: "Ḥayyeh rubda wa la ḍaif muḍḥa"—neither ash-grey snake nor mid-day guest. We were careful not to make a breach in our manners by outstaying our welcome, and our camp was up before the sun. To wake in that desert dawn was like waking in the heart of an opal. The mists lifting their heads out of the hollows, the dews floating in ghostly wreaths from the black tents, were shot through first with the faint glories of the eastern sky and then with the strong yellow rays of the risen sun. I sent a silver and purple kerchief to Fellaḥ ul 'Isa, "for the little son" who had played solemnly about the hearth, took grateful leave of Namrūd, drank a parting cup of coffee, and, the old sheikh holding my stirrup, mounted and rode away with Ḡablān. We climbed the Jebel el 'Alya and crossed the wide summit of the range; the landscape was akin to that of our own English border country but bigger, the sweeping curves more generous, the distances further away. The glorious cold air intoxicated every sense and set the blood throbbing—to my mind the saying about the Bay of Naples should run differently. See the desert on a fine morning and die—if you can. Even the stolid mules felt the breath of it and raced across the spongy ground ("Mad! the accursed ones!") till their packs swung round and brought them down, and twice we stopped to head them off and reload. The Little Heart, the highest peak of the Jebel Druze, surveyed us cheerfully the while, glittering in its snow mantle far away to the north.

At the foot of the northern slopes of the 'Alya hills we entered a great rolling plain like that which we had left to the south. We passed many of those mysterious rujm which start the fancy speculating on the past history of the land, and presently we caught sight of the scattered encampments of the Ḥassaniyyeh, who are good friends to the Da'ja and belong to the same group of tribes. And here we spied two riders coming across the plain and Ḉablān went out to greet them and remained some time in talk, and then returned with a grave face. The day before, the very day before, while we had been journeying peacefully from Ṭneib, four hundred horsemen of the Ṣukhūr and the Ḥoweiṭāt, leagued in evil, had swept these plains, surprised an outlying group of the Beni Ḥassan and carried off the tents, together with two thousand head of cattle. It was almost a pity, I thought, that we had come a day too late, but Ḉablān looked graver still at the suggestion, and said that he would have been forced to join in the fray, yes, he would even have left me, though I had been committed to his charge, for the Da'ja were bound to help the Beni Ḥassan against the Ṣukhūr. And perhaps yesterday's work would be enough to break the new-born truce between that powerful tribe and the allies of the 'Anazeh and set the whole desert at war again. There was sorrow in the tents of the Children of Ḥassan. We saw a man weeping by the tent pole, with his head bowed in his hands, everything he possessed having been swept from him. As we rode we talked much of ghazu (raid) and the rules that govern it. The fortunes of the Arab are as varied as those of a gambler on the Stock Exchange. One day he is the richest man in the desert, and next morning he may not have a single camel foal to his name. He lives in a state of war, and even if the surest pledges have been exchanged with the neighbouring

ARABS RIDING MARDŪF

tribes there is no certainty that a band of raiders from hundreds of miles away will not descend on his camp in the night, as a tribe unknown to Syria, the Beni Awājeh, fell, two years ago, on the lands south-east of Aleppo, crossing three hundred miles of desert, Mardūf (two on a camel) from their seat above Baghdad, carrying off all the cattle and killing scores of people. How many thousand years this state of things has lasted, those who shall read the earliest records of the inner desert will tell us, for it goes back to the first of them, but in all the centuries the Arab has bought no wisdom from experience. He is never safe, and yet he behaves as though security were his daily bread. He pitches his feeble little camps, ten or fifteen tents together, over a wide stretch of undefended and indefensible country. He is too far from his fellows to call in their aid, too far as a rule to gather the horsemen together and follow after the raiders whose retreat must be sufficiently slow, burdened with the captured flocks, to guarantee success to a swift pursuit. Having lost all his worldly goods, he goes about the desert and makes his plaint, and one man gives him a strip or two of goats' hair cloth, and another a coffee-pot, a third presents him with a camel, and a fourth with a few sheep, till he has a roof to cover him and enough animals to keep his family from hunger. There are good customs among the Arabs, as Namrūd said. So he bides his time for months, perhaps for years, till at length opportunity ripens, and the horsemen of his tribe with their allies ride forth and recapture all the flocks that had been carried off and more besides, and the feud enters on another phase. The truth is that the ghazu is the only industry the desert knows and the only game. As an industry it seems to the commercial mind to be based on a false conception of the laws of supply and demand, but as a game there is much to be said for it. The spirit of adventure finds full scope in it—you can picture the excitement of the night ride across the plain, the rush of the mares in the attack, the glorious (and comparatively innocuous) popping of rifles and the exhilaration of knowing yourself a fine fellow as you turn homewards with the spoil. It is the best sort of fantasia, as they say in the desert, with a spice of danger behind it. Not that the danger is alarmingly great: a considerable amount of amusement can be got without much bloodshed, and the raiding Arab is seldom bent on killing. He never lifts his hand against women and children, and if here and there a man falls it is almost by accident, since who can be sure of the ultimate destination of a rifle bullet once it is embarked on its lawless course? This is the Arab view of the ghazu; the Druzes look at it otherwise. For them it is red war. They do not play the game as it should be played, they go out to slay, and they spare no one. While they have a grain of powder in their flasks and strength to pull the trigger, they kill every man, woman and child that they encounter.

A TRAVELLING ENCAMPMENT OF THE 'AḲÊL

Knowing the independence of Arab women and the freedom with which marriages are contracted between different tribes of equal birth, I saw many romantic possibilities of mingled love and hatred between the Montagues and the Capulets. "Lo, on a sudden I loved her," says 'Antara, "though I had slain her kin." Ġablān replied that these difficult situations did indeed occur, and ended sometimes in a tragedy, but if the lovers would be content to wait, some compromise could be arrived at, or they might be able to marry during one of the brief but oft-recurring intervals of truce. The real danger begins when blood feud is started within the tribe itself and a man having murdered one of his own people is cast out a homeless, kinless exile to shelter with strangers or with foes. Such was Imr ul Ḳais, the lonely outlaw, crying to the night: "Oh long night, wilt thou not bring the dawn? yet the day is no better than thou."

A few miles further north the Ḥassaniyyeh encampments had not yet heard of yesterday's misfortune, and we had the pleasure of spreading the ill-news. Ġablān rode up to every group we passed and delivered his mind of its burden; the men in buckram multiplied as we went, and perhaps I had been wrong in accepting the four hundred of the original statement, for they had had plenty of time to breed during the twenty-four hours that had elapsed between their departure and our arrival. All the tents were occupied with preparations not for war but for feasting. On the morrow fell

A DESERT WELL

the great festival of the Mohammedan year, the Feast of Sacrifice, when the pilgrims in Mecca slaughter their offerings and True Believers at home follow their example. By every tent there was a huge pile of thorns wherewith to roast the camel or sheep next day, and the shirts of the tribe were spread out to dry in the sun after a washing which, I have reason to believe, takes place but once a year. Towards sunset we reached a big encampment of the Beni Ḥassan, where Ḍablān decided to spend the night. There was water in a muddy pool near at hand and a good site for our tents above the hollow in which the Arabs lay. None of the great sheikhs were camped there and, mindful of Namrūd's warnings, I refused all invitations and spent the evening at home, watching the sunset and the kindling of the cooking fires and the blue smoke that floated away into the twilight. The sacrificial camel, in gorgeous trappings, grazed among my mules, and after dark the festival was heralded by a prolonged letting off of rifles. Ḉablān sat silent by the camp fire, his thoughts busy with the merrymakings that were on foot at home. It went sorely against the grain that he should be absent on such a day. "How many horsemen," said he, "will alight

A DESERT WATER-COURSE

to-morrow at my father's tent! and I shall not be there to welcome them or to wish a good feast day to my little son!"

We were off before the rejoicings had begun. I had no desire to assist at the last moments of the camel, and moreover we had a long day before us through country that was not particularly safe. As far as my caravan was concerned, the risk was small. I had a letter in my pocket from Fellaḥ ul 'Isa to Nasīb el Aṭrash, the Sheikh of Ṣalkhad in the Jebel Druze. "To the renowned and honoured sheikh, Nasīb el Aṭrash," it ran (I had heard my host dictate it to Namrūd and seen him seal it with his seal), "the venerated, may God prolong his existence! We send you greetings, to you and to all the people of Ṣalkhad, and to your brother Jada'llah, and to the son of your uncle Muḥammad el Aṭrash in Umm er Rummān, and to our friends in Imtain. And further, there goes to you from us a lady of the most noble among the English. And we greet Muḥammada and our friends. . . . &c., (here followed another list of names), and this is all that is needful, and peace be with you." And beyond this letter I had the guarantee of my nationality, for the Druzes have not yet forgotten our interference on their behalf in 1860; moreover I was acquainted with several of the sheikhs of the Ṭurshān, to which powerful family Nasīb belonged. But Gablān was in a different case, and he was fully conscious of the ambiguity of his position. In spite of his uncle's visit to the Mountain, he was not at all certain how the Druzes would receive him; he was leaving the last outposts of his allies, and entering a border land by tradition hostile (he himself had no acquaintance with it but that which he had gathered on raiding expeditions), and if he did not find enemies among the Druzes he might well fall in with a scouring party of the bitter foes of the Da'ja, the Ḥaseneh or their like, who camp east of the hills.

After an hour or two of travel, the character of the country changed completely: the soft soil of the desert came to an end, and the volcanic rocks of the Ḥaurān began. We rode for some time up a gulley of lava, left the last of the Ḥassaniyyeh tents in a little open space between some mounds, and found ourselves on the edge of a plain that stretched to the foot of the Jebel Druze in an unbroken expanse, completely deserted, almost devoid of vegetation and strewn with black volcanic stones It has been said that the borders of the desert are like a rocky shore on which the sailor who navigates deep waters with success may yet be wrecked when he attempts to bring his ship to port. This was the landing which we had to effect. Somewhere between us and the hills were the ruins of Umm ej Jemāl, where I hoped to get into touch with the Druzes, but for the life of us we could not tell where they lay, the plain having just sufficient rise and fall to hide them Now Umm ej Jemāl has an evil name—I believe mine was the second European camp that had ever been pitched in it, the first having been that of a party of American archæologists who left a fortnight before I arrived—and

CAMELS OF THE ḤASENEH

Gablān's evident anxiety enhanced its sinister reputation. Twice he turned to me and asked whether it were necessary to camp there. I answered that he had undertaken to guide me to Umm ej Jemāl, and that there was no question but that I should go, and the second time I backed my obstinacy by pointing out that we must have water that night for the animals, and that there was little chance of finding it except

UMM EJ JEMĀL

in the cisterns of the ruined village. Thereupon I had out my map, and after trying to guess what point on the blank white paper we must have reached, I turned my caravan a little to the west towards a low rise from whence we should probably catch sight of our destination. Gablān took the decision in good part and expressed regret that he could not be of better service in directing us. He had been once in his life to Umm ej Jemāl, but it was at dead of night when he was out raiding. He and his party had stopped for half an hour to water their horses and had passed on eastward, returning by another route. Yes, it had been a successful raid, praise be to God! and one of the first in which he had engaged. Mikhāil listened with indifference to our deliberations, the muleteers were not consulted, but as we set off again Ḥabīb tucked his revolver more handily into his belt.

We rode on. I was engaged in looking for the rasīf, the paved Roman road that runs from Ḳal'at ez Zerka straight to Boṣrā, and also in wondering what I should do to protect if necessary the friend and guide whose pleasant companionship had enlivened our hours of travel and who should certainly come to no harm while he was with us. As we drew nearer to the rising ground we observed that it was crowned with sheepfolds, and presently we could see men gathering their flocks together and driving them behind the black walls, their hurried movements betraying their alarm. We noticed also some figures, whether mounted or on foot it was impossible to determine, advancing on us from a hollow to the left, and after a moment two puffs of smoke rose in front of them, and we heard the crack of rifles.

Ḡablān turned to me with a quick gesture.

"Ḍarabūna!" he said. "They have fired on us."

I said aloud: "They are afraid," but to myself, "We're in for it."

Ḡablān rose in his stirrups, dragged his fur-lined cloak from his shoulders, wound it round his left arm and waved it above his head, and very slowly he and I paced forward together. Another couple of shots were fired, and still we rode forward, Ḡablān waving his flag of truce. The firing ceased; it was nothing after all but the accepted greeting to strangers, conducted with the customary levity of the barbarian. Our assailants turned out to be two Arabs, grinning from ear to ear, quite ready to fraternise with us as soon as they had decided that we were not bent on sheep stealing, and most willing to direct us to Umm ej Jemāl. As soon as we had rounded the tell we saw it in front of us, its black towers and walls standing so boldly out of the desert that it was impossible to believe it had been ruined and deserted for thirteen hundred years. It was not till we came close that the rents and gashes in the tufa masonry and the breaches in the city wall were visible. I pushed forward and would have ridden straight into the heart of the town, but Ḡablān caught me up and laid his hand upon my bridle.

"I go first," he said. "Oh lady, you were committed to my charge."

And since he was the only person who incurred any risk and was well aware of the fact, his resolution did him credit.

We clattered over the ruined wall, passed round the square monastery tower which is the chief feature of the Mother of Camels (such is the meaning of the Arabic name), and rode into an open place between empty streets, and there was no one to fear and no sign of life save that offered by two small black tents, the inhabitants of which greeted us with enthusiasm, and proceeded to sell us milk and eggs in the most amicable fashion.

WATERING CAMELS

The Arabs who live at the foot of Ḥaurān mountains are called the Jebeliyyeh, the Arabs of the Hills, and they are of no consideration, being but servants and shepherds to the Druzes. In the winter they herd the flocks that are sent down into the plain, and in the summer they are allowed to occupy the uncultivated slopes with their own cattle.

I spent the hour of daylight that remained in examining the wonderful Nabatæan necropolis outside the walls. Monsieur Dussaud began the work on it five years ago; Mr. Butler and Dr. Littmann, whose visit immediately preceded mine, will be found to have continued it when their next volumes are given to the world. Having seen what tombs they had uncovered and noted several mounds that must conceal others, I sent away my companions and wandered in the dusk through the ruined streets of the town, into great rooms and up broken stairs, till Gablān came and called me in, saying that if a man saw something in a fur coat exploring those uncanny places after dark, he might easily take the apparition for a ghoul and shoot at it. Moreover, he wished to ask me whether he might not return to Ṭneib. One of the Arabs would guide us next day to the first Druze village, and Gablān would as soon come no nearer to the Mountain. I agreed readily, indeed it was a relief not to have his safety on my conscience. He received three napoleons for his trouble and a warm letter of thanks to deliver to Fellaḥ ul 'Isa, and we parted with many assurances that if God willed we would travel together again.

The stony foot of the Jebel Ḥaurān is strewn with villages deserted since the Mohammedan invasion in the seventh century. I visited two that lay not far from my path, Shabḥa and Shabḥīyyeh, and found them to be both of the same character as Umm ej Jemāl From afar they look like well-built towns with square towers rising above streets of three-storied houses. Where the walls have fallen they lie as they fell, and no hand has troubled to clear away the ruins. Monsieur de Vogüé was the first to describe the architecture of the Ḥaurān; his splendid volumes are still the principal source of information. The dwelling-houses are built round a court in which there is usually an outer stair leading to the upper story. There is no wood used in their construction, even the doors are of solid stone, turning on stone hinges, and the windows of stone slabs pierced with open-work patterns. Sometimes there are traces of a colonnaded portico, or the walls are broken by a double window, the arches of which are supported by a small column and a rough plain capital; frequently the lintels of the doors are adorned with a cross or a Christian monogram, but otherwise there is little decoration. The chambers are roofed with stone slabs resting on the back of transverse arches. So far as can be said with any certainty, Nabatæan inscriptions and tombs are the oldest monuments that have been discovered in the district; they are followed by many important remains of pagan Rome, but the really flourishing period seems to have been the Christian.

After the Mohammadan invasion, which put an end to the prosperity of the Ḥaurān uplands, few of the villages were re-inhabited, and when the Druzes came about a hundred and fifty years ago, they found no settled population. They made the Mountain their own, rebuilt and thereby destroyed the ancient towns, and extended their lordship over the plains to the south, though they have not established themselves in the villages of that debatable land which remains a happy hunting ground for the archæologist. The American expedition will make good use of the immense amount of material that exists there, and knowing that the work had been done by better hands than mine, I rolled up the measuring tape and folded the foot-rule. But I could not so far overcome a natural instinct as to cease from copying inscriptions, and the one or two (they were extremely few) that had escaped Dr. Littmann's vigilant eye and come by chance to me were made over to him when we met in Damascus.

STRIKING CAMP

To our new guide, Fendi, fell the congenial task of posting me up in the gossip of the Mountain. Death had been busy among the great family of the Turshān during the past five years. Fāiz el Aṭrash, Sheikh of Ḳreyeh, was gone, poisoned said some, and a week or two before my arrival the most renowned of all the leaders of the Druzes, Shibly Beg el Aṭrash, had died of a mysterious and lingering illness—poison again, it was whispered. There was this war and that on hand, a terrible raid of the Arabs of the Wādy Sirḥān to be avenged, and a score with the Ṣukhūr to be settled, but on the whole there was prosperity, and as much peace as a Druze would wish to enjoy. The conversation was interrupted by a little shooting at rabbits lying asleep in the sun, not a gentlemanly sport perhaps, but one that helped to fill and to diversify the pot. After a time I left the mules and Fendi to go their own way, and taking Mikhāil with me, made a long circuit to visit the ruined towns. We were just finishing lunch under a broken wall, well separated from the rest of the party, when we saw two horsemen approaching us across the plain. We swept up the remains of the lunch and mounted hastily, feeling that any greeting they might accord us was better met in the saddle. They stopped in front of us and gave us the salute, following it with an abrupt question as to where we were going. I answered: "To Ṣalkhād, to Nasīb el Aṭrash," and they let us pass without further remark. They were not Druzes, for they did not wear the Druze turban, but Christians from Ḳreyeh, where there is a large Christian community, riding down to Umm ej Jemāl to visit the winter quarters of their flocks, so said Fendi, whom they had passed a mile ahead. Several hours before we reached the present limits of cultivation, we saw the signs of ancient agriculture in the shape of long parallel lines of stones heaped aside from earth that had once been fruitful. They looked like the ridge and furrow of a gigantic meadow, and like the ridge and furrow they are almost indelible, the mark of labour that must have ceased with the Arab invasion. At the foot of the first spur of the hills, Tell esh Shīḥ (it is called after the grey-white Shīḥ plant which is the best pasturage for sheep), we left the unharvested desert and entered the region of ploughed fields—we left, too, the long clean levels of the open wilderness and were caught fetlock deep in the mud of a Syrian road. It led us up the hill to Umm er Rummān, the Mother of Pomegranates, on the edge of the lowest plateau of the Jebel Druze, as bleak a little muddy spot as you could hope to see. I stopped at the entrance of the village, and asked a group of Druzes where I should find a camping ground, and they directed me to an extremely dirty place below the cemetery, saying there was no other where I should not spoil the crops or the grass, though the crops, Heaven save the mark! were as yet below ground, and the grass consisted of a few brown spears half covered with melting snow. I could not entertain the idea of pitching tents so near the graveyard, and demanded to be directed to the house of Muḥammad el Aṭrash, Sheikh of Umm er Rummān. This prince of the Ṭurshān was seated upon his roof, engaged in directing certain agricultural operations that were being carried forward in the slough below. Long years had made him shapeless of figure and the effect was enhanced by the innumerable garments in which the winter cold had forced him to wrap his fat old body. I came as near as the mud would allow, and shouted:

MUḤAMMAD EL AṬRASH

"Peace be upon you, oh Sheikh!"

"And upon you peace!" he bawled in answer.

"Where in your village is there a dry spot for a camp?"

The sheikh conferred at the top of his voice with his henchmen in the mud, and finally replied that he did not know, by God! While I was wondering where to turn, a Druze stepped forward and announced that he could show me a place outside the town, and the sheikh, much relieved by the shifting of responsibility, gave me a loud injunction to go in peace, and resumed his occupations.

My guide was a young man with the clear cut features and the sharp intelligent expression of his race. He was endowed, too, like all his kin, with a lively curiosity, and as he hopped from side to side of the road to avoid the pools of mud and slush, he had from me all my story, whence I came and whither I was going, who were my friends in the Jebel Druze and what my father's name — very different this from the custom of the Arabs, with whom it is an essential point of good breeding never to demand more than the stranger sees fit to impart. In Aṭ Ṭabari's history there is a fine tale of a man who sought refuge with an Arab sheikh. He stayed on, and the sheikh died, and his son who ruled in his stead advanced in years, and at length the grandson of the original host came to his father and said: "Who is the man who dwells with us?" And the father answered: "My son, in my father's time he came, and my father grew old and died, and he stayed on under my protection, and I too have grown old; but in all these years we have never asked him why he sought us nor what is his name. Neither do thou ask." Yet I rejoiced to find myself once more among the trenchant wits and the searching koḥl-blackened eyes of the Mountain, where every question calls for a quick retort or a brisk parry, and when my interlocutor grew too inquisitive I had only to answer:

"Listen, oh you! I am not 'thou,' but 'Your Excellency,'" and he laughed and understood and took the rebuke to heart.

There are many inscriptions in Umm er Rummān, a few Nabatæan and the rest Cufic, proving that the town on the shelf of the hills was an early settlement and that it was one of those the Arabs re-occupied for a time after the invasion. A delighted crowd of little boys followed me from house to house, tumbling over one another in their eagerness to point out a written stone built into a wall or laid in the flooring about the hearth. In one house a woman caught me by the arm and implored me to heal her husband. The man was lying in a dark corner of the windowless room, with his face wrapped in filthy bandages, and when these had been removed a horrible wound was revealed, the track of a bullet that had passed through the cheek and shattered the jaw. I could do nothing but give him an antiseptic, and adjure the woman to wash the wound and keep the wrappings clean, and above all not to let him drink the medicine, though I felt it would make small odds which way he used it, Death had him so surely by the heel. This was the first of the long roll of sufferers that must pass before the eyes and catch despairingly at the sympathies of every traveller in wild places. Men and women afflicted with ulcers and terrible sores, with fevers and rheumatisms, children crippled from their birth, the blind and the old, there are none who do not hope that the unmeasured wisdom of the West may find them a remedy. You stand aghast at the depths of human misery and at your own helplessness.

The path of archæology led me at last to the sheikh's door, and I went in to pay him an official visit. He was most hospitably inclined now that the business of the day was over; we sat together in the maḳ'ad, the audience room, a dark and dirty sort of out-house, with an iron stove in the centre of it, and discussed the Japanese War and desert ghazus and other topics of the day, while Selmān, the sheikh's son, a charming boy of sixteen, made us coffee. Muḥammad is brother-in-law to Shibly and to Yahya Beg el Aṭrāsh, who had been my first host five years before when I had escaped to his village of 'Areh from the Turkish Mudir at Boṣrā, and Selmān is the only son of his father's old age and the only descendant of the famous 'Areh house of the Ṭurshān, for Shibly died and Yahya lives childless. The boy walked back with me to my camp, stepping lightly through the mud, a gay and eager figure touched with the air of distinction that befits one who comes of a noble stock. He had had no schooling, though there was a big Druze maktab at Ḳreyeh, fifteen miles away, kept by a Christian of some learning.

"My father holds me so precious," he explained, "that he will not let me leave his side."

"Oh Selmān," I began——

"Oh God!" he returned, using the ejaculation customary to one addressed by name.

"The minds of the Druzes are like fine steel, but what is steel until it is beaten into a sword blade?"

Selmān answered: "My uncle Shibly could neither read nor write."

I said: "The times are changed. The house of the Ṭurshān will need trained wits if it would lead the Mountain as it did before."

But that headship is a thing of the past Shibly is dead and Yahya childless, Muḥammad is old and Selmān undeveloped, Fāiz has left four sons but they are of no repute.

Nasīb is cunning but very ignorant, there is Muṣṭafa at Imtain, who passes for a worthy man of little intelligence, and Ḥamūd at Sweida, who is distinguished mainly for his wealth. The ablest man among the Druzes is without doubt Abu Tellāl of Shaḥba, and the most enlightened Sheikh Muḥammad en Naṣṣār.

The night was bitterly cold. My thermometer had been broken, so that the exact temperature could not be registered, but every morning until we reached Damascus the water in the cup by my bedside was a solid piece of ice, and one night a little tumbling stream outside the camp was frozen hard and silent. The animals and the muleteers were usually housed in a khān while the frost lasted. Muḥammad the Druze, who had returned to his original name and faith, disappeared the moment camp was pitched, and spent the night enjoying the hospitality of his relations. "For," said Mikhāil sarcastically, "every man who can give him a meal he reckons to be the son of his uncle."

I was obliged to delay my start next morning in order to profit by the sheikh's invitation to breakfast at a very elastic nine o'clock—two hours after sunrise was what was said, and who knows exactly when it may suit that luminary to appear? It was a pleasant party. We discussed the war in Yemen in all its bearings—theoretically, for I was the only person who had any news, and mine was derived from a *Weekly Times* a month old—and then Muḥammad questioned me as to why Europeans looked for inscriptions.

"But I think I know," he added. "It is that they may restore the land to the lords of it."

I assured him that the latest descendants of the former owners of the Ḥaurān had been dead a thousand years, and he listened politely and changed the subject with the baffled air of one who cannot get a true answer.

The young man who had shown us our camping ground rode with us to Ṣalkhad, saying he had business there and might as well have company by the way. His name was Ṣāleh; he was of a clerkly family, a reader and a scribe. I was so tactless as to ask him whether he were 'ākil, initiated —the Druzes are divided into the initiated and the uninitiated.

but the line of demarcation does not follow that of social pre-eminence, since most of the Ṭurshān are uninitiated. He gave me a sharp look, and replied :

" What do you think ? " and I saw my error and dropped the subject.

But Ṣāleh was not one to let slip any opportunity of gaining information. He questioned me acutely on our customs, down to the laws of marriage and divorce. He was vastly entertained at the English rule that the father should pay a man for marrying his daughter (so he interpreted the habit of giving her a marriage portion), and we laughed together over the absurdity of the arrangement. He was anxious to know Western views as to the creation of the world and the origin of matter, and I obliged him with certain heterodox opinions, on which he seized with far greater lucidity than that with which they were offered. We passed an agreeable morning, in spite of the mud and boulders of the road. At the edge of the snow wreaths a little purple crocus had made haste to bloom, and a starry white garlic—the Mountain is very rich in Spring flowers. The views to the south over the great plain we had crossed were enchanting ; to the north the hills rose in unbroken slopes of snow, Ḳuleib, the Little Heart, looking quite Alpine with its frosty summit half veiled in mist. Two hours after noon we reached Ṣalkhad, the first goal of our journey.

DESERT FLORA AND FAUNA

CHAPTER V

SALCAH, the city of King Og in Bashan, must have been a fortified place from the beginning of history. The modern village clusters round the base of a small volcano, on the top of which, built in the very crater, is the ruined fortress. This fortress and its predecessors in the crater formed the outpost of the Ḥaurān Mountains against the desert, the outpost of the earliest civilisation against the earliest marauders. The ground drops suddenly to the south and east, and, broken only by one or two volcanic mounds in the immediate neighbourhood, settles itself down into the long levels that reach Euphrates stream; straight as an arrow from a bow the Roman road runs out from Ṣalkhad into the desert in a line that no modern traveller has followed beyond the first two or three stages. The caravan track to Nejd begins here and passes by Kāf and Ethreh along the Wādi Sirḥan to Jōf and Ḥāil, a perilous way, though the Blunts pursued it successfully and Euting after them. Euting's description of it, done with all the learning and the minute observation of the German, is the best we have. Due south of Ṣalkhad there is an interesting ruined fort, Ḳal'at el Azrak, in an oasis where there are thickets full of wild boar: Dussaud visited it and has given an excellent account of his journey. No doubt there is more to be found still; the desert knows many a story that has not yet been told, and at Ṣalkhad it is difficult to keep your feet from turning south, so invitingly mysterious are those great plains.

I went at once to the house of Nasīb el Aṭrāsh and presented Fellāḥ ul 'Isa's letter. Nasīb is a man of twenty-seven, though he looks ten years older, short in stature and sleek, with shrewd features of a type essentially Druze and an expression that is more cunning than pleasant. He received me in his maḳ'ad, where he was sitting with his brother Jada'llah, a tall young man with a handsome but rather stupid face, who greeted me with "Bon jour," and then relapsed into silence, having come to the end of all the French he knew. Just as he had borrowed one phrase from a European tongue, so he had borrowed one article of dress from European wardrobes: a high stick-up collar was what he had selected, and it went strangely with his Arab clothes. There

THE CASTLE, ṢALKHAD

were a few Druzes drinking coffee in the maḳ'ad, and one other whom I instantly diagnosed as an alien. He turned out to be the Mudīr el Māl of the Turkish government—I do not know what his exact functions are, but his title implies him to be an agent of the Treasury. Ṣalkhad is one of three villages in Jebel Druze (the others being Sweida and 'Areh) where the Sultan has a Ḳāimaḳām and a telegraph station. Yūsef Effendi, Ḳāimaḳām, and Milḥēm Iliān, Mudīr el Māl, were considerably surprised when I turned up from the desert without warning or permission; they despatched three telegrams daily to the Vāli of Damascus, recounting all that I did and said, and though I was on the best of terms with both of them, finding indeed Milḥēm to be by far the most intelligent and agreeable man in the village, I fear I caused them much perturbation of mind. And here let me say that my experience of Turkish officials leads me to count them among the most polite and obliging of men. If you come to them with the proper certificates there is nothing they will not do to help you; when they stop you it is because they are obliged to obey orders from higher authorities; and even when you set aside, as from time to time you must, refusals that are always couched in language conciliatory to a fault, they conceal their just annoyance and bear you no ill will for the trouble you have caused them. The government agents at Ṣalkhad occupy an uneasy position. It is true that there has been peace in the Mountain for the past five years, but the Druzes are a slippery race and one quick to take offence. Milḥêm understood them well, and his appointment to the new post of Ṣalkhad is a proof of the Vāli's genuine desire to avoid trouble in the future. He had been at Sweida for many years before he came to Ṣalkhad; he was a Christian, and therefore not divided from the Druzes by the unbridged gulf of hatred that lies between them and Islām, and he was fully aware that Turkish rule in the Jebel Ḥaurān depends on how little demand is made on a people nominally subject and practically independent. Yūsef Effendi was not far behind him in the strength of his conviction on this head, and he had the best of reasons for realising how shadowy his authority was. There are not more than two hundred Turkish soldiers in all the Mountain; the rest of the Ottoman forces are Druze zaptiehs, well pleased to wear a government uniform and draw government pay, on the rare occasions when it reaches them, though they can hardly be considered a trustworthy guard if serious differences arise between their own people and the Sultan. To all outward appearance Nasīb and his brother were linked by the closest bonds of friendship with the Ḳāimaḳām; they were for ever sitting in his maḳ'ad and drinking his coffee, but once when

NASĪB EL AṬRASH

we happened to be alone together, Yūsef Effendi said pathetically in his stilted Turkish Arabic: "I never know what they are doing: they look on me as an enemy. And if they wish to disobey orders from Damascus, they cut the telegraph wire and go their own way. What power have I to prevent them?"

Nevertheless there are signs that the turbulent people of the Mountain have turned their minds to other matters than war with the Osmanli, and among the chief of these are the steam mills that grind the corn of Ṣalkhad and a few villages besides. A man who owns a steam mill is pledged to maintain the existing order. He has built it at considerable expense, he does not wish to see it wrecked by an invading Turkish army and his capital wasted; on the contrary, he hopes to make money from it, and his restless energies find a new and profitable outlet in that direction. My impression is that peace rests on a much firmer basis than it did five years ago, and that the Ottoman government has not been slow to learn the lessons of the last war—if only the Vāli of Damascus could have known how favourable an opinion his recent measures would force on the mind of the intriguing Englishwoman, he might have spared his telegraph clerks several hours' work.

A GROUP OF DRUZES

There could scarcely have been a better example of the freedom with which the Druzes control their own affairs than was offered by an incident that took place on the very evening of my arrival. It has already been intimated on the authority of Fendi that the relations between the Mountain and the Desert were fraught with the usual possibilities of martial incident, and we had not spent an afternoon in Ṣalkhad without discovering that the great raid that had occurred some months previously was the topic that chiefly interested Naṣīb and his brother. Not that they spoke of it in their conversations with me, but they listened eagerly when we told of the raid on the Ḥassaniyyeh and the part the Ṣukhūr had played in it, and they drew from us all we knew or conjectured as to the present camping grounds of the latter tribe, how far the raiders had come, and in which direction retreated. The muleteers overheard men whispering at the street corners, and their whispers were of warlike preparations; the groups round Mikhāīl's fire, ever a centre of social activity, spoke of injuries that could not be allowed to pass unnoticed, and one of the many sons of Muḥammad's uncle had provided that famished Beyrouti with a lunch flavoured with dark hints of a league between the Wādi Sirḥan and the Beni Ṣakhr which must be nipped in the bud ere it had assumed alarming proportions. The wave of the ghazu can hardly reach as far as Ṣalkhad itself, but the harm is done long before it touches that point, especially in the winter when every four-footed creature, except the mare necessary for riding, is far away in the southern plain.

My camp was pitched in a field outside the town at the eastern foot of the castle hill. The slopes to the north were deep in snow up to the ruined walls of the fortress, and even where we lay there were a few detached snowdrifts glittering under the full moon. I had just finished dinner, and was debating whether it were too cold to write my diary, when a sound of savage singing broke upon the night, and from the topmost walls of the castle a great flame leapt up into the sky. It was a beacon kindled to tell the news of the coming raid to the many Druze villages scattered over the plain below, and the song was a call to arms. There was a Druze zaptieh sitting by my camp fire; he jumped up and gazed first at me and then at the red blaze above us. I said:

FROM ṢALKHAD CASTLE, LOOKING SOUTH-EAST

"Is there permission to my going up?"

He answered: "There is no refusal. Honour us."

We climbed together over the half frozen mud, and by the snowy northern side of the volcano, edged our way in the darkness round the castle walls where the lava ashes gave beneath our feet, and came out into the full moonlight upon the wildest scene that eyes could see. A crowd of Druzes, young men and boys, stood at the edge of the moat on a narrow shoulder of the hill. They were all armed with swords and knives and they were shouting phrase by phrase a terrible song. Each line of it was repeated twenty times or more until it seemed to the listener that it had been bitten, as an acid bites the brass, onto the intimate recesses of the mind.

"Upon them, upon them! oh Lord our God! that the foe may fall in swathes before our swords!
Upon them, upon them! that our spears may drink at their hearts!
Let the babe leave his mother's breast!
Let the young man arise and be gone!
Upon them, upon them! oh Lord our God! that our swords may drink at their hearts. . . ."

So they sang, and it was as though the fury of their anger would never end, as though the castle walls would never cease from echoing their interminable rage and the night never again know silence, when suddenly the chant stopped and the singers drew apart and formed themselves into a circle, every man holding his neighbours by the hand. Into the circle stepped three young Druzes with bare swords, and strode round the ring of eager boys that enclosed them. Before each in turn they stopped and shook their swords and cried:

"Are you a good man? Are you a true man?"

And each one answered with a shout:

"Ha! ha!"

The moonlight fell on the dark faces and glittered on the quivering blades, the thrill of martial ardour passed from hand to clasped hand, and earth cried to heaven: War! red war!

And then one of the three saw me standing in the circle, and strode up and raised his sword above his head, as though nation saluted nation.

"Lady!" he said, "the English and the Druze are one."

I said: "Thank God! we, too, are a fighting race."

Indeed, at that moment there seemed no finer thing than to go out and kill your enemy.

And when this swearing in of warriors was over, we ran down the hill under the moon, still holding hands, and I, seeing that some were only children not yet full grown, said to the companion whose hand chance had put in mine:

"Do all these go out with you?"

He answered: "By God! not all. The ungrown boys must stay at home and pray to God that their day may soon come."

When they reached the entrance of the town, the Druzes leapt on to a flat house roof, and took up their devilish song. The fire had burnt out on the castle walls, the night struck suddenly cold, and I began to doubt whether if Milḥēm and the Vāli of Damascus could see me taking part in a demonstration against the Ṣukhur they would believe in the innocence of my journey; so I turned away into the shadow and ran down to my tents and became a European again, bent on peaceful pursuits and unacquainted with the naked primitive passions of mankind.

We had certain inquiries to make concerning our journey, and stores to lay in before we set out for the eastern side of the Mountain, where there are no big villages, and therefore we spent two days at Ṣalkhad. The great difficulty of the commissariat is barley for the animals. There had been enough for our needs at Umm er Rummān, but there was none at Ṣalkhad; it is always to be got at Sweida, which is the chief post of the Turkish government, but that was far away across the hills, and we decided to send down to Imtein, the path thither being bare of snow. It is worth recording that in the winter, when all the flocks are several hours away in the plain, it is impossible to buy a sheep in the Mountain, and the traveller has to make shift with such scraggy chickens as he may find. The want of foresight which had left our larder so ill-furnished affected Mikhāil considerably, for he prided himself on the roasting of a leg of mutton, and he asked me how it was that all the books I had with me had not hinted at the absence of the animal that could supply that delicacy. I answered that the writers of these works seemed to have been more concerned with Roman remains than with such weighty matters as roasts and stews, whereat he said firmly:

"When your Excellency writes a book, you will not say: Here there is a beautiful church and a great castle.' The

ḲREYEH

gentry can see that for themselves. But you shall say: 'In this village there are no hens.' Then they will know from the beginning what sort of country it is."

The first day of my visit I spent with Nasīb, watching him give orders for the grinding of the corn needed for the coming military expedition (to which we sedulously avoided any allusion), photographing him and the notables of his village, and lunching with him in his maḳ'ad on gritty brown-paper-like bread and dibs, a kind of treacle made from boiled grape juice, and a particularly nasty sort of soup of sour milk with scraps of fat mixed in it—*kirk* the Druzes call it and hold it in an unwarrantable esteem. In the afternoon Nasīb was riding some ten miles to the south, to settle a dispute that had arisen between two of his villages, and he invited me to accompany him; but I thought that there were probably other matters on hand, in which it might be awkward if a stranger were to assist, and I compromised by agreeing to go with him for an hour and turn aside to visit a shrine on top of a tell, the Weli of El Khuḍr, who is no other than our St. George. Nasīb rode out in style with twenty armed men by his side, himself arrayed in a long mantle of dark blue cloth embroidered in black, with a pale blue handkerchief tucked into the folds of the white turban that encircled his tarbūsh. The cavalcade looked very gallant, each man wrapped in a cloak and carrying his rifle across his knees. These rifles were handed to me one by one that I might read the lettering on them. They were of many different dates and origins, some antiquated pieces stolen from Turkish soldiers, the most French and fairly modern, while a few came from Egypt and were marked with V.R. and the broad arrow. Nasīb rode with me for a time and catechised me on my social status, whether I would ride at home with the King of England, and what was the extent of my father's wealth. His curiosity was not entirely without a motive; the Druzes are always hoping to find some very rich European whose sympathies they could engage, and who would finance and arm them if another war were to break out with the Sultan; but so contemptuous was he of the modest competence which my replies revealed, that I was roused to ask subsequently, by methods more tactful than those of Nasīb, what was wealth in the Mountain. The answer was that the richest of the Ṭurshān, Ḥamūd of Sweida, had an income of about 5000 napoleons. Nasīb himself was not so well off. He had some 1000 napoleons yearly. Probably it comes to him mainly in kind; all revenues are derived from land, and vary considerably with the fortunes of the agricultural year. The figures given me were, I should think, liberal, and depended on a reckoning according with the best harvest rather than with the mean.

Presently Nasīb fell behind and engaged in a whispered conversation with an old man who was his chief adviser, while the others crowded round me and told me tales of the desert and of great ruins to the south, which they were prepared to show me if I would stay with them. At the foot of the tell we met a group of horsemen waiting to impart to Nasīb some important news about the Arabs. Mikhāil and I stood aside, having seen our host look doubtfully at us out of the corners of his eyes. That the tidings were not good was all we heard, and no one could have learnt even that from Nasīb's crafty unmoved face and eyes concealed beneath

A DRUZE PLOUGHBOY

the lids as if he wished to make sure that they should not reveal a single flash of his thoughts. Here we left him, to his evident relief, and rode up the tell. Now there is never a prominent hill in the Jebel Druze but it bears a sanctuary on its summit, and the building is always one of those early monuments of the land that date back to the times before Druze or Turk came into it. What is their history? Were they erected to Nabatæan gods of rock and hill, to Drusāra and Allāt and the pantheon of the Semitic inscriptions whom the desert worshipped with sacrifice at the Ka'abah and on many a solitary mound? If this be so the old divinities still bear sway under changed names, still smell the blood of goats and sheep sprinkled on the black doorposts of their dwellings, still hear the prayers of pilgrims carrying green boughs and swathes of flowers. As at the Weli of El Khuḍr, there is always in the interior of the sanctuary an erection like a sarcophagus, covered with shreds of coloured rags, and when you lift the rags and peer beneath you find some queer block of tufa, worn smooth with libations and own brother to the Black Stone at Mecca. Near at hand there is a stone basin for water—the water was iced over that day, and the snow had drifted in through the stone doors and was melting through the roof, so that it lay in muddy pools on the floor.

The next day was exceedingly cold, with a leaden sky and a bitter wind, the forerunner of snow. Milḥēm Iliān came down to invite me to lodge with him, but I refused, fearing that I should feel the temperature of my tent too icy after his heated room. He stayed some time and I took the opportunity of discussing with him my plan of riding out into the Ṣafa, the volcanic waste east of the Jebel Druze. He was not at all encouraging, indeed he thought the project impossible under existing conditions, for it seemed that the Ghiāth, the tribe that inhabits the Ṣafa, were up in arms against the Government. They had waylaid and robbed the desert post that goes between Damascus and Baghdad, and were expecting retribution at the hands of the Vāli. If therefore a small escort of zaptiehs were to be sent in with me they would assuredly be cut to pieces. Milḥēm agreed, however, that it might be possible to go in alone with the Druzes though anything short of an army of soldiers would be useless, and he promised to give me a letter to Muḥammad en Naṣṣār, Sheikh of Ṣāleh, whom he described as a good friend of his and a man of influence and judgment. The Ghiāth are in the same position with regard to the Druzes as are the Jebeliyyeh; they cannot afford not to be on good terms with the Mountain, since they are dependent on the high pasturages during the summer.

Towards sunset I returned Milḥēm's visit. His room was full of people, including Nasīb newly returned from his expedition. They made me tell them of my recent experiences in the desert, and I found that all my friends were counted as foes by the Druzes and that they have no allies save the Ghiāth and the Jebeliyyeh—the Sherarāt, the Da'ja, the Beni Ḥassan, there was a score of blood against them all.

BOṢRA ESKI SHĀM

In the desert the word *gōm*, foe, is second to none save only that of *ḍaif*, guest, but in the Mountain it comes easily first. I said:

"Oh Nasīb, the Druzes are like those of whom Kureyt ibn Uneif sang when he said: 'A people who when evil bares its teeth against them, fly out to meet it in companies or alone.'"

The sheikh's subtle countenance relaxed for a second, but the talk was drifting too near dangerous subjects, and he rose shortly afterwards and took his leave. His place was filled by new comers (Milḥēm's coffee-pots must be kept boiling from dawn till late at night), and presently one entered whom they all rose to salute. He was a Kurdish Agha, a fine old man with a white moustache and a clean-shaven chin, who comes down from Damascus from time to time on some business of his own. Milḥēm is a native of Damascus, and had much to ask and hear; the talk left desert topics and swung round to town dwellers and their ways and views.

"Look you, your Excellencies," said a man who was making coffee over the brazier, "there is no religion in the towns as there is in country places."

"Yes," pursued Milḥēm—

"May God make it Yes upon you!" ejaculated the Kurd.

"May God requite you, oh Agha! You may find men in the Great Mosque at Damascus at the Friday prayers and a few perhaps at Jerusalem, but in Beyrout and in Smyrna the mosques are empty and the churches are empty. There is no religion any more."

"My friends," said the Agha, "I will tell you the reason. In the country men are poor and they want much. Of whom should they ask it but of God? There is none other that is compassionate to the poor save He alone. But in the towns they are rich, they have got all they desire, and why should they pray to God if they want nothing? The lady laughs—is it not so among her own people?"

I confessed that there was very little difference in this matter between Europe and Asia and presently left the party to pursue their coffee drinking and their conversation without me.

Late at night some one came knocking at my tent and a woman's voice cried to me:

"Lady, lady! a mother's heart (are not the English merciful?) listen to the sorrow of a mother's heart and take this letter to my son!"

I asked the unseen suppliant where her son was to be found.

"In Tripoli, in Tripoli of the West. He is a soldier and an exile, who came not back with the others after the war. Take this letter, and send it by a sure hand from Damascus, for there is no certainty in the posts of Ṣalkhad."

I unfastened the tent and took the letter, she crying the while:

"The wife of Nasīb told me that you were generous. A mother's heart, you understand, a mother's heart that mourns!"

So she departed weeping, and I sent the mysterious letter by the English post from Beyrout, but whether it ever reached Tripoli of the West and the Druze exile we shall not know.

The Ḳāimaḳām came out to see us off next morning and provided us with a Druze zaptieh to show us the way to Ṣāleh. The wind was searchingly cold, and the snow was reported to lie very deep on the hills, for which reason we took the lower road by Ormān, a village memorable as the scene of the outbreak of the last war. Milḥēm had entrusted my guide, Yūsef, with the mail that had just come in to Ṣalkhad; it consisted of one letter only, and that was for a Christian, an inhabitant of Ormān, whom we met outside the village. It was from Massachusetts, from one of his three sons who had emigrated to America and were all doing well, praise be to God! They had sent him thirty liras between them the year before: he bubbled over with joyful pride as we handed him the letter containing fresh news of them. At Ormān the road turned upwards—I continue to call it a road for want of a name bad enough for it. It is part of the Druze system of defence that there shall be no track in the Mountain wide enough for two to go abreast or smooth enough to admit of any pace beyond a stumbling walk, and it is the part that is the most successfully carried out. We were soon in snow, half melted, half frozen, concealing the holes in the path but not firm enough to prevent the animals from breaking through into them.

Occasionally there were deep drifts on which the mules embarked with the utmost confidence only to fall midway and scatter their packs, while the horses plunged and reared till they almost unseated us. Mikhāil, who was no rider, bit the slush several times. The makers of the Palestine Exploration map have allowed their fancy to play freely over the eastern slopes of the Jebel Druze. Hills have hopped along for miles, and villages have crossed ravines and settled themselves on the opposite banks, as, for instance, Abu Zreik, which stands on the left bank of the Wādi Rājil, though the map places it on the right. At the time it all seemed to fit in with the general malevolence of that day's journey, and our misery culminated when we entered on an interminable snow field swept by a blizzard of cutting sleet. At the dim end of it, quite unapproachably far away, we could just see through the sleet the slopes on which Ṣāleh stands, but as we plodded on mile after mile (it was useless to attempt to ride on our stumbling animals and far too cold besides) we gradually came nearer, and having travelled seven hours to accomplish a four hours' march, we splashed and waded late in the afternoon though the mounds of slush and pools of water that did duty as streets. There was not a dry place in all the village,

THE VILLAGE GATEWAY, ḤABRĀN

and the snow was falling heavily; clearly there was nothing to be done but to beat at the door of Muḥammad en Naṣṣār, who has an honoured reputation for hospitality, and I made the best of my way up steps sheeted with ice to his maḳ'ad.

If Providence owed us any compensation for the discomforts of the day, it paid us, or at least it paid me, full measure and running over, by the enchanting evening that I spent in the sheikh's house. Muḥammad en Naṣṣār is a man full of years and wisdom who has lived to see a large family of sons and nephews grow up round him, and to train their quick wits by his own courteous and gracious example. All the Druzes are essentially gentlefolk; but the house of the sheikhs of Ṣāleh could not be outdone in good breeding, natural and acquired, by the noblest of the aristocratic races, Persian or Rajputs, or any others distinguished beyond their fellows. Milḥēm's letter was quite unnecessary to ensure me a welcome; it was enough that I was cold and hungry and an Englishwoman. The fire in the iron stove was kindled, my wet outer garments taken from me, cushions and carpets spread on the divans under the sheikh's directions, and all the band of his male relations, direct and collateral, dropped in to enliven the evening. We began well. I knew that Oppenheim had taken his escort from Ṣāleh when he went into the Ṣafa, and I happened to have his book with me—how often had I regretted that a wise instinct had not directed my choice towards Dussaud's two admirable volumes, rather than to Oppenheim's ponderous work, packed with information that was of little use on the present journey! The great merit of the book lies in the illustrations, and fortunately there was among them a portrait of Muḥammad en Naṣṣār with his two youngest children. Having abstracted Kiepert's maps, I was so generous as to present the tome to one of the family who had accompanied the learned German upon his expedition. It has remained at Ṣāleh to be a joy and a glory to the sheikhs, who will look at the pictures and make no attempt to grapple with the text, and the hole in my bookshelves is well filled by the memory of their pleasure.

We talked without ceasing during the whole evening, with a brief interval when an excellent dinner was brought in. The old sheikh, Yūsef the zaptieh, and I partook of it together, and the eldest of the nephews and cousins finished up the ample remains. The topic that interested them most at Ṣāleh was the Japanese War—indeed it was in that direction that conversation invariably turned in the Mountain, the reason being that the Druzes believe the Japanese to belong to their own race. The line of argument which has

A DRUZE MAK'AD, ḤABRĀN

led them to this astonishing conclusion is simple. The secret doctrines of their faith hold out hopes that some day an army of Druzes will burst out of the furthest limits of Asia and conquer the world. The Japanese had shown indomitable courage, the Druzes also are brave; the Japanese had been victorious, the Druzes of prophecy will be unconquerable: therefore the two are one and the same. The sympathy of every one, whether in Syria or in Asia Minor, is on the side of the Japanese, with the single exception of the members of the Orthodox Church, who look on Russia as their protector. It seems natural that the Ottoman government should rejoice to witness the discomfiture of their secular foes, but it is more difficult to account for the pleasure of Arab, Druze (apart from the secret hope of the Druzes above mentioned), and Kurd, between whom and the Turk there is no love lost. These races are not wont to be gratified by the overthrow of the Sultan's enemies, a class to which they themselves generally belong. At bottom there is no doubt a certain *Schadenfreude*, and the natural impulse to favour the little man against the big bully, and behind all there is that curious link which is so difficult to classify except by the name of a continent, and the war appeals to the Asiatic because it is against the European. However eagerly you may protest that the Russians cannot be considered as a type of European civilisation, however profoundly you may be convinced that the Japanese show as few common characteristics with Turk or Druze as they show with South Sea Islander or Esquimaux, East calls to East, and the voice wakes echoes from the China Seas to the Mediterranean.

We talked also of the Turk. Muḥammad had been one of the many sheikhs who were sent into exile after the Druze war; he had visited Constantinople, and his experiences embraced Asia Minor also, so that he was competent to hold an opinion on Turkish characteristics. In a blind fashion, the fashion in which the Turk conducts most of his affairs, the wholesale carrying off of the Druze sheikhs and their enforced sojourn for two or three years in distant cities of the Empire, has attained an end for which far-sighted statesmanship might have laboured in vain. Men who would otherwise never have travelled fifty miles from their own village have been taught perforce some knowledge of the world; they have returned to exercise a semi-independence almost as they did before, but their minds have received, however reluctantly, the impression of the wide extent of the Sultan's dominions, the infinite number of his resources, and the comparative unimportance of Druze revolts in an empire which yet survives though it is familiar with every form of civil strife. Muḥammad had been so completely convinced that there was a world beyond the limits of the Mountain that he had attempted to push two of his six sons out into it by putting them into a Government office in Damascus. He had failed because, even with his maxims in their ears, the boys were too headstrong. Some youthful neglect of duty, followed by a sharp rebuke from their superior, had sent them hurrying back to the village where they could be independent sheikhs, idle and respected. Muḥammad took in a weekly sheet published in Damascus, and the whole family followed with the keenest interest such news of foreign politics, of English politics in particular, as escaped the censor's pencil. Important events sometimes eluded their notice—or that of the editor—for my hosts asked after Lord Salisbury and were deeply grieved to hear he had been dead some years. The other name they knew, besides Lord Cromer's, which is known always and everywhere, was that of Mr. Chamberlain, and thus there started in the maḳ'ad at Ṣāleh an animated debate on the fiscal question, lavishly illustrated on my part with examples drawn from the Turkish gumruk, the Custom House. It may be that my arguments were less exposed to contradiction than those which most free traders are in a position to use, for the whole of Ṣāleh rejected the doctrines of protection and retaliation (there was no half-way-house here) with unanimity.

There was only one point which was not settled with perfect satisfaction to all, and that was my journey to the Ṣafa. I have a shrewd suspicion that Milḥēm's letter, which had been handed to me sealed, so that I had not been able to read it, was of the nature of that given by Prætus to Bellerophon when he sent him to the King of Lycia, and that if Muḥammad was not commanded to execute the bearer on arrival, he was strongly recommended to discourage her project. At any rate, he was of opinion that the expedition could not be accomplished unless I would take at least twenty Druzes as escort, which would have involved so much preparation and expense that I was obliged to abandon the idea,

At ten o'clock I was asked at what hour I wished to sleep. and, to the evident chagrin of those members of the company who had not been riding all day in the snow, I replied that the time had come. The sons and nephews took their departure, wadded quilts were brought in and piled into three beds one on each of the three sides of the immense divan, the sheikh, Yūsef and I tucked ourselves up, and I knew no more till I woke in the sharp frost of the early dawn. I got up and went out into the fresh air. Ṣāleh was fast asleep in the snow; even the little stream that tumbled in and out of a

Roman fountain in the middle of the village was sleeping under a thick coat of ice. In the clear cold silence I watched the eastern sky redden and fade and the sun send a long shaft of light over the snow field through which we had toiled the day before. I put up a short thanksgiving appropriate to fine weather, roused the muleteers and the mules from their common resting place under the dark vaults of the khān, ate the breakfast which Muḥammad en Naṣṣār provided, and took a prolonged and most grateful farewell of my host and his family. No better night's rest and no more agreeable company can have fallen to the lot of any wanderer by plain and hill than were accorded to me at Ṣāleh.

LINTEL, EL KHURBEH

CHAPTER VI

My objective that day was the village of Umm Ruweik on the eastern edge of the Druze hills. Remembering the vagaries of the map, I took with me one of Muḥammad en Naṣṣār's nephews as a guide, Fāiz was his name, and he was brother to Ghishghāsh, the Sheikh of Umm Ruweik. I had singled him out the night before as being the pleasantest member of the pleasant circle in the maḳ'ad, and in a four days' acquaintance there was never an incident that caused me to regret my choice. He was a man with features all out of drawing, his nose was crooked, his mouth was crooked, you would not have staked anything upon the straight setting of his eyes; his manner was particularly gentle and obliging, his conversation intelligent, and he was full of good counsel and resource. We had not ridden very far along the lip of the hills, I gazing at the eastern plain as at a Promised Land that my feet would never tread, before Fāiz began to develop a plan for leaving the mules and tents behind at Umm Ruweik and making a dash across the Ṣafa to the Ruḥbeh, where lay the great ruin of which the accounts had fired my imagination. In a moment the world changed colour, and Success shone from the blue sky and hung in golden mists on that plain which had suddenly become accessible.

Our path fell rapidly from Ṣāleh, and in half an hour we were out of the snow and ice that had plagued us for the last day and night; half an hour later when we reached the Wādi Buṣān, where the swift waters turned a mill wheel, we had left the winter country behind. Ṣāneh, the village on the north side of the Wādi Buṣān, looked a flourishing place and contained some good specimens of Ḥaurān architecture —I remember in particular a fine architrave carved with a double scroll of grapes and vine leaves that fell on either side of a vase occupying the centre of the stone. It was at Ṣãneh that we came onto the very edge of the plateau and saw the great plain of the Ṣafa spread out like a sea beneath us. The strange feature of it was that its surface was as black as a black tent roof, owing to the sheets of lava and volcanic stone that were spread over it. At places there were patches of yellow, which I afterwards discovered to be the earth on which

THE WALLS OF KANAWĀT

the lumps of tufa lay revealed by their occasional absence, and these the Arabs call the Beiḍa, the White Land, in contradistinction to the Ḥarra, the Burnt Land of lava and tufa. In the Ṣafa the White Land is almost as arid as the Burnt, though generally the word Beiḍa means arable, for I heard Fāiz shout to the muleteers: "Come off the Beiḍa!" when the mules had strayed into a field of winter wheat. The literary word for desert bears a puzzling resemblance to this other, as for instance in Mutanabbi's verse.

"Al lail w'al khail w'al beida ta'rafuni:"
Night and my steed and the desert know me—
And the lance thrust and battle, and parchment and the pen."

The Ṣafa ran out to a dark mass of volcanoes, lying almost due north and south, but we were so high above them that their elevation was not perceptible. Beyond them again we could see a wide stretch of Beiḍa which was the Ruḥbel

ḲANAWĀT, THE BASILICA

plain. To the east and south on the immensely distant horizon a few little volcanic cones marked the end of the Ḥaurān outcrop of lava and the beginning of the Ḥamād, the waterless desert that reaches to Baghdad. To the north were the hills round Dmer, and still further north the other range bounding the valley ten miles wide that leads to Palmyra, and these ran back to the slopes of Anti-Libanus, snow-capped, standing above the desert road to Ḥomṣ. We turned east to Shibbekeh, a curious place built above a valley the northern bank of which is honeycombed with caves, and north to Sheikhly and Rāmeh on the southern brink of a very deep gully, the Wādi esh Shām, down which are the most easterly of the inhabited villages, Fedhāmeh and Ej Jeita. The settlements on this side of the Mountain have an air of great antiquity. The cave villages may have existed long before Nabatæan times; possibly they go back to the prehistoric uncertainties of King Og, or the people whom his name covered, when whole towns were quarried out underground, the most famous example being Dera'a in the Ḥaurān plain south of Mezērib. We left Mushennef to the west, not without regrets on my part that I had not time to revisit it, for mirrored in its great tank is one of the most charming of all the temples of the Jebel Druze, not excepting the magnificent monuments of Ḳanawāt. El Ajlāt, north of the Wādi esh Shām, is perched on top of a tell high enough to touch the February snow line, and another valley leads down from it to the Ṣafa—I heard of a ruin and an inscription in its lower course but did not visit them We got to Umm Ruweik about four o'clock, and pitched tents on the edge of the mountain shelf, where I could see through my open tent door the whole extent of the Ṣafa.

Sheikh Ghishghāsh was all smiles. Certainly I could ride out to the Ruḥbeh if I would take him and his son Aḥmed and Fāiz with me. He scoffed at the idea of a larger escort. By the Face of the Truth, the Ghiāth were his servants and his bondmen, they would entertain us as the noble should be entertained and provide us with luxurious lodgings. I dined with Ghishghāsh (he would take no refusal), and concluded that he was an easy tempered, boastful, and foolish man, extremely talkative, though all that he said was not worth one of Fāiz's sentences. Fāiz fell into comparative silence in his company, and Aḥmed too said little, but that little was sensible and worth hearing. Ghishghāsh told great tales of the Ṣafa and of what it contained, the upshot of which was that beyond the ruins already known there was nothing till you travelled a day's journey east of the Ruḥbeh, but that there you came to a quarry and a ruined castle like the famous White Ruin of the Ruḥbeh which we were going to see, but smaller and less well preserved. And beyond that stretched the Ḥamād, with no dwellings in it and no rujm—even the bravest of the Arabs were forced to desert it in the summer owing to the total lack of water. My heart went out to the mysterious castle east of the Ruḥbeh, unvisited, I believe, by any traveller; but it was too distant a journey to be accomplished on the spur of the moment without preparation. "When you next return, oh lady——." Yes, when I return. But I shall not on a future occasion rely on the luxurious entertainment of the Ghiāth.

After consultation I decided that Mikhāil and Ḥabīb should accompany us, the latter at his special request. He would ride his best mule, he said, and she could keep pace with any mare and carry besides the rugs and the five chickens which we took with us to supplement the hospitality of the Ghiāth. I had a fur coat strapped behind my saddle and, as usual, a camera and a note-book in my saddle-bags. We rode down the steep slopes of the hills for an hour, three other Druze horsemen joining us as we went. I presently discovered that the sheikhs had added them to the stipulated escort, but I made no comment. One of the three was a relative of Ghishghāsh, his name Khittāb; he had travelled with Oppenheim and proved to be an agreeable companion. We passed through the ploughland of Ghishghāsh's village and then down slopes almost barren, though they yielded enough pasturage for his flocks of sheep shepherded by Arabs, and at the foot of the hill we entered a shallow stony valley wherein was a tiny encampment surrounded by more herds that quarried their dinner among the boulders. After an hour of the valley, which wound between volcanic

ḲANAWĀT, DOORWAY OF THE BASILICA

H

rocks, we came out onto the wide desolation of the Ṣafa. It is almost, but not quite, flat. The surface breaks into low gentle billowings, just deep enough to shut out the landscape from the horseman in the depression, so that he may journey for an hour or more and see nothing but a sky-line of black stones a few feet above him on either side. The billowings have an ordered plan; they form continuous waterless valleys,

ḲANAWÂT, A TEMPLE

each one of which the Arabs know by a name. Valley and ridge alike are covered with blocks of tufa, varying from six inches across to two feet or more, and where there is any space between them you can perceive the hard yellow soil, the colour of sea sand, on which they lie. An extremely scanty scrub pushes its way between the stones, ḥamad and shīḥ and ḥajeineh, and here and there a tiny geranium, the starry garlic and the leaves of the tulip, but generally there is no room even for the slenderest plants, so closely do the stones lie together. They are black, smooth and edgeless, as though they had been waterworn; when the sun shines the air dazzles above them as it dazzles above a sheet of molten metal, and in the summer the comparison must hold good in other respects, for the pitiless heat is said to be almost unendurable. It would be difficult to cross the Ṣafa if it were not for the innumerable minute paths that intersect it. At first the rider is not aware of them, so small and faint they are, but presently as he begins to wonder why there is always just enough space before him for his horse to step in, he realises that he is following a road. Hundreds of generations of passing feet have pushed aside the tufa blocks ever so little and made it possible to travel through that wilderness of stones.

We rode by the depression called the Ghadīr el Gharz, and at the end of two hours we met one in rags, whose name was Heart of God. He was extremely glad to see us, was Heart of God, having been a friend of the family for years (at least eighty years I should judge), and extremely surprised when he discovered me in the cavalcade. There his surprise ceased, for when he heard I was English it conveyed nothing further to him, his mind being unburdened with the names and genealogies of the foreigner. He told us there was water close at hand and that Arab tents were not more than two hours away, and bade Ghishghāsh go in peace, and might there be peace also upon the stranger with him. In the matter of the tents he lied, did Heart of God, or we misunderstood him; but we found the water, a muddy pool, and lunched by it, sharing it with a herd of camels. Water in the Ṣafa there is none fit to drink according to European canons, and for that matter there is none in the Jebel Druze. There are no springs in the hills; the water supply is contained in open tanks, and the traveller may consider himself fortunate if he be not asked to drink a liquid in which he has seen the mules and camels wallowing. Under the most favourable conditions it is sure to be heavily laden with foreign ingredients which boiling will not remove, though it renders them comparatively innocuous. The tea made with this fluid has a body and a flavour of its own; it is the colour of muddy coffee and leaves a sediment at the bottom of the cup. Mikhāil carried an earthenware jar of boiled water for me from camp to camp, and having brought him to use this precaution by refusing to drink of the pools and tanks we might meet by the way, I had no difficulty in continuing the system in the Ṣafa. He and the Druzes and the muleteers drank what they found,

THE TEMPLE, MASHENNEF

whether in the Mountain or in the Ṣafa, and they did not appear to suffer from any ill effect. Probably the germs contained in their careless draughts were so numerous and so active that they had enough to do in destroying one another.

We rode on and on over all the stones in the world, and even Ghishghāsh fell silent or spoke only to wonder where the tents of the Ghiāth might be. Khittāb opined that when we reached the Ḳantarah, the Arch, we should catch sight of them, and I pricked up my ears at a name that seemed to imply some sort of construction. But the Ḳantarah was nothing more than a rise in the ground, a little higher than the rest and no less stony. There are many such; leading up to the crest of most of them is a track by which the Arabs creep on their stomachs to look out for foes, hidden themselves behind the small black pile that has been erected as a permanent bastion on the summit. In summer the Ṣafa is swept with raiders. Big tribes like the 'Anazeh ride through to deal a sudden blow at some enemy to the south or north, harrying the Ghiāth as they pass, and since there are exceedingly few places where water is to be found in the unparalleled heat of the stony waste, the raiders and such men of the Ghiāth as are still in the plain have no choice but to frequent at dusk the same muddy holes, and the days and nights of the Ghiāth are dogged in consequence by constant terror till the great tribes go east again to the Ḥamād. There was no sign of tents to be seen from the Ḳantarah, and it began to seem probable that we should spend a waterless night among the stones under the clear frosty sky, when about an hour before sunset Khittāb exclaimed that he could see the smoke of camp fires to the north-west. We rode a good way back, making a semicircle of our course, and got to the tents at nightfall after a journey of nine hours. With the goats and camels who were returning home after a laborious day's feeding we stumbled in over the stones, and very miserable the little encampment looked, though it had been so eagerly desired. A couple of hundred pounds would be a handsome price for all the worldly goods of all the Ghiāth, they have nothing but the black tents and a few camels and the coffee-pots, and if they had more it would be taken from them in a midsummer ghazu. They live by bread alone—shirāk the thin flaps that are like brown paper—and for the whole length of their days they wander among the stones in fear of their lives, save for the month or two when they come up to the Jebel Druze for the pasturage.

We scattered, being a large party, and Ghishghāsh, my servants and I went to the house of the sheikh, whose name was Understanding. His two sons, Muḥammad and Ḥamdān, lighted a fire of thorn and camel dung that smoked abominably, and we sat round and watched the coffee making. Muḥammad, being the eldest, officiated. He was skilful in the song of the pestle, and beat out a cheerful tattoo upon the mortar. His face was dark and thin and his white teeth shone when he smiled; he was dressed airily in dirty white cotton garments, a cotton kerchief fell from the camel's hair rope on his head down on to his bare breast, and he spoke in a guttural speech which was hard to follow. Our dinner was of shirāk and dibs; the Ghiāth are too poor to kill a sheep for their guest, even when he is a personage so important as Ghishghāsh. He, foolish man, was in his element. He preened himself and swelled with pride, combed out his long moustache before the admiring gaze of his hosts and talked without ceasing until far into the night, silly talk, thought I, who longed to be allowed to sleep. I had a rug to cover me and my saddle for a pillow, and I lay in a corner by the sāḥah, the division against the women's quarter, and at times I listened to a conversation which was not particularly edifying, and at times I cursed the acrid, pungent smoke. Towards the middle of the night I was awakened by the moon that shone with a frosty brilliance into the tent. The fire had burnt down and the smoke had blown out; the Arabs and the Druzes were lying asleep round the cold hearth; a couple of mares stood peacefully by the tent pole and gazed with wise eyes upon their masters within, and beyond them a camel lay chumping among the black stones. The strange and silent beauty of a scene as old as the world caught at the heart and spurred the fancy even after sleep had fallen upon it again.

Before dawn Mikhāil had succeeded in making me a cup

of tea over the fitful blaze of the thorns, and as the sun rose we got into the saddle, for we had far to go. "God's bright and intricate device" had clothed the black plain in exquisite loveliness. The level sun towards which we were riding cast a halo of gold round every stone, the eastern ranges of volcanoes stood in clear cut outline against the cloudless sky, and to the north-west the snows of Anti-Libanus and Hermon gleamed incredibly bright above the glittering blackness of the foreground. One of the Arabs was added to our party as a guide; 'Awāḍ was his name. He rode a camel, and from that point of vantage conversed with us in a raucous shout, as though to bridge the immense distance between rākib and fāris, a camel rider and one who rides a mare. We were all shivering as we set out in the chill dawn, but 'Awāḍ turned the matter into a jest by calling out from his camel: "Lady, lady! do you know why I am cold? It is because I have four wives in the house!" And the others laughed, for he had the reputation of being a bit of a Don Juan, and such funds as he possessed went to replenishing his harem rather than his wardrobe.

I think we must speedily have re-entered the Ghadīr el Gharz. After two hours' riding we crossed some rising ground to the south-west of the Tulūl es Ṣafa, the line of volcanoes, and cantered across a considerable stretch of stoneless yellow ground, Beiḍa, till we came to the southern end of the lava bed. The lava lay on our left hand like a horrible black nightmare sea, not so much frozen as curdled, as though some hideous terror had arrested the flow of it and petrified the lines of shrinking fear upon its surface. But it was long long ago that a mighty hand had lifted the Gorgon's head before the waves of the Tulūl es Ṣafa. Sun and frost and æons of time had splintered the original forms of the volcanoes, rent the lava beds, shattered the precipices and obliterated the features of the hills. One or two terebinths had found a foothold in the crevices, but when I passed they were still bare and grey and did nothing to destroy the general sense of lifelessness.

As we rode round these frontiers of death I became aware that we were following a track almost as old as the hills themselves, a little thread of human history leading us straight through that forbidding land. 'Awāḍ kept talking of a stone which he called El 'Ablā, a word that denotes a white rock visible from afar, but I was so much used to names signifying nothing that I paid no attention until he stopped his camel and shouted:

"Oh lady! here it is. By the Face of God, this is El 'Ablā."

It was no more nor less than a well stone. It bore the groove of the rope worn a couple of inches deep into it, and must have served a respectable time, since this black rock is extremely hard, but there was no modern well within miles of it. Close at hand was a big heap of stones and then another and another, two or three in every quarter of a mile, and when I looked closely I perceived that they were built, not thrown together. Some of them had been opened by Arabs seeking for treasure, and where the topmost layers had been thus removed a square shallow space lay revealed in the centre of the mound, carefully constructed of half-dressed blocks. 'Awāḍ said that as far as he knew nothing had ever been found in these places, whatever they might have contained formerly. Clearly the mounds were made to mark the line of that ancient road through the wilderness. 'Awāḍ stopped again a few hundred yards further at some black rocks almost flush with the ground, and they were like the open pages of a book in which all the races that had passed that way had written their names, in the queer script that the learned call Safaitic, in Greek, in Cufic, and in Arabic. Last of all the unlettered Bedouin had scrawled their tribe marks there.

"By Shuraik son of Naghafat son of Na'fīs (?) son of Nu'mān," so ran one of them; and another: "By Būkhālih son of Ṭhann son of An'am son of Rawāḳ son of Būkhālih He found the inscription of his uncle and he longed after him and . . . ." And there was another in a label which I did not copy sufficiently well to admit of its being deciphered with certainty. Probably it contains two names connected by "ibn," "son of." Above the names are seven straight lines which, according to Dussaud's ingenious suggestion, may represent the seven planets.* The Greek letters spelt the word Hanelos, which is John, a Semitic name written possibly by its owner in the foreign script that he had learnt while he served under the Roman eagles; the Cufic sentences were pious ejaculations calling down a blessing on the traveller who had paused to inscribe them. So each man according to his kind had left his record and departed into the mists of time, and beyond these scratches on the black rocks we know nothing of his race, nor of his history, nor of the errand that brought him into the inhospitable Ghadīr el Gharz. As I copied the phrases they seemed like the murmur of faint voices from out the limbo of the forgotten past, and Orpheus with his lute could not have charmed the rocks to speak more clearly of the generations of the dead. All the Ṣafa is full of these whisperings; shadows that are nothing but a name quiver in the quivering air above the stones, and call upon their God in divers tongues.

I copied in haste, for there was no time to lose that day. The Druzes stood round me impatiently, and 'Awāḍ shouted, "Yallah, yallah! ya sitt," which being interpreted means, "Hurry up!" We rode on to the eastern limit of the Ṣafa, turned the corner of the lava bed, and saw the yellow plain of the Ruḥbeh before us. I know, because I have observed it from the Jebel Druze, that it stretches for a great distance to the east; but, when we reached it, it seemed no wider than half a mile, and beyond it lay a wonderful lake of bluish misty water. The little volcanoes far away to the east rose like islands out of the sea, and were mirrored in the water at their feet; yet as we rode towards that inland flood, its shores retreated before us, for it was but a phantom sea whereat the phantom hosts of the Ṣafa may fitly assuage their thirst. Then on the brink of the lava hills we caught sight of a grey tower, and in the plain below it we saw a domed and whitewashed shrine, and these were the Khirbet el Beiḍa and the Mazār of Sheikh Serāk. Sheikh Serāk inherits his position as guardian

* Dussaud, "Mission Scientific," p. 64. The translation of the inscriptions I owe to the kindness of Dr. Littmann, who will include the original copies in his "Semitic Inscriptions."

of the Ruḥbeh from Zeus Saphathenos, who is in turn the direct heir to the god El, the earliest divinity of the Ṣafa. His business is to watch over the crops, which in good years the Arabs sow round his soul's dwelling place; he is respected by Moslem and by Druze alike, and he holds a well-attended yearly festival which had fallen about a fortnight before I came. The shrine itself is a building of the Haurān type, with

ḲAL'AT EL BEIḌA

a stone roof supported on transverse arches. Over the doors there is a carved lintel taken from the ruins of the White Castle.

But I could scarcely stay while my men assembled here, so eager was I to see the Ḳal'at el Beiḍa—Khirbeh or Ḳal'ah, ruin or castle, the Arabs call it either indifferently. I left the Druzes to pay such respects as were due to Zeus Saphathenos or whoever he might be, and cantered off to the edge of the lava plateau. A deep ditch lay before the lava, so full of water that I had to cross it by a little bridge of planks; Ḥabīb was there watering his mule, that admirable mule which walked as fast as the mares, and, entrusting my horse to him, I hastened on over the broken lava and into the fortress court. There were one or two Arabs sauntering through it, but they paid as little attention to me as I did to them. This was it, the famous citadel that guards a dead land from an unpeopled, the Ṣafa from the Ḥamād. Grey white on the black platform rose the walls of smoothly dressed stones, the ghostly stronghold of a world of ghosts. Whose hands reared it, whose art fashioned the flowing scrolls on door-post and lintel, whose eyes kept vigil from the tower, cannot yet be decided with any certainty. Hanelos and Shuraik and Būkhālih may have looked for it as they rounded the corner of the Wādi el Gharz, and perhaps the god El took it under his protection, and perhaps the prayers of the watchman were turned to some distant temple, and offered to the deities of Greece and Rome. A thousand unanswered, unanswerable, questions spring to your mind as you cross the threshold.

ḲAL'AT EL BEIḌA

De Vogüé and Oppenheim and Dussaud have described the Khirbet el Beiḍa, and any one who cares to read their words may know that it is a square enclosure with a round tower at each corner, a round bastion between the towers and a rectangular keep against the south wall; that its doorways are carved with wonderful flowing patterns, scrolls and leaves and flowers, with animals striding through them; and that it is probably an outlying fortress of Rome, built between the second and fourth centuries. The fact remains that we are not certain of its origin, any more than we are certain of the origin of the ruins near it at Jebel Sēs, or of Mshitta, or of any of the buildings in the western desert. There are resemblances between them all, and there are marked differences, just as there are resemblances between Ḳal'at el Beiḍa and the architecture of the Ḥaurān, and yet what stonecutter of the Mountain would have let his imagination so outstrip the classic rule as did the man who set the images of the animals of the desert about the doors of the White Castle? There is a breath of something that is strange to neighbouring art, a wilder, freer fancy, not so skilled as that which created the tracery of Mshitta, cruder, and probably older. It is all guess work; the desert may give up its secrets, the history of the Ṣafa and the Ruḥbeh may be pieced together from the lettered rocks, but much travel must be accomplished first and much excavation on the Syrian frontiers, in Hira perhaps, or in Yemen. I would only remark that the buildings at Ḳal'at el Beiḍa cannot as they stand belong to one and the same period. The keep is certainly a later work than the curtain walls of the fort. While these are built with mortar, like the Roman camp at Ḳasṭal and the fortress at Muwaḳḳar, the keep is of dry masonry resembling that which is universal in the Ḥaurān, and in its walls are set carved stones which were assuredly not executed for the positions they occupy. Even the decoration about the main door of the keep is of borrowed stones; the two superimposed carved blocks of the lintel do not fit each other, and neither fits the doorway. But the only conclusion I venture to draw is, that the two suggestions of origin that have been made by archæologists, the one that the place was a Roman camp, the other that it was the Ghassānid fortress, may both be true.

The edge of the lava plateau lies a few feet above the plain. Along this natural redoubt are other buildings besides the White Castle, but none of them are of the same architectural interest. Their walls are roughly made of squared tufa blocks laid dry, whereas the castle is of a grey stone, and part of it is constructed with mortar. The only building of any importance that I visited lay a little to the north and had been roofed after the Ḥaurān manner with stone slabs laid on transverse arches. At intervals along the lava bed there were small towers like sentry boxes guarding the approach to the castle, and these, too, were of dry masonry.

A couple of hours' halt was all that we could allow ourselves, for we had to be in sight of our encampment before the dusk closed in at the risk of passing the night in the open Ṣafa. So after devouring hastily the remains of the five chickens we had brought from Umm Ruweik, flavoured by stalks of wild onions that 'Awāḍ had found in the lava, we set off homewards. We just accomplished the ride of 4¾ hours in time, that is we saw the smoke of the camp fires before night fell, and got our direction thereby. A series of spaces cleared of stones led us to the camp. These open places are the marāḥ (tent marks) of the 'Anazeh, who used to camp in the Ṣafa before the Druzes established themselves in the Mountain over a hundred years ago. The marāḥ, therefore, have remained visible after at least a century, and will remain, probably, for many centuries more. There was a strong cold wind that evening, and the main wall of the tent had been shifted round to shelter us the better; but for all that we passed

KAL'AT EL BEIḌA, DOOR OF KEEP

a comfortless night, and the cold woke me several times to an uneasy sense of having fallen asleep on an ant hill. How the Arabs contrive to collect so many fleas among so few possessions is an insoluble mystery. There was hardly a suitable place for them to lodge in, except the tent walls themselves, and when those walls are taken down they must show skill and agility beyond the common wont of fleas in order to get themselves packed up and carried off to the next camping ground, but that they are equal to the task every one knows who has spent a night in a house of hair. After two nights with the Ghiāth our own tents seemed a paradise of luxury when we returned to them the next afternoon, and a bath the utmost height to which a Sybaritic life could attain, even when taken in a temperature some degrees below freezing point.

During our ride homewards an incident occurred which is worth recording, as it bears on Druze customs. The sect, as has been remarked before, is divided into initiated and uninitiated. To the stranger the main difference between the two is that the initiated abstain from the use of tobacco, and I had noticed in the evening I spent at Ṣāleh that none of Muḥammad en Naṣṣār's family smoked. I was therefore surprised when Fāiz, finding himself alone with Mikhāil and me, begged the former for a cigarette, and I apologised for having omitted to offer him one before, saying that I had understood smoking to be forbidden to him. Fāiz blinked his crooked eyes, and replied that it was as I had said, and that he would not have accepted a cigarette if another Druze had been in sight, but that since none of his co-religionists were present he felt himself at liberty to do as he pleased. He begged me, however, not to mention to his brother this lapse from virtue. That night in the maḳ'ad of Umm Ruweik the three sheikhs and I laid many plans for a further exploration of the Ṣafa, settled the number of camels I was to take with me, and even the presents which were to reward the escort at the end of the journey. Fāiz and Aḥmed and Khittāb shall certainly be of the expedition if the selecting of it lies in my hands.

Next morning at 8.30 we started on our three days' ride to

MOULDINGS FROM ḲALA'AT EL BEIDA AND FROM PALMYRA.
THE UPRIGHT BLOCK IS FROM ḲALA'AT EL BEIḌA

Damascus. Of Umm Ruweik I need only add that it took exactly four days to scrape together sufficient money among the inhabitants for the changing of a gold piece. We had brought a bag of silver and copper coins with us from Jerusalem, but when it was exhausted we had the utmost difficulty in paying our debts — this is also one of the Hints to Travellers that Mikhāil urged me to embody in the book I was to write. We rode by enchanting slopes, covered where the snow had melted with the sky-blue Iris Histrio, and spent an hour or two at Shakka, which was one of the principal scenes of de Vogüé's archæological work. The basilica which figures as almost perfect in his book is now fallen completely into ruin, only the façade remaining, but the Kaisarīeh still stands, and the monastery which he believes to be one of the oldest monastic buildings in existence. We rode by Ḥīt, an interesting village containing a fine pre-Arabic house in which the sheikh lives, and camped at Bathaníyyeh in a frost that sent me shivering to bed. It was here that a running stream was completely frozen. Next day I made a circuit to visit Ḥayāt, where there is a lovely Kalybeh, published by de Vogüé, and a castle, that I might fill up some gaps in my former journey and see what sort of buildings are to be found on the

A GATEWAY, SHAKKA

northern slopes of the mountain, if I could do no more. The old villages are rapidly filling up, and in a few years little trace of their monuments will remain. So we came down into the plain, joined the Lejā road from Shahbah to Damascus at Laḥīteh, and pursued our mules to Brāk, the furthest village of the Ḥaurān. There is a military post at Brāk held by a score of soldiers; just before we reached it we met a little Druze girl who cowered by the roadside and wept with fear at the sight of us. "I am a maid!" she cried, "I am a maid!" Her words threw an ominous shadow upon the Turkish *régime* under which we were now to find ourselves again. Almost opposite the fort we passed two Druzes returning from Damascus. They gave me a friendly greeting, and I said:

"Are you facing to the Mountain?"

They said: "By God! may God keep you!"

I said: "I come from thence—salute it for me," and they answered:

"May God salute you! go in peace!"

It is never without a pang that the traveller leaves the Druze country behind, and never without registering a vow to return to it as soon as may be.

Having passed under the protection of the Sultan, I found that my road next day lay across a really dangerous bit of country. The Circassians and Turks of Brāk (the Turks were charming people from the northern parts of Asia Minor) dissuaded me strongly from taking the short cut across the hills to Damascus, so strongly that I had almost abandoned the idea. They said the hills were infested by robbers and probably empty of Arab encampments at this time of year, so that the robbers had it all their own way. Fortunately next morning we heard of a company of soldiers who were said to be riding to Damascus across the hills, and the report encouraged us to take the same path. We never saw them, and I do not believe that they had any real existence; on the other hand, we did see some black tents which gave us confidence at the worst bit of the road, and the robbers must have been otherwise engaged for they did not appear. But I noted with interest, firstly, that desert life comes to within an hour or two of Damascus, a fact I had not been able to observe before when I went by the high road, and secondly that the Sultan's peace, if peace it can be called, ceases almost at the walls of the chief city of Syria. We crossed the Nahr el 'Awāj, which is the Pharpar, and reached soon after midday the Circassian village of Nejḥā, where I stopped to lunch under a few poplars, the first grove of trees I had seen

THE SHEIKH'S HOUSE, ḤAYĀT

since we left Salt. Whether you ride to Damascus by a short cut or by a high road, from the Ḥaurān or from Palmyra, it is always further away than any known place. Perhaps it is because the traveller is so eager to reach it, the great and splendid Arab city set in a girdle of fruit trees and filled with the murmur of running water. But if he have only patience there is no road that will not end at last; and we, too, at the last came to the edge of the apricot gardens and then to the Bawābet Ullah, the Gates of God, and so passed into the Meidān, the long quarter of shops and khāns stretching out like the handle to a great spoon, in the bowl of which lie the minarets and domes of the rich quarters. By four o'clock I was lodged in the Hotel Victoria, and had a month's post of letters and papers in my hands.

CHAPTER VII

WHEN I had come to Damascus five years before, my chief counsellor and friend—a friend whose death will be deplored by many a traveller in Syria—was Lütticke, head of the banking house of that name and honorary German consul. It was a chance remark of his that revealed to me the place that the town had and still has in Arab history. "I am persuaded," said he, "that in and about Damascus you may see the finest Arab population that can be found anywhere. They are the descendants of the original invaders who came up on the first great wave of the conquest, and they have kept their stock almost pure."

Above all other cities Damascus is the capital of the desert. The desert stretches up to its walls, the breath of it is blown in by every wind, the spirit of it comes through the eastern gates with every camel driver. In Damascus the sheikhs of the richer tribes have their town houses; you may meet Muḥammad of the Ḥaseneh or Bassān of the Beni Rashīd peacocking down the bazaars on a fine Friday, in embroidered cloaks and purple and silver kerchiefs fastened about their brows with camels' hair ropes bound with gold. They hold their heads high, these Lords of the Wilderness, striding through the holiday crowds, that part to give them passage, as if Damascus were their own town. And so it is, for it was the first capital of the Bedouin khalifs outside the Ḥejāz, and it holds and remembers the greatest Arab traditions. It was almost the first of world-renowned cities to fall before the irresistible chivalry of the desert which Muḥammad had called to arms and to which he had given purpose and a battle-cry, and it was the only one which remained as important under the rule of Islām as it had been under the empire of Rome. Mu'āwiyah made it his capital, and it continued to be the chief city of Islām until the fall of the house of Ummayah ninety years later. It was the last of Moslem capitals that ruled in accordance with desert traditions. Persian generals placed the Beni Abbās upon their throne in Mesopotamia, Persian and Turkish influences were dominant in Baghdad, and with them crept in the fatal habits of luxury which the desert had never known, nor the early khalifs who milked their own goats and divided the spoils of their victories among the Faithful. The very soil of Mesopotamia exhaled emanations fatal to virility. The ancient ghosts of Babylonian and Assyrian palace intrigue rose from their muddy graves, mighty in evil, to overthrow the soldier khalif, to strip him of his armour and to tie him hand and foot with silk and gold. Damascus had been innocent of them; Damascus, swept by the clean desert winds, had ruled the empire of the Prophet with some of the Spartan vigour of early days. She was not a parvenue like the capitals on the Tigris; she had seen kings and emperors within her walls, and learnt the difference between strength and weakness, and which path leads to dominion and which to slavery.

IN THE PALMYRENE DESERT

When I arrived I was greeted with the news that my journey in the Ḥaurān had considerably agitated the mind of his Excellency Nāzim Pasha, Vāli of Syria; indeed it was currently reported that this much exercised and delicately placed gentleman had been vexed beyond reason by my sudden appearance at Ṣalkhad and that he had retired to his bed when I had departed beyond the reach of Yūsef Effendi's eye, though some suggested that the real reason for his Excellency's sudden indisposition was a desire to avoid taking part in the memorial service to the Archduke Serge. Be that as it may, he sent me on the day of my arrival a polite message expressing his hope that he might have the pleasure of making my acquaintance.

I confess my principal feeling was one of penitence when I was ushered into the big new house that the Vāli has built for himself at the end of Ṣalaḥiyyeh, the suburb of Damascus that stretches along the foot of the bare hills to the north of the town. I had a great wish to apologise, or at any rate to prove to him that I was not to be regarded as a designing enemy. These sentiments were enhanced by the kindness with which he received me, and the respect with which he inspires those who come to know him. He is a man of a nervous temperament, always on the alert against the difficulties with which his vilayet is not slow to provide him, conscientious, and I should fancy honest, painfully anxious to reconcile interests that are as easy to combine as oil with vinegar, the corner of his eye fixed assiduously on his royal master who will take good care that so distinguished a personality as Nāzim Pasha shall be retained at a considerable distance from the shores of the Bosphorus. The Vāli has been eight years in Damascus, the usual term of office being five, and he has evidently made up his mind that in Damascus he will remain, if no ill luck befall him, for he has built himself a large house and planned a fine garden, the laying out of which distracts his mind, let us hope, from preoccupations that can seldom be pleasant. One of his safeguards is that he has been actively concerned with the construction of the Ḥejāz railway, in which the Sultan takes the deepest interest, and until it is completed or abandoned he is sufficiently useful to be kept at his post.* The bazaar, that is public opinion, does not think that it will be abandoned, in spite of the opposition of the Sherīf of Mecca and all his clan, who will never be convinced of the justice of the Sultan's claim to the khalifate of Islām nor willing to bring him into closer touch with the religious capitals. The bazaar backs the Sultan against the Sherīf and all other adversaries, sacred or profane. The wheels of the Turk grind slowly and often stop, but in the end they grind small, especially when the grist is Arab tribes rendered peculiarly brittle by their private jealousies and suspicions

* Since I wrote these sentences, a turn of the political wheel has brought him down, and he is now reduced to an unimportant post in the island of Rhodes.

THE GREAT MOSQUE AND THE ROOFS OF THE BAZAAR FROM THE FORT

and pretensions. Turkish policy is like that of which Ibn Kulthūm sang when he said:

When our mill is set down among a people they are as flour before our coming.
Our meal cloth is spread eastwards of Nejd and the grain is the whole tribe of Ḳuda'a.
Like guests you alighted at our door and we hastened our hospitality lest you should turn on us.
We welcomed you and hastened the welcoming: yea, before the dawn, and our mills grind small.

A CORN MARKET

Nāzim Pasha, though he has been eight years in Syria, talks no Arabic. We in Europe, who speak of Turkey as though it were a homogeneous empire, might as well when we speak of England intend the word to include India, the Shan States, Hongkong and Uganda. In the sense ot a land inhabited mainly by Turks there is not such a country as Turkey. The parts of his dominions where the Turk is in a majority are few; generally his position is that of an alien governing, with a handful of soldiers and an empty purse, a mixed collection of subjects hostile to him and to each other. He is not acquainted with their language, it is absurd to expect of him much sympathy for aspirations political and religious which are generally made known to him amid a salvo of musketry, and if the bullets happen to be directed, as they often are, by one unruly and unreasonable section of the vilayet at another equally unreasonable and unruly, he is hardly likely to feel much regret at the loss of life that may result. He himself, when he is let alone, has a strong sense of the comfort of law and order. Observe the internal arrangements of a Turkish village, and you shall see that the Turkish peasant knows how to lay down rules of conduct and how to obey them. I believe that the best of our own native local officials in Egypt are Turks who have brought to bear under the new *régime* the good sense and the natural instinct for government for which they had not much scope under the old. It is in the upper grades that the hierarchy of the Ottoman Empire has proved so defective, and the upper grades are filled with Greeks, Armenians, Syrians, and personages of various nationalities generally esteemed in the East (and not without reason) untrustworthy. The fact that such men as these should inevitably rise to the top, points to the reason of the Turk's failure. He cannot govern on wide lines, though he can organise a village community; above all he cannot govern on foreign lines, and unfortunately he is brought more and more into contact with foreign nations. Even his own subjects have caught the infection of progress. The Greeks and Armenians have become merchants and bankers, the Syrians merchants and landowners; they find themselves hampered at every turn by a government which will not realise that a wealthy nation is made up of wealthy subjects. And yet, for all his failure, there is no one who would obviously be fitted to take his place. For my immediate purpose I speak only of Syria, the province with which I am the most familiar. Of what value are the pan-Arabic associations and the inflammatory leaflets that they issue from foreign printing presses? The answer is easy: they are worth nothing at all. There is no nation of Arabs; the Syrian merchant is separated by a wider gulf from the Bedouin than he is from the Osmanli, the Syrian country is inhabited by Arabic speaking races all eager to be at each other's throats, and only prevented from fulfilling their natural desires by the ragged half fed soldier who draws at rare intervals the Sultan's pay. And this soldier, whether he be Kurd or Circassian or Arab from Damascus, is worth a good deal more than the hire he receives. Other armies may mutiny, but the Turkish army will stand true to the khalif; other armies may give way before suffering and privation and untended sickness, but that of the Sultan will go forward as long as it can stand, and fight as long as it has arms, and conquer as long as it has leaders. There is no more wonderful and pitiful sight than a Turkish regiment on the march: greybeards and half-fledged youths, ill-clad and often barefoot, pinched and worn—and indomitable. Let such as watch them salute them as they pass: in the days when war was an art rather than a science, of that stuff the conquerors of the world were made.

THE ḲUBBET EL KHAZNEH

But I have left the Governor of Syria waiting far too long. We talked, then, in French, a language with which he was imperfectly acquainted, and from time to time a Syrian gentleman helped him in Turkish over the stiles and pitfalls of the foreign tongue. The Syrian was a rich Maronite landowner of the Lebanon, who happened to be in good odour at Government House though he had but recently spent a year in prison. He had accompanied me upon my visit and was then and there appointed by the Vāli to be my cicerone in Damascus; Selīm Beg was his name. The talk was principally of archæology, I purposely insisting on my interest in that subject as compared with the politics of the Mountain and the Desert, to which we thus avoided any serious allusion. The Vāli was affability itself. He presented me with certain photographs of the priceless manuscripts of the Kubbet el Khazneh in the Great Mosque, now closed for ever to the public eye, and promised me the rest of the series. To that end a bowing personage took my English address and noted it carefully in a pocket book, and I need scarcely say that that was the last any one heard of the matter. Presently the Vāli announced that Madame Pasha and the children were waiting to see me, and I followed him upstairs into a sunny room with windows opening on to a balcony from which you could see all Damascus and its gardens and the hills beyond. There is only one Madame Pasha, and she is a pretty, sharp-featured Circassian, but there was another (gossip says the favourite) who died a year ago. The children were engaging. They recited French poems to me, their bright eyes quick to catch and to respond to every expression of approbation or amusement; they played tinkling polkas, sitting very upright on the music stool with their pig-tails hanging down their velvet backs. The Pasha stood in the window and beamed upon them, the Circassian wife smoked cigarettes and bowed whenever she caught my eye, a black slave boy at the door grinned from ear to ear as his masters and mistresses, who were also his school-mates and his play-fellows, accomplished their tasks. I came away with a delightful impression of pretty smiling manners and vivacious intelligence, and expressed my pleasure to the Pasha as we went down stairs.

"Ah!" said he politely, "if I could have them taught English! But what will you? we cannot get an Englishwoman to agree with our customs, and I have only the Greek lady whom you saw to teach them French."

I had indeed noticed the Greek woman, an underbred little person, whose bearing could not escape attention in the graceful company upstairs, but I was not slow to expatiate on the excellence of the French she spoke—may Heaven forgive me! The Pasha shook his head.

"If I could get an Englishwoman!" said he. Unfor-

THE TEKKIYYAH OF NAKSH PENDI

tunately I had no one to suggest for the post, nor would he have welcomed a suggestion.

Before I left, two distinguished personages arrived to have audience of the Vāli. The first was a man by complexion almost a negro, but with an unmistakable look of race and a sharp quick glance. He was the Amīr 'Abdullah Pasha, son of 'Abd ul Ḳādir, the great Algerian, by a negro slave. The second was Sheikh Ḥassan Nakshibendi, hereditary chief—pope, I had almost said—of an orthodox order of Islām famous in Damascus, where its principal Tekyah is situated. (Now a Tekyah is a religious institution for the housing of mendicant dervishes and other holy persons, something like a monastery, only that there is no vow of chastity imposed upon its members, who may have as many wives as they choose outside the Tekyah; Sheikh Ḥassan himself had the full complement of four.) All the wily ecclesiastic's astuteness shone from the countenance of this worthy. I do not know that his wits were especially remarkable, but his unscrupulousness must have supplemented any deficiencies, or his smile belied him. The meeting with these two accomplished my introduction to Damascus society. Both of them extended to me a warm invitation to visit them in their houses, the Tekyah or anywhere I would, and I accepted all, but I went to the Amīr 'Abdullah first.

GATE OF THE TEKYAH

Or rather, I went first to the house of his elder brother, the Amīr 'Ali Pasha, because it was there that 'Abd ul Ḳādir had lived, and there that he had sheltered, during the black days of the massacres in 1860, a thousand Christians. About his name there lingers a romantic association of courage and patriotism, crowned by a wise and honoured age full of authority and the power lent by wealth, for the 'Abd ul Ḳādir family own all the quarter in which they reside. The house, like any great Damascus house, made no show from the outside. We entered through a small door in a narrow winding street by a dark passage, turned a couple of corners and found ourselves in a marble court with a fountain in the centre and orange trees planted round. All the big rooms opened into this court, the doors were thrown wide to me, and coffee and sweetmeats were served by the groom of the chambers, while I admired the decoration of the walls and the water that bubbled up into marble basins and flowed away by marble conduits. In this and in most of the Damascene palaces every window sill has a gurgling pool in it, so that the air that blows into the room may bring with it a damp freshness. The Amīr 'Ali was away, but his major domo, who looked like a servant *de bonne maison* and had the respectful familiarity of manner that the Oriental dependant knows so well how to assume, showed us his master's treasures, the jewelled sabre presented to the old Amīr by Napoleon III, 'Abd ul Ḳādir's rifles, and a pair of heavy, silver-mounted swords sent as a gift last year by 'Abd ul 'Aziz ibn er Rashīd—there is a traditional friendship, I learnt, between the Algerian family and the Lords of Ḥāil. He showed us, too, pictures of 'Abd ul Ḳādir; the Amīr leading his cavalry, the Amīr at Versailles coming down the steps of the palace with Napoleon, bearing himself as one who wins and not as one who loses, the Amīr as an old man in Damascus, always in the white Algerian robes that he never abandoned, and always with the same grave and splendid dignity of countenance. And last I was led over a little bridge, that crossed a running stream behind the main court, into a garden full of violets, through which we passed to stables as airy, as light and as dry as the best European stables could have been. In the stalls stood two lovely Arab mares from the famous studs of the Ruwalla and a well-bred mule almost as valuable as they. There was a sad-looking man who accompanied us upon our round, though he did not seem to belong to the establishment; his face was so gloomy that it arrested my attention, and I asked Selīm Beg who he was. A Christian, he answered, of a rich family, who had been persecuted to change his religion and had sought sanctuary with the Amīr 'A'i. I heard no more of his story, but he fitted into the picture that 'Abd ul Ḳādir's dwelling-place left upon the mind: the house of gentlefolk, well kept by well-trained servants, provided with the amenities of life and offering protection to the distressed.

On the following morning I went to see the Amīr 'Abdullah, who lived next door to his brother. I found there a nephew of 'Abdullah's, the Amīr Ṭāhir, son of yet another brother, and my arrival was greeted with satisfaction because there happened to be staying with them a distinguished guest whom I should doubtless like to see. He was a certain Sheikh Ṭāhir ul Jezāiri, a man much renowned for his learning and for his tempestuous and revolutionary politics. Summoned hastily into the divanned and carpeted upper room in which we were sitting, he entered like a whirlwind, and establishing himself by my side poured into my ear, and into all other ears in the vicinity, for he spoke loud, his distress at not being permitted by the Vāli to associate freely with gifted foreigners such as the American archæologists or even myself ("God forbid!" I murmured modestly), and a great many other grievances besides. When this topic had run comparatively dry, he sent the Amīr Ṭāhir to seek for some publications of his own with which he presented me. They dealt with Arabic and the allied languages, such as Nabatæan, Safaitic and Phœnician, the alphabetical signs of which he had arranged very carefully and well in comparative tables, though he had not an idea of the signification of any one of the tongues except his own. A curious and typical example of oriental scholarship was Sheikh Ṭāhir, but from the samples I had of his conversation I am not sure that the sympathies of those who respect peace and order would not be with the Vāli. Presently another notable dropped in, Muṣṭafa Pasha el Barāzi, a member of one of the four leading families of Ḥamāh, and the whole company fell to talking of their own concerns, Syrian politics and other matters, while I listened and looked out of window over the Amīr's garden and the stream at its foot, and wondered what had made me so fortunate as to be taking part in a Damascene morning call. At length the Amīr 'Abdullah and his nephew took me aside and discussed long and earnestly a great project which I had broached to them and which I will not reveal here. And when the visit was over Selīm and Muṣṭafa and I went out and lunched at an excellent native restaurant in the Greek bazaar, sitting cheek by jowl with a Bedouin from the desert and eating the best of foods and the choicest of Damascus cream tarts for the sum of eighteenpence between the three of us, which included the coffee and a liberal tip.

There was another morning no less pleasant when I went with the faithful Selīm to pay my respects on a charming old man, the most famous scribe in all the city, Muṣṭafa el Asbā'i was his name. He lived in a house decorated with the exquisite taste of two hundred years ago inlaid with coloured marbles and overlaid with gesso duro worked in patterns like the frontispiece of an illuminated Persian manuscript and painted in soft rich colours in which gold and golden brown predominated. We were taken through the reception rooms into a little chamber on an upper floor where Muṣṭafa was wont to sit and write those texts that are the pictures of the Moslem East. It was hung round with examples from celebrated hands ancient and modern, among which I recognised that of my friend Muḥammad 'Ali, son of Beha Ullaḥ the Persian prophet, to my mind the most skilful penman of our day, though Oriental preference goes out to another Persian of the same religious sect, Mushḳin Kalam, and him also I count among my friends. We sat on cushions and drank coffee, turning over the while exquisite manuscripts of all dates and countries, some written on gold and some on silver, some on brocade and some on supple parchment (several of these last being pages of Kufic texts abstracted from the Ḳubbet el Khazneh before it was closed), and when we rose to go Muṣṭafa presented me with three examples of his own art, and I carried them off rejoicing.

Later in the afternoon we drove out to the valley of the Barada, Selīm and I, and called on a third son of 'Abd ul

Ḳādir: "Amir Omar, princ d'Abd ul Kadir" ran his visiting card, printed in the Latin character. He is the country gentleman of the family. 'Ali has been carried into spheres of greater influence by his marriage with a sister of 'Izzet Pasha, the mighty Shadow behind the Throne in Constantinople; 'Abdullah has always a thousand schemes on hand that keep him to the town, but 'Umar is content to hunt and shoot and tend his garden and lead the simple life. So simple was it that we found him in a smoking cap and a dressing gown and carpet slippers walking the garden alleys. He took us into his house, which, like the other houses of his family, was full of flowers, and up to a pavilion on the roof, whither his pointer followed us with a friendly air of companionship. There amid pots of hyacinths and tulips we watched the sun set over the snowy hills and talked of desert game and sport.

MUSHḲIN KALAM

Nor let me, amid all this high company, forget my humbler friends: the Afghan with black locks hanging about his cheeks, who gave me the salute every time we met (the Amīr of Afghanistan has an agent in Damascus to look after the welfare of his subjects on the pilgrimage); the sweetmeat seller at the door of the Great Mosque, who helped me once or twice through the mazes of the bazaars and called to me each time I passed him: "Has your Excellency no need of your

Dragoman to-day?"; or the dervishes of Sheikh Ḥassan's Tekyah, who invited me to attend the Friday prayers. Not least the red-bearded Persian who keeps a tea shop in the Corn Market and who is a member of the Beha'i sect among which I have many acquaintances. As I sat drinking glasses of delicious Persian tea at his table, I greeted him in his own tongue and whispered: "I have been much honoured by the Holy Family at Acre." He nodded his head and smiled and answered: "Your Excellency is known to us," and when I rose to go and asked his charge he replied: "For you there is never anything to pay." I vow there is nothing that so warms the heart as to find yourself admitted into the secret circle of Oriental beneficence—and few things so rare.

Upon a sunny afternoon I escaped from the many people who were always in waiting to take me to one place or another and made my way alone through the bazaars, ever the most fascinating of loitering grounds, till I reached the doors of the Great Mosque. It was the hour of the afternoon prayer. I left my shoes with a bed-ridden negro by the entrance and wandered into the wide cloister that runs along the whole of the west side of the Mosque. A fire some ten years ago, and the reparations that followed it, have robbed the Mosque of much of its beauty, but it still remains the centre of interest to the archæologist, who puzzles over the traces of church and temple and Heaven knows what besides that are to be seen embedded in its walls and gates. The court was half full of afternoon shadow and half of sun, and in the golden light troops of little boys with green willow switches in their hands were running to and fro in noiseless play, while the Faithful made their first prostrations before they entered the Mosque. I followed them in and watched them fall into long lines down nave and aisle from east to west. All sorts and grades of men stood side by side, from the learned doctor in a fur-lined coat and silken robes to the raggedest camel driver from the desert, for Islām is the only republic in the world and recognises no distinctions of wealth or rank. When they had assembled to the number of three or four hundred the chant of the Imām began. "God!" he cried, and the congregation fell with a single movement upon their faces and remained a full minute in silent adoration till the high chant began again. "The Creator of this world and the next, of the heavens and of the earth, He who leads the r ghteous in the true path and the wicked to destruction : God!" And as the almighty name echoed through the colonnades where it had sounded for near two thousand years, the listeners prostrated themselves again, and for a moment all the sanctuary was silence.

SWEETMEAT SELLERS

That night I went to an evening party at the invitation of Shekīb el Arslān, a Druze of a well known family of the Lebanon and a poet foreby—have I not been presented with a copy of his latest ode? The party was held in the Maidān, at the house of some corn merchants, who are agents to the Ḥaurān Druzes in the matter of corn selling and know the politics of the Mountain well. There were twelve or fourteen persons present, Shekīb and I and the corn merchants (dressed as befits well-to-do folk in blue silk robes and embroidered yellow turbans) and a few others, I know not who they were. The room was blessedly empty of all but carpets and a divan and a brazier, and this was noteworthy, for not even the 'Abd ul Ḳādir houses are free from blue and red glass vases and fringed mats that break out like a hideous disease in the marble embrazures and on the shelves of the gesso duro cupboards. Shekīb was a man of education and had experience of the world; he had even travelled once as far as London. He talked in French until one of our hosts stopped him with:

"Oh, Shekīb! you know Arabic, the lady also. Talk therefore that we can understand."

His views on Turkish politics were worth hearing.

"My friends," said he, "the evils under which we suffer are due to the foreign nations who refuse to allow the Turkish empire to move in any direction. When she fights they take the fruits of her victory from her, as they did after the war with the Greeks. What good is it that we should conquer the rebellious Albanians? the Bulgarians alone would gain advantage and the followers of our Prophet (*sic*, though he was a Druze) could not live under the hand of the Bulgarians as they would not live under the hand of the Greeks in Crete. For look you, the Moslems of Crete are now dwelling at Ṣalaḥiyyeh as you know well, and Crete has suffered by their departure."

There was so much truth in this that I who listened wished that the enemies of Turkey could hear and would deeply ponder the point of view of intelligent and well-informed subjects of the Ottoman Empire.

My last day in Damascus was a Friday. Now Damascus on a fine Friday is a sight worth travelling far to see. All the male population dressed in their best parade the streets, the sweetmeat sellers and the auctioneers of second-hand clothes drive a roaring trade, the eating shops steam with dressed meats of the most tempting kind, and splendidly caparisoned mares are galloped along the road by the river Abana. Early in the afternoon I had distinguished visitors. The first to wait on me was Muḥammad Pasha, Sheikh of Jerūd, an oasis half way upon the road to Palmyra. Jerūdi is the second greatest brigand in all the land, the greatest (no one disputes him the title) being Fayyāḍ Agha of Ḳaryatein, another oasis on the Palmyra road. Fayyāḍ, I fancy, is an evil rogue, though he had been polite enough to me when I had passed his way, but Jerūdi's knavery is of a different brand. He is a big, powerful man with a wall eye; he was a mighty rider and raider in his day, for he has Arab blood in his veins, and his grandfather was of the high stock of the 'Anazeh, but he has grown old and heavy and gouty, and his desire is for peace, a desire difficult to attain, what with his antecedents and the outlying position of Jerūd, which makes it the natural resort of all the turbulent spirits of the desert. He must keep on terms both with his Arab kin and with the government, each trying to use his influence with the other, and he the while seeking to profit from both, with his wall eye turned towards the demands of the aw, and his good eye fixed on his own advantage,

COURT OF THE GREAT MOSQUE

if I understand him. Justly irate consuls have several times demanded of the Vāli his immediate execution; but the Vāli, though he not infrequently signifies his disapproval of some markedly outrageous deed by a term of imprisonment, can never be brought to take the further step, saying that the government has before now found Jerūdi a useful man, and no doubt the Vāli is the best judge. To his great sorrow Muḥammad Pasha has no sons to inherit his very considerable wealth, and the grasshopper, in the shape of a tribe of expectant nephews, has come to be a burden on his years. Recently he married a daughter of Fayyāḍ's house, a girl of fifteen, but she has not brought him children. A famous tale about him is current in Damascus, a tale to which men do not, however, allude in his presence. At the outbreak of the last Druze war

Jerūdi happened to be enjoying one of his interludes of adhesion to the powers that be, and because he knew the Mountain well he was sent with thirty or forty men to scout and report, the army following upon his heels. It happened that as he passed through a hamlet near Ormān, his old acquaintance, the sheikh of the village, saw him, and invited

THRESHING-FLOOR OF ḲARYATEIN

him in to eat. And as he sat in the maḳ'ad awaiting his dinner he heard the Druzes discussing outside whether they had not better profit by this opportunity to kill him as an officer of the Turkish army; and he desired earnestly to go away from that place, but he could not, the rules of polite society making it incumbent upon him to stay and eat the dinner that was a-cooking. So when it came he despatched it with some speed, for the discussion outside had reached a stage that inspired him with the gravest anxiety, and having eaten he mounted his horse and rode away before the Druzes had reached a conclusion. And as he went he found himself suddenly between two fires; the Turkish army had come up and the first battle of the war had begun. He and his men, discouraged and perplexed, took refuge behind some rocks, and, as best they might, they made their way back one by one to the extreme rear of the Turkish troops. The Druzes have composed a song about this incident; it begins:

Jerudi's golden mares are famed,
And fair the riders in their stumbling flight!
Muḥammad Pasha, tell thy lord
Where are his soldiers, where his arms!

This piece is not often sung before him.

My next visitor was Sheikh Ḥassan Nakshibendi, he of the sleek and cunning clerical face. He contrived to make

THE TEKYAH OF NAKSHIBENDI

good use even of the ten minutes he spent in the inn parlour, for noticing a gaudy ring on Selīm Beg's finger he asked to see it, and liked it so well that he put it in his pocket saying that Selīm would certainly wish to give a present to his khānum, the youngest of his wives, whom he had married a year or two before. Selīm replied that in that case we must go at once to his house in Ṣalaḥiyyeh that the present might be offered, and both Sheikh Ḥassan and Muḥammad Pasha having their victorias at the door, we four got into them and drove off to Ṣalaḥiyyeh through the bright holiday streets. At the door of the house Selīm announced that I ought first to take leave of the Vāli, who lived close at hand, and borrowed Jerūdi's carriage that we might go in style. Then said Selīm to Muḥammad Pasha:

"Are you not coming with us?" But the question was put in sarcasm, for he knew well that Jerūdi was going through a period of disgrace and that he had but recently emerged from a well-merited imprisonment.

Jerūdi shook his head and drawing near to us, seated in his victoria, he whispered:

"Say something in my favour to the Pasha."

We laughed and promised to speak for him, though Selīm confided to me as we drove away that when he had been in disgrace ("entirely owing to the intrigues of my enemies"), not a man had come forward to help him, while now that he was in favour every one begged for his intervention; and he drew his frock coat round him and lent back against the cushions of Jerūdi's carriage with the air of one who is proudly conscious that he is in a position to fulfil scriptural injunctions to the letter.

Nāzim Pasha was on his doorstep taking leave of the commander-in-chief. When he saw us he came down the steps and called us in with the utmost friendliness. The second visit to his house (he had been to see me in between) was much less formal than the first. We talked of the Japanese War, a topic never far from the lips of my interlocutors, great or small, and I made bold to ask him his opinion.

"Officially," said he, "I am neutral."

"But between friends?"

"Of course I am on the side of the Japanese," he answered. And then he added: "It is you who have gained by their victory."

I replied: "But will you not also gain?"

He answered gloomily: "We have not gained as yet. Not at all in Macedonia."

Then he asked how I had enjoyed my visit to Damascus. Selīm replied hastily:

"To-day she has had a great disappointment."

The Vāli looked concerned.

"Yes," continued Selīm, "she had hoped to see a chief of brigands, and she has found only a peaceful subject of your Excellency."

"Who is he?" said Nāzim

"Muḥammad Pasha Jerūdi," answered Selīm. The good word had been spoken very skilfully.

When we returned to Sheikh Ḥassan's house we related this conversation to the subject of it, and Jerūdi pulled a wry face, but expressed himself satisfied. Sheikh Ḥassan then took me to see his wife—his fifth wife, for he had divorced one of the legal four to marry her. He has the discretion to keep a separate establishment for each, and I do not question that he is repaid by the resulting peace of his hearths. There

OUTSIDE DAMASCUS GATES

were three women in the inner room, the wife and another who was apparently not of the household, for she hid her face under the bed-clothes when Sheikh Ḥassan came in, and a Christian, useful in looking after the male guests (there were others besides Jerūdi and Selīm) and in doing commissions in the bazaars, where she can go more freely than her sister Moslems. The harem was shockingly untidy. Except when the women folk expect your visit and have prepared for it, nothing is more forlornly unkempt than their appearance. The disorder of the rooms in which they live may partly be accounted for by the fact that there are neither cupboards nor drawers in them, and all possessions are kept in large green and gold boxes, which must be unpacked when so much as a pocket-handkerchief is needed, and frequently remain unpacked. Sheikh Ḥassan's wife was a young and pretty woman, though her hair dropped in wisps about her face and neck, and a dirty dressing-gown clothed a figure which had, alas! already fallen into ruin.

But the view from Nakshibendi's balcony is immortal. The great and splendid city of Damascus, with its gardens and its domes and its minarets, lies spread out below, and beyond it the desert, the desert reaching almost to its gates. And herein is the heart of the whole matter.

This is what I know of Damascus; as for the churches and the castles, the gentry can see those for themselves.

A WATER-SELLER

CHAPTER VIII

THE Vāli had inquired of me closely whither I was going from Damascus, and when I told him that Ba'albek was my goal he had replied that he must certainly send a small body of armed men to guard so distinguished a traveller. Thereupon I had answered quickly, so as to avoid further discussion, that I should go by train. But as I had in reality no intention of adopting that means of progression it was necessary to make an early start if I would journey alone. We left the city on a bright and sunny morning; the roads were full of cheerful wayfarers, and our horses tugged at the bits after the week's rest. We passed by the Amīr 'Umar's house in the Wādi Barada, and saw that nobleman enjoying the morning sun upon his roof. He shouted down to me an invitation to enter, but I replied that there was business on hand, and that he must let me go.

"Go in peace!" he answered. "Please God some day we may ride together."

"Please God!" said I, and "God requite you!"

A mile or two further we came to a parting of the ways and I altered my route and struck straight into the Anti-Libanus the better to avoid the attentions of all the official personages who had been warned to do me honour. We rode up the beautiful valley of the Barada, which is full of apricots (but they were not yet in flower), crossed the river above Suḳ Wādi Barada, a splendid gorge, and journeyed over a plain between snowy mountains to Zebdāny, famous for its apples. Here we pitched a solitary camp in a green meadow by a spring, the snowy flanks of Hermon closing the view to the south and the village scattered over the hill slopes to the north, and no one in Zebdāny paid any attention to the two small tents. Next day we crossed the Anti-Libanus in a howling wind; a very lovely and enjoyable ride it was nevertheless, but a long stage of eight and a quarter hours. There were Latin inscriptions cut at intervals in the rocks all down the valley that falls into the Yaḥfūfa at Jānta —I imagine we were on the Roman road from Damascus to Ba'albek. The last long barren miles were done in driving rain and we arrived wet through at Ba'albek. It was almost too windy to pitch a camp, and yet my soul revolted against the thought of a hotel; fortunately, Mikhāil suggested a resource. He knew, said he, a decent Christian woman who lived at the entrance of the village and who would doubtless give us a lodging. It happened as he had predicted. The Christian woman was delighted to see us. Her house contained a clean empty room which was speedily made ready for my camp furniture, Mikhāil established himself and his cooking gear in another, the wind and the rain beat its worst against the shutters and could do us no harm.

The name of my hostess was Kurunfuleh, the Carnation Flower, and she was wife to one Yūsef el 'Awais, who is at present seeking his fortune in America, where she wishes to join him. I spent an hour or two with her and her son and daughter and a few relations who had dropped in for a little talk and a little music, bringing their lutes with them. They told me that they were very anxious about their future. The greater part of the population of Ba'albek and round about belongs to an unorthodox sect of Islām, called the Metāwileh, which has a very special reputation for fanaticism and ignorance. These people, when they heard of the Japanese victories, would come and shake their fists at their Christian neighbours, saying: "The Christians are suffering defeat! See now, we too will shortly drive you out and seize your goods." Mikhāil joined in, and declared that it was the same thing at Jerusalem. There, said he (I know not with what truth), the Moslems had sent a deputation to the Mufti, saying: "The time has come for us to turn the Christians out." But the Mufti answered: "If you raise a disturbance the nations of Europe will step in, for Jerusalem is the apple of their eye" (so the Mufti affirmed), "and they will take the whole land and we shall be worse off than before." I tried to com-

SUḲ WĀDI BARADA L

fort Kurunfuleh by saying that it was improbable that the Christians of Syria should suffer persecution, the country being so well known and so much frequented by tourists, who would not fail to raise an outcry. The yearly stream of tourists is, in fact, one of the best guarantees of order. Now Kurunfuleh was a Lebanon woman, and I asked her why she did not return to her own village, where she would be under the direct protection of the Powers and exempt from danger. She said:

"Oh lady, the house here is taken in my husband's name, and I cannot sell it unless he return, nor yet leave it empty, and moreover the life in the Lebanon is not like the life in the plain, and I, being accustomed to other things, could not endure it. There no one has any business but to watch his neighbour, and if you put on a new skirt the village will whisper together and mock at you saying, 'Hast seen the lady?' Look you, I will show you what it is like to live in the Lebanon. I eat meat in Ba'albek once a day, but they once a month. They take an onion and divide it into three parts, using one part each evening to flavour the burghul (cracked wheat), and I throw a handful of onions into the dish every night. Life pinches in the Lebanon."

Life pinches so straitly that all of the population that can scrape together their passage money are leaving for the United States, and it is next to impossible to find labour to cultivate the corn, the mulberry and the vine. There is no advancement, to use the Syrian phrase. The Lebanon province is a *cul de sac*, without a port of its own and without commerce. True, you need not go in fear of death, but of what advantage is an existence that offers no more than the third of an onion at supper time? As usual, the Sublime Porte has been too many for the Powers. It has accorded all they asked, oh yes, and gladly, but the concessions that seemed to lay open the path of prosperity have in reality closed the gates for ever upon those who should have profited by them.

Next day the rain had not abated. I received the Commissioner of Police, who had run me to earth—he proved to be a charming man—and paid a visit to a large family of

Portuguese who were staying at the hotel hard by my lodging. Monsieur Luiz de Sommar, with his wife and daughters and nephews, had come up from Jerusalem to Damascus by the Jebel Druze. I had heard of their arrival at Sweida while I was at Ṣalkhad, and had wondered how they had gained admission. The story was curious and it redounds to the credit of Monsieur de Sommar, while it shows how eager the Government still is to keep the Mountain free from the prying eyes of tourists. The Portuguese family had met Mr. Mark Sykes at 'Ammān, and he had advised them to change their route so as to pass through Ḳanawāt in the Jebel Druze, saying they would have no difficulty in obtaining permission to do so. Monsieur de Sommar went guilelessly forward, but when he reached Sweida, which is the chief post of the Government, the Ḳāimaḳām stopped him and intimated politely but firmly that he must return the way he had come. He replied as firmly that he would not, and sent telegrams to his Consul in Damascus and his Minister at Constantinople. Thereupon followed an excited exchange of messages, the upshot of which was that he was to be allowed to proceed to Ḳanawāt if he would take a hundred zaptiehs with him. The country, said the Ḳāimaḳām, was extremely dangerous—that country through which, as I know well, a woman can ride with no escort but a Druze boy, and might ride alone, even if she had her saddle-bags full of gold. But Monsieur de Sommar was a man of judgment. He replied that he was quite willing to take the hundred zaptiehs, but not one piastre piece should they receive from him. Thus countered, the Ḳāimaḳām changed his note and diminished the escort till it numbered twenty, with which guard the de Sommars reached Ḳanawāt in safety. I congratulated them on their exploit, and myself on having sought my permit from Fellaḥ ul 'Isa, and not from the Vāli of Syria.

In spite of the rain, the day at Ba'albek was not mis-spent. Since my last visit the Germans had excavated the Temple of the Sun and laid bare altars, fountains, bits of decoration and foundations of churches, which were all of the deepest interest. Moreover, the great group of temples and enclosing walls set between the double range of mountains, Lebanon and

BA'ALBEK

Anti-Libanus, produces an impression second to none save the Temple group of the Athenian Acropolis, which is easily beyond a peer. The details of Ba'albek are not so good as those at Athens; the matchless dignity and restraint of that glory among the creations of architects are not to be approached, nor is the splendid position on the hill top overlooking the blue

THE GREAT COURT, BA'ALBEK

sea and the Gulf of Salamis to be rivalled. But in general effect Ba'albek comes nearer to it than any other mass of building, and it provides an endless source of speculation to such as busy themselves with the combination of Greek and Asiatic genius that produced it and covered its doorposts, its architraves and its capitals with ornamental devices infinite in variety as they are lovely in execution. For the archæologist there is neither clean nor unclean. All the works of the human imagination fall into their appointed place in the history of art, directing and illuminating his own understanding of it. He is doubly blest, for when the outcome is beautiful to the eyes he returns thanks; but, whatever the result, it is sure to furnish him with some new and unexpected link between one art and another, and to provide him with a further rung in the ladder of history. He is thus apt to be well satisfied with what he sees, and above all, he does not say: "Alas, alas! these dogs of Syrians! Phidias would have done so and so;" for he is glad to mark a new attempt in the path of artistic endeavour, and a fresh breath moving the acanthus leaves and the vine scrolls on capital and frieze.

Our departure from Ba'albek was marked by a regrettable occurrence—my dog Kurt was found to have disappeared in the night. Unlike most Syrian pariah dogs, he was of a very friendly disposition, he was also (and in this respect he did not differ from his half-fed clan) insatiably greedy; the probability was, therefore, that he had been lured away with a bone and shut up till we were safely out of the road. Ḥābib set off in one direction through the village, Mikhāil in another, while the Commissioner of Police, who had appeared on the agitated scene, tried to pour balm upon my wounded feelings. After a few minutes Ḥābib reappeared with Kurt, all wag, behind him on a chain. He had found him, he explained breathlessly, in the house of one who had thought to steal him, fastened with this very chain:

"And when Kurt heard my voice he barked, and I went into the yard and saw him. And the lord of the chain demanded it of me, and by God! I refused to give it him and struck him to the earth with it instead. God curse him for a thievish Metawīleh! And so I left him."

I have, therefore, the pleasure to record that the Metāwileh are as dishonest a sect as rumour would have them to be, but that their machinations can be brought to nought by vigilant Christians.

We rode down the wide and most dreary valley between Lebanon and Anti-Libanus. I might have gone by train to Ḥomṣ, and eke to Ḥamāh, but I preferred to cross from side to side of the valley as the fancy took me, and visit such places of interest as the country had to show, and this could only be done on horseback. North of Ba'albek all Syria was new to me; it marked an epoch, too, that we had reached the frontier of the Palestine Exploration Map. I now had recourse to Kiepert's small but excellent sheet, which I had abstracted from the volume of Oppenheim that had been left at Ṣāleh.

COLUMNS OF THE TEMPLE OF THE SUN, BA'ALBEK

There is no other satisfactory map until, at a line some thirty miles south of Aleppo, Kiepert's big Kleinasien 1-400,000 begins; when the American Survey publishes its geographical volume the deficiency will, I hope, be rectified. After four and a half hours we came to Lebweh, where one of the principal sources of the Orontes bursts out of the earth in a number of springs, very beautiful to see; and here we were overtaken by two soldiers who had been sent after us by the Ḳāimaḳām with a polite inquiry as to whether I would not like an escort. I sent one back and kept the other, fearing to hurt the Ḳāimaḳām's feelings; Derwīsh was the man's name, helpful and pleasant he proved, as indeed were all in the long series of his successors who accompanied us until I stepped into the train at Konia. Some of them added greatly to the pleasure of the journey, telling me many tales of their experiences and adventures as we rode together hour by hour. They enjoyed the break in garrison life that was thus afforded them, and they enjoyed also the daily fee of a mejideh (4*s.* roughly) which was so much more certain than the Sultan's pay. I gave them besides a little tip when they reached the term of their services, and they fed themselves and their horses on provisions and grain that I shrewdly suspect were taken from the peasantry by force, a form of official exaction that the traveller is powerless to prevent.

At Lebweh are the ruins of a temple built in the massive masonry of Ba'albek. A podium of four great courses of stones crowned by a simple moulding, a mere splay face, is all that is left of it. The village belongs to a man called Asad Beg, a rich Metawīleh and brother to a certain Dr. Haida, who is a ubiquitous person well known in north Syria. I never go to Damascus without meeting him and never meet him without satisfaction, for he is well read in Arabic literature and exceptionally intelligent. He has recently been engaged in some job on the Mecca railway, and he is, so far as I know, the only example in his sect of a man who has received a good education and risen to a certain distinction.

We pitched camp at Rās Ba'albek, where there is an excellent spring in a gorge of the barren eastern hills an hour and a half from Lebweh. The frost had ceased to pinch us of a morning, praise be to God! but it was still cold. When we rose at dawn the sleet was beating against the tents and we rode all day in the devil's own wind. This was March 8; Spring travels slowly into Northern Syria. I sent my camp by the direct path and rode with Derwīsh to a monument that stands on some rising ground in the middle of the Orontes valley and which in that desolate expanse is seen for a day's journey on either side. It is a tall tower of massive stonework capped by a pyramid and decorated with pilasters and a rough frieze carved in low relief with hunting scenes and trophies of arms. The Syrians call it Ḳāmu'a Hurmul, the Tower of Hurmul, after the village close by, and the learned are of opinion that it commemorates some great battle of the Roman conquest, but there is no inscription to prove them right or wrong. It lies two hours to the west of Rās Ba'albek. Buffeted by the furious wind we rode on another hour and a half to a line of little mounds protecting the air-holes of an underground water channel—a Ḳanāt it would be called in Persian, and I believe is so called in Arabic. Another two and a half hours brought us to Ḳṣeir, the mules came up a quarter of an hour later, and we camped hard by the cemetery outside the ugly mud-built town. The wind dropped after sunset, and peace, moral and physical, settled down upon the camp. Even Mikhāil's good humour had been somewhat disturbed by the elements, but Ḥābib had come in as smiling as ever, and I am glad to remember that I, feeling my temper slipping from me down the gale, had preserved the silence of the philosopher. Muḥammad the Druze was no longer with us, for he had been left behind in Damascus. Whether through his own fault or by reason of a conspiracy against him among the others, difficulties and quarrels were always arising, and it was better to sacrifice one member of the staff and preserve the equanimity of the caravan. My contract with him ceased at Damascus; we parted on the best of terms, and his place was taken by a succession of hirelings, indistinguishable, as far as I was concerned, the one from the other.

The valley of the Orontes was formerly an Arab camping ground and is still frequented in dry seasons by a few skeikhs of the Ḥaseneh and of the 'Anazeh, particularly by the

TEMPLE OF JUPITER, BA'ALBEK

Ruwalla branch of the latter tribe, but the bulk of the Bedouin have been driven out by cultivation. The Ḳāmu'a Hurmul bears the record of them in the shape of ancient tribe marks. It was more curious to reflect that we were in the southern headquarters of the Hittites, whoever they may have been; the famous examples of their as yet undecyphered script which were found at Ḥamāh are now lodged in the museum at Constantinople, where they have baffled all the efforts of the learned. The present population of Ḳṣeir is composed partly of Christians and partly of the members of a sect called the Noṣairiyyeh. They are not recognised by Islām as orthodox, though, like all the smaller sects, they do their best to smooth away the outward differences between themselves and the dominant creed. They keep the tenets of their faith secret as far as possible, but Dussaud has pried into the heart of them and found them full of the traces of Phœnician tradition. Living apart in mountain fastnesses that have remained almost inviolate, the Noṣairiyyeh have held on to the practices of ancient Semitic cults, and they occupy an honourable position in the eyes of Syriologists as the direct descendants of paganism, while remaining themselves profoundly ignorant of their ancestry. Native report speaks ill of their religion, following the invariable custom by which people whisper scandal of what they are not allowed to understand, and I was told that the visible signs of it as expressed by the conduct of the sect left everything to be desired. Dussaud has, however, washed away the stain that lay upon their faith, and my experience of their dealings with strangers leads me to adopt an attitude of benevolent neutrality. I spent five days in the mountains west of Ḥomṣ and a week near Antioch, in which districts they are chiefly to be found, and had no reason to raise a complaint. Kurt was not so well pleased with the company in which he found himself at Ḳṣeir. He kept up a continual barking all night; I could almost have wished him back in the courtyard of the Metawīleh.

Next day the weather was gloriously fine. With Mikhāil I made a long circuit that I might visit Tell Nebi Mendu, which is the site of Kadesh on the Orontes, the southern capital of the Hittites. Kadesh in its day must have been a fair city.

The mound on which it was built rises out of a great corn-growing plain; to the south the wide valley of the Orontes runs up between the twin chains of Lebanon, to the west the Jebel Noṣairiyyeh protect it from the sea, and between the ranges of Lebanon and the Noṣairiyyeh mountains there is a smiling lowland by which merchants and merchandise might pass down to the coast. Northwards to the horizon stretch the plains of Coelo Syria; the steppes of the Palmyrene desert bound the view to the east. The foot of the tell is washed by the young and eager Orontes (the Rebellious is the meaning of its Arabic name), and in the immediate foreground lies the lake of Ḥomṣ, six miles long. The mound of Kadesh is approached by grassy swards, and among willow trees a mill-wheel turns merrily in the rushing stream. The site must have been inhabited almost continuously from Hittite times, for history tells of a Seleucid city, Laodocia ad Orontem, and there are traces of a Christian town. Each succeeding generation has built upon the dust of those that went before, and the mound has grown higher and higher, and doubtless richer and richer in the traces of them that lived on it. But it cannot be excavated thoroughly owing to the miserable mud hovels that have inherited the glories of Laodocia and Kadesh, and to the little graveyard at the northern end of the village which, according to the Moslem prejudice, must remain undisturbed till Gabriel's trump rouses the sleepers in it. I noticed fragments of columns and of very rough capitals lying about among the houses, but my interest, while I stood upon the mound, was chiefly engaged in picturing the battle fought at Kadesh by the Hittite king against the Pharaoh of his time, which is recorded in a famous series of hieroglyphs in Egypt. A quarter of an hour's ride to the north of Tell Nebi Mendu there is a singular earthwork which is explained by the Arabs as being the Sefinet Nuḥ (Noah's Ark) and by archæologists as an Assyrian fortification, and the one account of its origin has as much to support it as the other. It is a heap of earth, four-square, its sides exactly oriented to the points of the compass, standing some forty to fifty feet above the level of the plain and surrounded by a ditch, the angles of which are still sharp. We rode to the top of it, and found it to be an immense

CAPITALS IN THE TEMPLE OF JUPITER, BA'ALBEK

platform of solid earth, about an eighth of a mile square, the four corners raised a little as if there had been towers upon them, and tower and rampart and platform were alike covered with springing corn. Whoever raised it, Patriarch or Assyrian, must have found it mighty tiresome to construct, but until a few trenches have been cut across it the object that directed

FOUNTAIN IN THE GREAT COURT, BA'ALBEK

his labours will rest undetermined. We rode down to the lake and lunched by the lapping water on a beach of clean shells. There are two mounds close to the shores, another a mile or two out of Ḥomṣ, while the castle of Ḥomṣ itself was built upon a fourth. They have all the appearance of being artificial, and probably contain the relics of towns that were sisters to Kadesh. The fertile plain east of the Orontes must always have been able to support a large population, larger perhaps in Hittite days than in our own. The day's ride had lasted from 9.30 to 2 o'clock, with three-quarters of an hour at Tell Nebi Mendu and half an hour by the lake.

We approached Ḥomṣ through the cemeteries. That it should be preceded by a quarter of a mile of graves is not a peculiarity of Ḥomṣ, but a constant feature of oriental towns.

Every city is guarded by battalions of the dead, and the life of the town moves in and out through a regiment of turbaned tombstones. It happened to be a Thursday when we came to Ḥomṣ, and Thursday is the weekly Day of All Souls in the Mohammedan world. Groups of veiled women were laying flowers upon the graves or sitting on the mounds engaged in animated chat—the graveyard is the pleasure ground of Eastern women and the playground of the children, nor do the gloomy associations of the spot affect the cheerfulness of the visitors. My camp was pitched in the outskirts of the city on a stretch of green grass below the ruins of barracks built by Ibrahim Pasha and destroyed immediately after his death by the Syrians, who were desirous of obliterating every trace of his hated occupation. All was ready for me, water boiling for tea and a messenger from the Ḳāimaḳām in waiting to assure me that my every wish should have immediate attention, in spite of which I do not like the town of Ḥomṣ and never of free will shall I camp in it again. This resolution is due to the behaviour of the inhabitants, which I will now describe.

The conduct of the Ḳāimaḳām was unexceptionable. I visited him after tea, and found him to be an agreeable Turk, with a little of the Arabic tongue and an affable address. There were various other people present, turbaned muftis and grave senators—we had a pleasant talk over our coffee. When I rose to go the Ḳāimaḳām offered me a soldier to escort me about the town, but I refused, saying that I had nothing to fear, since I spoke the language. I was wrong: no knowledge of Arabic would be sufficient to enable the stranger to express his opinion of the people of Ḥomṣ. Before I was well within the bazaar the persecution began. I might have been the Pied Piper of Hamelin from the way the little boys flocked upon my heels. I bore their curiosity for some time, then I adjured them, then I turned for help to the shopkeepers in the bazaars. This was effective for a while, but when I was so unwary as to enter a mosque, not only the little boys but every male inhabitant of Ḥomṣ (or so it seemed to my fevered imagination) crowded in after me. They were not annoyed, they had no wish to stop me, on the contrary they desired eagerly that I should go on for a long time, that they might have a better opportunity of watching me; but it was more than I could bear, and I fled back to my tents, pursued by some two hundred pairs of inquisitive eyes, and sent at once for a zaptieh. Next morning I was wiser and took the zaptieh with me from the first. We climbed to the top of the castle mound to gain a general idea of the town. Though it has no particular architectural beauty, Ḥomṣ has a character of its own. It is built

FRAGMENT OF ENTABLATURE, BA'ALBEK

of tufa, the big houses standing round courtyards adorned with simple but excellent patterns of white limestone let into the black walls. Sometimes the limestone is laid in straight courses, making with the tufa alternate bars of black and white like the façade of Siena cathedral. The mind is carried back the more to Italy by the minarets, which are tall square towers, for all the world like the towers of San Gimignano, except that those of Ḥomṣ are capped by a white cupola, very pretty and effective. All that remained of the castle was Arabic in origin, and so were the fortifications round the town, save at one place to the east, where the Arab work seemed to rest on older foundations. I saw no mass of building of pre-Mohammedan date but one, a brick ruin outside the Tripoli gate which was certainly Roman, the sole relic of the Roman city of Emesa. The castle mound is also outside the town, and when I had completed my general survey we entered by the western gate and went sight-seeing. This is a process which takes time, for it is constantly interrupted by pressing invitations to come in and drink coffee. We passed by the Turkmān Jāmi'a, where there are a couple of Greek inscriptions built into the minaret and a sarcophagus, carved with bulls' heads and garlands, that serves as a fountain. The zaptieh was of opinion that I could not do better than pay my respects to the Bishop of the Greek Orthodox Church, and to his palace I went, but found that I was still too early to see his lordship. I was entertained, however, on jam and water and coffee, and listened to the lamentations of the Bishop's secretary over the Japanese victories. The Greek Orthodox Church held penitential services each time that they received the news of a Russian defeat, and at that moment they were kept busy entreating the Almighty to spare the enemies of Christendom. The secretary deputed a servant to show me the little church of Mār Eliās, which contains an interesting marble sarcophagus with Latin crosses carved on the body of it and Greek crosses on the lid, a later addition, I fancy, to a classical tomb. Outside the church I met one called 'Abd ul Wahhāb Beg, whom I had seen at the Serāya when I was calling on the Ḳāimaḳām, and he invited me into his house, a fine example of the domestic architecture of Ḥomṣ, the harem court being charmingly decorated with patterns in limestone and basalt. When I came out, the zaptieh, who had grasped what sort of sight it was I wished to see, announced that he would take me to the house of one Ḥassan Beg Nā'i, which was the oldest in Ḥomṣ. Thither we went, and as we passed through the narrow but remarkably clean streets I noticed that in almost every house there was a loom, whereon a weaver was weaving the striped silk for which Ḥomṣ is famous, while down most of the thoroughfares were stretched the silken yarns. The zaptieh said that the workers were paid by the piece, and earned from seven to twelve piastres a day (one to two shillings), a handsome wage in the East. Living was cheap, he added; a poor man could rent his house, that is a single room, for a hundred piastres a year, and feed his family on thirty to forty piastres a week or even less if he had not many children.

BASILICA OF CONSTANTINE, BA'ALBEK

Ḥassan Beg Nā'i was a red-haired and red-bearded man, with a hard-featured face of a Scotch lowland type. He was not at all pleased to see me, but, at the instance of the zaptieh, he slouched out of his bachelor quarters, where he was drinking a Friday morning cup of coffee with his friends, took me across the street to his harem, and left me with his womenkind, who were as friendly as he was surly. They were, indeed, delighted

A STONE IN THE QUARRY, BA'ALBEK

to have a visitor, for Ḥassan Beg is a strict master, and neither his wife nor his mother nor any woman that is his is allowed to put her nose out of doors, not even to take a walk through the graveyard or to drive down to the meadow by the Orontes on a fine summer afternoon. The harem had been a very beautiful Arab house on the model of the houses of Damascus. There were plaster cupolas over the rooms and over the liwān (the audience hall at the bottom of the court), but the plaster was chipping away and the floors and staircases crumbled beneath the feet of those that trod them. A marble column with an acanthus capital was built into one wall, and on the floor of the liwān stood a big marble capital, simple in style but good of its kind. It had been converted into a water basin, and may have done duty as a font before the Arabs took Emesa and after the earlier buildings of the Roman town had begun to fall into decay and their materials to be put to other uses. I passed as I went home a fine square minaret, built of alternate bands of black and white. The mosque or the Christian church to which the tower belonged had fallen; it is reputed, said my zaptieh, to be the oldest tower in the town. The mosque at the entrance of the bazaar was certainly a church of no mean architectural merit.

There was nothing more to see in Ḥomṣ, and as the afternoon was fine I rode down to the meadow by the Orontes, the fashionable resort of all holiday makers in spring and summer. The course of the Orontes leaves Ḥomṣ a good mile to the south-west, and the water supply is both bad and insufficient, being derived from a canal that begins at the northern end of the lake. The Marj ul 'Asi, the meadow of the Orontes, is a good type of the kind of place in which the Oriental, be he Turk or Syrian or Persian, delights to spend his leisure. "Three things there are," says an Arabic proverb, "that ease the heart from sorrow: water, green grass and the beauty of women." The swift Orontes stream flowed by swards already starred with daisies, where Christian ladies, most perfunctorily veiled, alighted from their mules under willow trees touched with the first breath of spring. The river turned a great Na'oura, a Persian wheel, which filled the air with its pleasant rumbling. A coffee maker had set up his brazier by the edge of the road, a sweetmeat seller was spreading out his wares by the waterside, and on a broader stretch of grass a few gaily dressed youths galloped and wheeled Arab mares. The East made holiday in her own simple and satisfactory manner, warmed by her own delicious sun.

The rest of the afternoon was devoted to society and to fruitless attempts to escape from the curiosity of the townsfolk. It was a Friday afternoon, and no better way of spending it occurred to them than to assemble to the number of many hundreds round my tents and observe every movement of every member of the camp. The men were bad enough, but the women were worse and the children were the worst of all. Nothing could keep them off, and the excitement reached a

RĀS UL 'AIN, BA'ALBEK

climax when 'Abd ul Ḥamed Pasha Druby, the richest man in Ḥomṣ, came to call, bringing with him the Ḳāḍi Muḥammad Sāid ul Khāni. I could not pay as much attention to their delightful and intelligent conversation as it deserved, owing to the seething crowd that surrounded us, but an hour later I returned their call at the Pasha's fine new house at the gate of the town, accompanied thither by at least three hundred people. I must have breathed a sigh of relief when the door closed upon my escort, for as I established myself in the cool and quiet liwān, 'Abd ul Ḥamed said :

CEDARS OF LEBANON

"Please God the populace does not trouble your Excellency; for if so we will order out a regiment of soldiers."

I murmured a half-hearted refusal of his offer, though I would have been glad to have seen those little boys shot down by volleys of musketry, and the Pasha added reflectively :

"The Emperor of the Germans when he was in Damascus gave orders that no one was to be forbidden to come and gaze on him."

With this august example before me I saw that I must bear the penalties of greatness and foreignness without complaint.

The talk turned on religious beliefs. I began by asking about the Noṣairiyyeh, but the Ḳāḍi pursed his lips and answered:

"They are not pleasant people. Some of them pretend to worship 'Ali and some worship the sun. They believe that when they die their souls pass into the bodies of other men or even animals, as it is in the faiths of India and of China."

THE ḲĀMU'A HURMUL

I said: "I have heard a story that they tell of a man who owned a vineyard, and the man died and left it to his son. Now the young man worked in the vineyard until the time of the harvest, and when the grapes were ripe a wolf entered in, and every evening he ate the fruit. And the young man tried to hunt him forth, and every evening he returned. And one night the wolf cried aloud: 'Shall I not eat of the grapes who planted the vines?' And the young man was astounded and he said: 'Who art thou?' The wolf replied: 'I am thy father.' The young man answered: 'If thou art indeed my father, where did'st hide the pruning knife, for I have not found it since thy soul left thy body!' Then the wolf took him to the place where the pruning knife lay concealed, and he believed and knew it was his father."

AN EASTERN HOLIDAY

The Ḳāḍi dismissed the evidence.

"Without doubt they are mighty liars," said he.

I asked him next whether he had any acquaintance with the Behā'is. He answered:

"As for the Behā'is and others like them, your Excellency knows that the Prophet (may God give him peace!) said that there were seventy-two false creeds and but one true, and I

A STREET IN ḤOMṢ

can tell you that of the seventy-two there are certainly fifty in our country."

I replied that it appertained to prophets alone to distinguish the true from the false, and that we in Europe, where there were none to help us, found it a difficult task.

"In Europe," said the Ḳāḍi, "I have heard that the men of science are your prophets."

"And they make answer that they know nothing," I observed. "Their eyes have explored the stars, yet they cannot tell us the meaning of the word infinity."

"If you speak of the infinite sky," remarked the Ḳāḍi, "we know that it is occupied by seven heavens."

"And what beyond the seventh heaven?"

"Does not your Excellency know that the number one is the beginning of all things?" said he. "When you have told me what comes before the number one, I will tell you what lies beyond the seventh heaven."

The Pasha laughed and said that if the Ḳāḍi had finished his argument he would like to ask me what was the current opinion in Europe in the matter of thought-reading. "For," said he, "a month ago a ring of price was stolen in my house and I could not find the thief. Now a certain Effendi among my friends, hearing of my case, came to me and said: 'I know a man in the Lebanon skilful in these things.' I said: 'Do me the kindness to send for him.' And the man came, and he sought in Ḥomṣ, until he found a woman gifted with second sight, and he worked spells on her until she spoke and said: 'The thief is so-and-so, and he has taken the ring to his house.' And we sought in the house and found the jewel. This is my experience, for the event happened under my eyes."

I replied that thought-readers in the Lebanon made a better use of their gifts than any I had heard of in London, and the Pasha said meditatively:

"It may be that the woman of the bazaar had a complaint against the man in whose house we found the ring—God alone knows, may His name be exalted!"

And so we left it.

When I returned to my tent I found a visiting card on my table, bearing the name and title, "Hanna Khabbāz, the preacher of the Protestant Church at Homs." Beneath this inscription was written the following message: "Madam,—My wife and I are ready to do any service you need in the name of Christ and the humanity. We should like to visit you if you kindly accept us. I am, your obedient servant." I sent word that I would kindly accept them if they would come at once, and they appeared before sundown, two friendly people, very eager to offer me hospitality, of which I had no opportunity to take advantage. I regretted it the less because the Pasha and the Ḳāḍi had been good enough company for one afternoon, and when I look back on the tumultuous visit to Ḥomṣ, the hour spent with those two courteous and well-bred Mohammadans stands out like the memory of a sheltered spot in a gale of wind.

CHAPTER IX

We left next day at an early hour, but the people of Ḥomṣ got up to see us off. Nothing save the determination to afford them no more amusement than I could help kept me outwardly calm. In a quarter of an hour we had passed beyond the Tripoli Gate, and the Roman brickwork, and beyond the range of vision of the furthest sighted of the little boys; the peaceful beauty of the morning invaded our senses, and I turned to make the acquaintance of the companions with whom the Ḳāimaḳām had provided me. They were four in number, and two of them were free and two were bound. The first two were Kurdish zaptiehs; one was charged to show me the way to Ḳal'at el Ḥuṣn, and the other to guard over the second pair of my fellow travellers, a couple of prisoners who had been on the Ḳāimaḳām's hands for some days past, waiting until he could find a suitable opportunity, such as that afforded by my journey, to send them to the fortress in the Jebel Noṣairiyyeh, and so to the great prison at Tripoli. They were clad, poor wretches, in ragged cotton clothes and handcuffed together. As they trudged along bravely through dust and mud, I proffered a word of sympathy, to which they replied that they hoped God might prolong my life, but as for them it was the will of their lord the Sultan that they should tramp in chains. One of the Kurds interrupted with the explanation :

"They are deserters from the Sultan's army: may God reward them according to their deeds! Moreover, they are Ismailis from Selemiyyeh, and they worship a strange god who lives in the land of Hind. And some say she is a woman, and for that reason they worship her. And every year she sends an embassy to this country to collect the money that is due to her, and even the poorest of the Ismailis provide her with a few piastres. And yet they declare that they are Muslims: who knows what they believe? Speak, oh Khuḍr, and tell us what you believe."

The prisoner thus addressed replied doggedly:

"We are Muslims;" but the soldier's words had given me a clue which I was able to follow up when the luckless pair crept close to my horse's side and whispered:

"Lady, lady! have you journeyed to the land of Hind?"

"Yes," said I.

"May God make it Yes upon you! Have you heard there of a great king called the King Muḥammad?"

Again I was able to reply in the affirmative, and even to add that I myself knew him and had conversed with him, for their King Muḥammad was no other than my fellow subject the Agha Khān, and the religion of the prisoners boasted a respectable antiquity, having been founded by him whom we call the Old Man of the Mountain. They were the humble representatives of the dreaded (and probably maligned) sect of the Assassins.

Khuḍr caught my stirrup with his free hand and said eagerly:

"Is he not a great king?"

But I answered cautiously, for though the Agha Khān is something of a great king in the modern sense, that is to say he is exceedingly wealthy, it would have been difficult to explain to his disciples exactly what the polished, well-bred man of the world was like whom I had last met at a London dinner party, and who had given me the Marlborough Club as his address. Not that these things, if they could have understood them, would have shocked them; the Agha Khān is a law unto himself, and if he chose to indulge in far greater excesses than dinner parties his actions would be sanctified by the mere fact that they were his. His father used to give letters of introduction to the Angel Gabriel, in order to secure for his clients a good place in Paradise; the son, with his English education and his familiarity with European thought, has refrained from exercising this privilege, though he has not ceased to hold, in the opinion of his followers, the keys of heaven. They show their belief in him in a substantial manner by subscribing, in various parts of Asia and Africa, a handsome income that runs yearly into tens of thousands.

We rode for about an hour through gardens, meeting bands of low-caste Arabs jogging into Ḥoms on their donkeys with milk and curds for the market, and then we came to the plain beyond the Orontes, which is the home of these Arabs. The plain had a familiar air; it was not dissimilar from the country

COFFEE BY THE ROAD-SIDE

in the Druze hills, and like the Ḥaurān it was covered with black volcanic stones. It is a vast quarry for the city of Ḥoms. All the stones that are used for building are brought from beyond the river packed on donkeys. They are worth a metalīk in the town (now a metalīk is a coin too small to possess a European counterpart), and a man with a good team can earn up to ten piastres a day. In the Spring the only Arabs who camp in the Wa'r Ḥoms, the Stony Plain of Ḥoms, are a despised race that caters for the needs of the city, for, mark you. no Bedouin who respected himself would earn a livelihood by selling curds or by any other means except battle; but in the summer the big tribes such as the Ḥaseneh settle there for a few months, and after the harvest certain of the 'Anazeh who feed their camels upon the stubble. These great folk are much like salmon in a trout stream coming in from the open sea and bullying the lesser fry. When we passed in March there was a good deal of standing water in the plain, and grass and flowers grew between the stones; and as we journeyed westward, over ground that rose gradually towards the hills, we came into country that was like an exquisite garden of flowers. Pale blue hyacinths lifted their clustered bells above the tufa blocks, irises and red anemones and a yellow hawksweed and a beautiful purple hellebore dotted the grass—all the bounties of the Syrian Spring were scattered on that day beneath our happy feet. For the first five hours we followed the carriage road that leads to Tripoli, passing the khān that marks the final stage before the town of Ḥomṣ, and the boundary line between the vilayets of Damascus and of Beyrout; then we turned to the right and entered a bridle-path that lay over a land of rolling grass, partly cultivated and fuller of flowers than the edges of the road had been. The anemones were of every shade of white and purple, small blue irises clustered by the path and yellow crocuses by the banks of the stream. In the eyes of one who had recently crossed southern Syria the grass was even more admirable than the flowers. The highest summits of the Jebel Noṣairiyyeh are clad with a verdure that no fertile slope in Samaria or Judæa can boast. The path mounted a little ridge and dropped down to a Kurdish village, half Arab tent and half mud-built wall. The inhabitants must have been long in Syria, for they had forgotten their own tongue and spoke nothing but Arabic, though, like the two zaptiehs, they spoke with the clipped accent of the Kurd. Beyond the village a plain some three miles wide, the Bḳei'a, stretched to the foot of the steep buttress of the Noṣairiyyeh hills, and from the very top of the mountain frowned the great crusader fortress towards which we were going. The sun shone on its turrets, but a black storm was creeping up behind it; we could hear the thunder rumbling in the hills, and jagged lightning shot through the clouds behind the castle. The direct road across the Bḳei'a was impassable for horsemen, owing to the flooded swamps, which were deep enough, said the villagers, to engulf a mule and its load; we turned therefore reluctantly to the right, and edged round the foot of

ḲALA'AT EL ḤUSN

the hills. Before we had gone far we met two riders sent out to welcome us by the Ḳāimaḳām of Ḳal'at el Ḥuṣn, and as they joined us the storm broke and enveloped us in sheets of rain. Splashing through the mud and drenched with rain we reached the foot of the hills at five o'clock, and here I left my caravan to follow the road, and with one of the Ḳāimaḳām's horsemen climbed by a steep and narrow bridle-path straight up to the hill-top. And so at sunset we came to the Dark Tower and rode through a splendid Arab gateway into a vaulted corridor, built over a winding stair. It was almost night within; a few loopholes let in the grey dusk from outside and provided the veriest apology for daylight. At intervals we passed doorways leading into cavernous blackness. The stone steps were shallow and wide but much broken; the horses stumbled and clanked over them as we rode up and up, turned corner after corner, and passed under gateway after gateway until the last brought us out into the courtyard in the centre of the keep. I felt as though I were riding with some knight of the Fairy Queen, and half expected to see written over the arches: "Be bold!" "Be bold!" "Be not too bold!" But there was no magician in the heart of the castle—nothing but a crowd of villagers craning their necks to see us, and the Ḳāimaḳām, smiling and friendly, announcing that he could not think of letting me pitch a camp on such a wet and stormy night, and had prepared a lodging for me in the tower.

The Ḳāimaḳām of Ḳal'at el Ḥuṣn is a distinguished man of letters. His name is 'Abd ul Ḥamid Beg Rāfi'a Zādeh, and his family comes from Egypt, where many of his cousins are still to be found. He lives in the topmost tower of the keep, where he had made ready a guest chamber commodiously fitted with carpets and a divan, a four-post bedstead and a mahogany wardrobe with looking-glass doors of which the glass had been so splintered in the journey a-camel back from Tripoli that it was impossible to see the smallest corner of one's face in it. I was wet through, but the obligations of good society had to be fulfilled, and they demanded that we should sit down on the divan and exchange polite phrases while I drank glasses of weak tea. My host was preoccupied and evidently disinclined for animated conversation—for a good reason, as I subsequently found—but on my replying to his first greeting he heaved a sigh of relief, and exclaimed:

"Praise be to God! your Excellency speaks Arabic. We had feared that we should not be able to talk with you, and I had already invited a Syrian lady who knows the English tongue to spend the evening for the purpose of interpreting."

We kept up a disjointed chat for an hour while the damp soaked more and more completely through my coat and skirt, and it was not until long after the mules had arrived and their packs had been unloaded that the Ḳāimaḳām rose and took his departure, saying that he would leave me to rest. We had, in fact, made a long day's march; it had taken the muleteers eleven hours to reach Ḳal'at el Ḥuṣn. I had barely had time to change my wet clothes before a discreet knocking at the inner door announced the presence of the womenfolk. I opened at once and admitted a maid servant, and the wife of the Ḳāimaḳām, and a genteel lady who greeted me in English of the most florid kind. This last was the Sitt Ferīdeh, the Christian wife of the Government land surveyor, who is also a Christian. She had been educated at a missionary school in Tripoli, and I was not long left in ignorance of the fact that she was an authoress, and that her greatest work was the translation of the "Last Days of Pompeii" into Arabic. The Ḳāimaḳām's wife was a young woman with apple cheeks, who would have been pretty if she had not been inordinately fat. She was his second wife; he had married her only a month or two before, on the death of his first, the mother of his children. She was so shy that it was some time before she ventured to open her lips in my presence, but the Sitt Ferīdeh carried off the situation with a gushing volubility, both in English and in Arabic, and a cheerful air of emphasising by her correct demeanour the fervour of her Christianity. She was a pleasant and intelligent woman, and I enjoyed her company considerably more than that of my hostess. The first word that the Khānum ventured to utter was, however, a welcome one, for she asked when I would please to dine. I replied with enthusiasm that no hour could be too early for me, and we crossed a muddy courtyard and entered a room in which a bountiful meal had been spread out. Here we were joined by an ancient dame who was presented to me as "a friend who has come to gaze upon your Excellency," and we all sat down to the best of dinners eaten by one at least of the party with the best of sauces. A thick soup and four enormous dishes of meat and vegetables, topped by a rice pudding, composed the repast. When dinner

ḲAL'AT EL ḤUṢN, INTERIOR OF THE CASTLE

was over we returned to my room, a brazier full of charcoal was brought in, together with hubble-bubbles for the ladies, and we settled ourselves to an evening's talk. The old woman refused to sit on the divan, saying that she was more accustomed to the floor, and disposed herself neatly as close as possible to the brazier, holding out her wrinkled hands over the glowing coals. She was clad in black, and her head was covered by a thick white linen cloth, which was bound closely above her brow and enveloped her chin, giving her the air of some aged prioress of a religious order. Outside the turret room the wind howled; the rain beat against the single window, and the talk turned naturally to deeds of horror and such whispered tales of murder and death as must have startled the shadows in that dim room for many and many a century. A terrible domestic tragedy had fallen upon the Ḳāimaḳām ten days before: his son had been shot by a schoolfellow at Tripoli in some childish quarrel—the women seemed to think it not unusual that a boy's sudden anger should have such consequences. The Ḳāimaḳām had been summoned by telegraph; he had ridden down the long mountain road with fear clutching at his heart, only to find the boy dead, and his sorrow had been almost more than he could bear. So said the Sitt Ferīdeh.

The ancient crone rocked herself over the brazier and muttered:

"Murder is like the drinking of milk here! God! there is no other but Thou."

A fresh gust of wind swept round the tower, and the Christian woman took up the tale.

"This Khānum," said she, nodding her head towards the figure by the brazier, "knows also what it is to weep. Her son was but now murdered in the mountains by a robber who slew him with his knife. They found his body lying stripped by the path."

The mother bent anew over the charcoal, and the glow flushed her worn old face.

"Murder is like the spilling of water!" she groaned. "Oh Merciful!"

It was late when the women left me. One of them offered to pass the night in my room, but I refused politely and firmly.

Next day I was wakened by thunder and by hailstones rattling against my shutters. There was nothing for it but to spend another twenty-four hours under the Ḳāimaḳām's roof and be thankful that we had a roof to spend them under. I explored the castle from end to end, with immense satisfaction to the eternal child that lives in the soul of all of us and takes more delight in the dungeons and battlements of a fortress than in any other relic of antiquity. Ḳal'at el Ḥuṣn is so large that half the population of the village is lodged in the vaulted substructures of the keep, while the garrison occupies the upper towers. The walls of the keep rise from a moat inside the first line of fortifications, the line through which we had passed the night before by the vaulted gallery. The butcher of the castle lodged by the gateway of the inner wall; every morning he killed a sheep on the threshold, and those who went out stepped across a pool of blood as though some barbaric sacrifice were performed daily at the gate. The keep contained a chapel, now converted into a mosque,

WINDOWS OF THE BANQUET HALL

and a banquet hall with Gothic windows, the tracery of which was blocked with stones to guard those who dwelt within against the cold. The tower in which I was lodged formed part of the highest of the defences and rose above three stories of vaults. A narrow passage from it along the top of the wall led into a great and splendid chamber, beyond which was a round tower containing a circular room roofed by a fourfold vault, and lighted by pointed windows with rosettes and mouldings round the arches. The castle is the "Kerak of the Knights" of Crusader chronicles. It belonged to the Hospitallers, and the Grand Master of the Order made it his residence. The Egyptian Sultan Malek eḍ Dāher took it from them, restored it, and set his exultant inscription over the main gate. It is one of the most perfect of the many fortresses which bear witness to the strange jumble of noble ardour, fanaticism, ambition and crime that combined to make the history of the Crusades—a page whereon the Christian nations cannot look without a blush nor read without the unwilling pity exacted by vain courage. For to die in a worthless cause is the last extremity of defeat. Kerak is closely related to the military architecture of southern France, yet it bears traces of an Oriental influence from which the great Orders were not immune, though the Templars succumbed to it more completely than the Hospitallers. Like the contemporary Arab fortresses the walls increased in thickness towards the foot to form a sloping bastion of solid masonry which protected them against the attacks of sappers, but the rounded towers with their great projection from the line of the wall were wholly French in character. The Crusaders are said to have found a castle on the hill top and taken it from the Moslims, but I saw no traces of earlier work than theirs. Parts of the present structure are later than their time, as, for instance, a big building by the inner moat, on the walls of which were carved lions not unlike the Seljuk lion.

After lunch I waded down the muddy hill to the village and called on the Sitt Ferīdeh and her husband. There were another pair of Christians present, the man being the Sāḥib es Sandūḳ, which I take to be a kind of treasurer. The two men talked of the condition of the Syrian poor. No one, said the land surveyor, died of hunger, and he proceeded to draw up the yearly budget of the average peasant. The poorest of the fellaḥīn may earn from 1000 to 1500 piastres a year (£7 to £11), but he has no need of any money except to pay the capitation tax and to buy himself a substitute for military service. Meat is an unknown luxury; a cask of semen (rancid butter) costs 8*s.* or 10*s.* at most; it helps to make the burghul and other grains palatable, and it lasts several months. If the grain and the semen run low the peasant has only to go out into the mountains or into the open country, which is no man's land, and gather edible leaves or grub up roots. He builds his house with his own hands, there are no fittings or furniture in it, and the ground on which it stands costs nothing. As for clothing, what does he need ? a couple of linen shirts, a woollen cloak every two or three years, and a cotton kerchief for the head. The old and the sick are seldom left uncared for; their families look after them if they have families, and if they are without relations they can always make a livelihood by begging, for no one in the East refuses to give something when he is asked, though the poor can seldom give money. Few of the fellaḥīn own land of their own ; they work for hire on the estates of richer men. The chief landowners round Ḳal'at el Ḥuṣn are the family of the Danādisheh, who come from Tripoli. Until quite recently the government did not occupy the castle ; it belongs to the family of the Zā'bieh, who have owned it for two hundred years, and still live in some rooms on the outer wall. The Treasurer broke in here and said that even the Moslem population hated the Ottoman government, and would infinitely rather be ruled by a foreigner, what though he were an infidel—preferably by the English, because the prosperity of Egypt had made so deep an impression on Syrian minds.

KAL'AT EL ḤUṢN, WALLS OF THE INNER ENCEINTE

That evening the Ḳāimaḳām sent me a message asking whether I would choose to dine alone or whether I would honour him and his wife, and I begged to be allowed to take the latter alternative. In spite of a desire, touchingly evident, to be a good host, he was sad and silent during the earlier stages of the dinner, until we hit upon a subject that drew him from the memory of his sorrow. The mighty dead came out to help us with words upon their lips that have lifted the failing hearts of generations of mankind. The Ḳāimaḳām was well acquainted with Arabic literature; he knew the poets of the Ignorance by heart, and when he found that I had a scanty knowledge of them and a great love for them he quoted couplet after couplet. But his own tastes lay with more modern singers; the tenth-century Mutanabbi was evidently one of his favourite authors. Some of the old fire still smoulders in Mutanabbi's verse; it burnt again as the Ḳāimaḳām recited the famous ode in which the poet puts from him the joys of youth:

> "Oft have I longed for age to still the tumult in my brain,
> And why should I repine when my prayer is fulfilled?
> We have renounced desire save for the spear-points,
> Neither do we dally, except with them.
> The most exalted seat in the world is the saddle of a swift horse,
> And the best companion for all time is a book."

"Your Excellency," concluded the Ḳāimaḳām, "must surely hold that couplet in esteem."

When we returned to the guest chamber he asked whether he should not read his latest poem, composed at the request of the students of the American College at Beyrout (the most renowned institution of its kind in Syria) to commemorate an anniversary they were about to celebrate. He produced first the students' letter, which was couched in flattering terms, and then his sheets of manuscript, and declaimed his verses with the fine emphasis of the Oriental reciter, pausing from time to time to explain the full meaning of a metaphor or to give an illustration to some difficult couplet. His subject was the praise of learning, but he ended inconsequently with a fulsome panegyric on the Sultan, a passage of which he was immensely proud. As far as I could judge it was not very great poetry, but what of that? There is no solace in misfortune like authorship, and for a short hour the Ḳāimaḳām forgot his grief and entered into regions where there is neither death nor lamentation. I offered him sympathy and praise at suitable points and could have laughed to find myself talking the same agreeable rubbish in Arabic that we all talk so often in English. I might have been sitting in a London drawing-room, instead of between the bare walls of a Crusader tower, and the world is after all made of the one stuff throughout.

It was still raining on the following morning and I had dressed and breakfasted in the lowest spirits when of a sudden

FELLAHIN ARABS

some one waved a magic wand, the clouds were cleared away, and we set off at half-past seven in exquisite sunshine. At the bottom of the steep hill on which the castle stands there lies in an olive grove a Greek monastery. When I reached it I got off my horse and went in, as was meet, to salute the Abbot, and, behold! he was an old acquaintance whom I had met at the monastery of Ma'alūla five years earlier on my return from Palmyra. There were great rejoicings at this fortunate coincidence, and much jam and water and coffee were consumed in the celebration of it. The monastery has been rebuilt, except for a crypt-like chapel, which they say is 1200 years old. The vault is supported by two pairs of marble columns, broken off below the capital and returned into the wall, a scheme more curious than attractive. The capitals are in the form of lily heads of a Byzantine type. By the altar screen, a good piece of modern wood carving, there are some very beautiful Persian tiles. In the western wall of the monastery I was shown a door so narrow between the jambs that it is scarcely possible to squeeze through them, impossible, said the monks, for any one except he be pure of heart. I did not risk my reputation by attempting to force the passage.

We rode on through shallow wooded valleys full of flowers; the fruit trees were coming into blossom and the honeysuckle into leaf, and by a tiny graveyard under some budding oaks we stopped to lunch. Before us lay the crucial point of our day's march. We could see the keep of Ṣāfiṭa Castle on the opposite hill, but there was a swollen river between, the bridge had been swept away, and report said that the ford was impassable. When we reached the banks of the Abrash we saw the river rushing down its wide channel, an unbroken body of swirling water through which no loaded mule could pass. We rode near two hours down stream, and were barely in time with the second bridge, the Jisr el Wād, which was in the last stage of decrepitude, the middle arch just holding together. The hills on the opposite bank were covered with a low scrub, out of which the lovely iris stylosa lifted its blue petals, and the scene was further enlivened by a continuous procession of white-robed Noṣairis making their way down to the bridge. I had a Kurdish zaptieh with me, 'Abd ul Mejīd, who knew the mountains well, and all the inhabitants of them. Though he was a Mohammedan he had no feeling against the Noṣairis, whom he had always found to be a harmless folk, and every one greeted him with a friendly salutation as we passed. He told me that the white-robed companies were going to the funeral feast of a great sheikh much renowned for piety, who had died a week ago. The feast on such occasions is held two days after the funeral, and when the guests have eaten of the meats each man according to his ability pays tribute to the family of the dead, the sums varying from one lira upwards to five or six. To have a reputation for holiness in the Jebel Noṣairiyyeh is as good as a life insurance with us.

Owing to our long circuit we did not reach Ṣāfiṭa till four. I refused the hospitality of the Commandant, and pitched my tents on a ridge outside the village. The keep which we had seen from afar is all that remains of the White Castle of the Knights Templars. It stands on the top of the hill with the village clustered at its foot, and from its summit are visible the Mediterranean and the northern parts of the Phœnician coast. I saw a Phœnician coin among the antiquities offered me for sale, and the small bronze figure of a Phœnician god—Ṣāfiṭa was probably an inland stronghold of the merchant nation. The keep was a skilful architectural surprise. It contained, not the vaulted hall or refectory that might have been expected, but a great church which had thus occupied the very heart of the fortress. A service was being held when we entered and all the people were at their prayers in a red glow of sunset that came through the western doors. The inhabitants of Ṣāfiṭa are most of them Christians, and many speak English with a strong American accent picked up while they were making their small fortunes in the States. Besides the accent, they had acquired a familiarity of address that did not please me, and lost some of the good manners to which they had been born. 'Abd ul Mejīd, the smart non-commissioned officer, accompanied me through the town, saved me from the clutches of the Americanised Christians, twirled his fierce military moustaches at the little boys who thought to run after us, and followed their retreat with extracts from the finest vocabulary of objurgation that I have been privileged to hear.

Late in the evening two visitors were announced, who turned out to be the Ẓābit (Commandant) and another official sent by the Ḳāimaḳām of Drekish to welcome me and bring me down to his village. We three rode off together in the early morning with a couple of soldiers behind us, by a winding path through the hills, and after two hours we came to a valley full of olive groves, with the village of Drekish on the slopes above them. At the first clump of olive trees we found three worthies in frock coats and tarbushes waiting to receive us; they mounted their horses when we approached and fell into the procession, which was further swelled as we ascended the village street by other notables on horseback, till it reached the sum total of thirteen. The Ḳāimaḳām met us at the door of his house, frock-coated and ceremonious, and led me into his audience-room where we drank coffee. By this time the company consisted of some thirty persons of importance. When the official reception was over my host took me into his private house and introduced me to his wife, a charming Damascene lady, and we had a short conversation, during which I made his better acquaintance. Riẓa Beg el 'Ābid owes his present position to the fact that he is cousin to 'Izzet Pasha, for there is not one of that great man's family but he is at least Ḳāmaiḳām. Riẓa Beg might have climbed the official ladder unaided; he is a man of exceptionally pleasant manners, amply endowed with the acute intelligence of the Syrian. The family to which he and 'Izzet belong is of Arab origin. The members of it claim to be descended from the noble tribe of the Muwāli, who were kin to Harūn er Rashīd, and when you meet 'Izzet Pasha it is as well to congratulate him on his relationship with that Khalif, though he knows, and he knows also that you know, that the Muwāli repudiate his claims with scorn and count him among the descendants of their slaves, as his name 'Ābid (slave), may show. Slaves or freemen, the members of the 'Ābid house have climbed so cleverly that they have set their feet upon the neck of Turkey, and will remain in that precarious position until 'Izzet falls from favour. Riẓa Beg pulled a grave face when I alluded to his high connection, and observed that power such as that enjoyed by his family was a serious matter, and how gladly would he retire into a less prominent position than that of Ḳāimaḳām! Who knew but that the Pasha too would not wish to exchange the pleasures of Constantinople for a humbler and a safer sphere—a supposition that I can readily believe to be well grounded, since 'Izzet, if rumour speaks the truth, has got all that a man can reasonably expect from the years during which he has enjoyed the royal condescension. I assured the Kāimaḳām that I should make a point of paying my respects to the Pasha when I reached Constantinople, a project that I ultimately carried out with such success that I may now reckon myself, on 'Izzet's own authority, as one of those who will enjoy his life-long friendship.

By this time lunch was ready, and the Khānum having retired, the other guests were admitted to the number of four, the Ẓābit, the Ḳāḍi and two others. It was a copious, an excellent and an entertaining meal. The conversation flowed merrily round the table, prompted and encouraged by the Ḳāimaḳām, who handled one subject after the other with the polished ease of a man of the world. As he talked I had reason to observe once more how fine and subtle a tongue is modern Syrian Arabic when used by a man of education. The Ḳāḍi's speech was hampered by his having a reputation for learning to uphold, which obliged him to confine himself to the dead language of the Ḳur'an. As I took my leave the Ḳāimaḳām explained that for that night I was still to be his guest. He had learnt, said he, that I wished to camp at the ruined temple of Ḥuṣn es Suleimān, and had despatched my caravan thither under the escort of a zaptieh, and sent up servants and provisions, together with one of his cousins to see to my entertainment. I was to take the Ẓābit with me, and Rā'ib Effendi el Ḥelu, another of the luncheon party, and he hoped that I should be satisfied. I thanked him profusely for his kindness, and declared that I should have known his Arab birth by his generous hospitality.

Our path mounted to the top of the Noṣairiyyeh hills and followed along the crests, a rocky and beautiful track. The hills were extremely steep, and bare of all but grass and flowers except that here and there, on the highest summits, there was a group of big oaks with a white-domed Noṣairi mazār shining through their bare boughs. The Noṣairis have neither mosque nor church, but on every mountain top they build a shrine that marks a burial-ground. These high-throned dead, though they have left the world of men, have not ceased from their good offices, for they are the protectors of the trees rooted among their bones, trees which, alone among their kind, are allowed to grow untouched.

Ḥuṣn es Suleimān lies at the head of a valley high up in the mountains. A clear spring breaks from under its walls and flows round a natural platform of green turf, on which we pitched our tents. The hills rise in an amphitheatre behind the temple, the valley drops below it, and the gods to whom it was dedicated enjoy in solitude the ruined loveliness of their shrine. The walls round the temenos are overgrown with ivy, and violets bloom in the crevices. Four doorways lead into the court, in the centre of which stand the ruins of the temple, while a little to the south of the cella are the foundations of an altar, bearing in fine Greek letters a dedication that recounts how a centurion called Decimus of the Flavian (?) Legion, with his two sons and his daughter, raised an altar of brass to the god of Baitocaicē and placed it upon a platform of masonry in the year 444. The date is of the Seleucid era and corresponds to A.D. 132. It is regrettable that Decimus did not see fit to mention the name of the god, which remains undetermined in all the inscriptions. The northern gateway is a triple door, lying opposite to a second rectangular enclosure, which contains a small temple in antis at the south-east corner, and the apse of a sanctuary in the northern wall. This last sheltered perhaps the statue of the unknown god, for there are steps leading up to it and the bases of columns on either side. As at Ba'albek, the Christians sanctified the spot by the building of a church, which lay across the second enclosure at right angles to the northern sanctuary. The masonry of the outer walls of both courts is very massive, the stones being sometimes six or eight feet long. The decoration is much more austere than that of Ba'albek, but certain details so intimately recall the latter that I am tempted to conjecture that the same architect may have been employed at both places, and that it was he who cut on the under side of the architraves of Baitocaicē the eagles and cherubs that he had used to adorn the architrave of the Temple of Jupiter. The peasants say that there are deep vaults below both temple and court. The site must be well worthy of careful excavation, though no additional knowledge will enhance the beauty of the great shrine in the hills.

The Ḳāimaḳām had not fallen short of his word. Holocausts

THE TEMPLE AT ḤUSN ES SULEIMĀN

of sheep and hens had been offered up for us, and after my friends and I had feasted, the soldiers and the muleteers made merry in their turn. The camp fires blazed brightly in the clear sharp mountain air, the sky was alive with stars, the brook gurgled over the stones; and the rest was silence, for Kurt was lost. Somewhere among the hills he had strayed away, and he was gone never to return. I mourned his loss, but slept the more peacefully for it ever after.

NORTH GATE, ḤUṢN ES SULEIMÂN

All my friends and all the soldiers rode with us next day to the frontier of the district of Drekish and there left us after having hounded a reluctant Noṣairi out of his house at 'Ain esh Shems and bidden him help the zaptieh who accompanied us to find the extraordinarily rocky path to Masyād. After they had gone I summoned Mikhāil and asked him what he had thought of our day's entertainment. He gave the Arabic equivalent for a sniff and said:

"Doubtless your Excellency thinks that you were the guest of the Ḳāimaḳām. I will tell you of whom you were the guest. You saw those fellaḥīn of the Noṣairiyyeh, the miserable ones, who sold you antīcas at the ruins this morning? They were your hosts. Everything you had was taken from them without return. They gathered the wood for the fires, the hens were theirs, the eggs were theirs, the lambs were from their flocks, and when you refused to take more saying, 'I have enough,' the soldiers seized yet another lamb and carried it off with them. And the only payment the fellaḥīn received were the metalīks you gave them for their old money. But if you will listen to me," added

Mikhāil inconsequently, "you shall travel through the land of Anatolia and never take a quarter of a mejīdeh from your purse. From Ḳāimaḳām to Ḳāimaḳām you shall go, and everywhere they shall offer you hospitality—that sort does not look for payment, they wish your Excellency to say a good word for them when you come to Constantinople. You shall sleep in their houses, and eat at their tables, as it was when I travelled with Sacks. . . ."

THE CITY GATE, MASYĀD

But if I were to tell all that happened when Mikhāil travelled with Mark Sykes I should never get to Masyād.

The day was rendered memorable by the exceptional difficulty of the paths and by the beauty of the flowers. On the hill tops grew the alpine cyclamen, crocuses, yellow, white and purple, and whole slopes of white primroses; lower down, irises, narcissus, black and green orchids, purple orchis and the blue many-petalled anemone in a boscage of myrtle. When we reached the foot of the steepest slopes I sent the unfortunate Noṣairi home with a tip, which was a great deal more than he expected to get out of an adventure that had begun with a command from the soldiery. At three we reached Masyād and camped at the foot of the castle.

Now Masyād was a disappointment. There is indeed a great castle, but, as far as I could judge, it is of Arab workmanship, and the walls round the town are Arab also. A Roman road from Ḥamāh passes through Masyād, and there must be traces of Roman settlement in the town, but I saw none. I heard of a castle at Abu Kbesh on the top of the hills, but it was said to be like Masyād, only smaller, and I did not go up to it. The castle of Masyād has an outer wall and an inner keep reached by a vaulted passage like that of Ḳal'at el Ḥuṣn. The old keep is almost destroyed, and has been replaced by jerry-built halls and chambers erected by the Ismailis some hundreds of years ago when they held the place, so I was told by an old man called the Emir Muṣṭafa Milḥēm, who belonged to the sect and served me as guide. He also said that his family had inhabited the castle for seven or eight hundred years, but possibly he lied, though it is true that the Ismailis have held it as long. Built into the outer gateways are certain capitals and columns that must have been taken from Byzantine structures. There are some old Arabic inscriptions inside the second gate which record the names of the builders of that part of the fortifications, but they are much broken. I was told afterwards that I ought to have visited a place called Deir es Sleb, where there are two churches and a small castle. It is not marked in the map, and I heard nothing of it until I had left it far behind. I saw bits of the rasīf, the Roman road, as I travelled next day to Ḥamāh. At the bridge over the river Sarut, four and a half hours from Masyād, there is a curious mound faced to the very top with a rough wall of huge stones. Mikhāil found a Roman coin in the furrows of the field at the foot of it. From the river we had two and a half hours of tedious travel that were much lightened by the presence of a charming old Turk, a telegraph official, who joined us at the bridge and told me his story as we rode.

CAPITAL AT MASYĀD

" Effendim, the home of my family is near Sofia. Effendim,

you know the place? Māsha'llah, it is a pleasant land! Where I lived it was covered with trees, fruit trees and pines in the mountains and rose gardens in the plain. Effendim, many of us came here after the war with the Muscovite for the reason that we would not dwell under any hand but that of the Sultan, and many returned again after they had come. Effendim? for what cause? They would not live in a country without trees; by God, they could not endure it."

Thus conversing we reached Ḥamāh.

CAPITAL AT MASYAD

A NA'OURA, ḤAMAH

CHAPTER X

You do not see Ḥamāh until you are actually upon it—there is no other preposition that describes the attitude of the new comer. The Orontes at this point flows in a deep bed and the whole city lies hidden between the banks. The monotonous plain of cornfields stretches before you without a break until you reach a veritable entanglement of graveyards—the weekly All Souls' Day had come round again when we arrived, and the cemeteries were crowded with the living as well as with the dead. Suddenly the plain ceased beneath our feet, and we stood on the edge of an escarpment, with the whole town spread out before us, the Orontes set with gigantic Persian wheels, and beyond it the conical mound on which stood the fortresses of Hamath and Epiphaneia and who knows what besides, for the site is one of the oldest in the world. Two soldiers started from the earth and set about to direct me to a camping ground, but I was tired and cross, a state of mind that does sometimes occur on a journey, and the arid spots between houses to which they took us seemed particularly distasteful. At length the excellent Turk, who had not yet abandoned us, declared that he knew the very place that would please me; he led us along the edge of the escarpment to the extreme northern end of the city, and here showed us a grassy sward which was as lovely a situation as could be desired. The Orontes issued from the town below us amid gardens of flowering apricot trees, the golden evening light lay behind the minarets, and a great Na'oura ground out a delicious song of the river.

Ḥamāh is the present terminus of the French railway,* and the seat of a Muteserrif. The railway furnished me with a guide and companion in the shape of a Syrian station-master, a consequential half-baked little man, who had been educated in a missionary school and scorned to speak Arabic when he could stutter in French. He announced that his name was Monsieur Kbēs and his passion archæology, and, that he might the better prove himself to be in the van of modern thought, he attributed every antiquity in Ḥamāh to the Hittites, whether it were Byzantine capital or Arab enlaced decoration. With the Muteserrif I came immediately into collision by reason of his insisting on providing me with eight soldiers to guard my camp at night, a preposterous force, considering that two had been ample in every country district. So numerous a guard would have been an intolerable nuisance, for they would have talked all night and left the camp no peace, and I sent six of them away, in spite of their protestations that they must obey superior orders. They reconciled the Muteserrif's commands with mine by spending the night in a ruined mosque a quarter of a mile away, where they were able to enjoy excellent repose unbroken by a sense of responsibility.

For picturesqueness Ḥamāh is not to be outdone by any town in Syria. The broad river with its water wheels is a constant element of beauty, the black and white striped towers of the mosques an exquisite architectural feature, the narrow, partly vaulted streets are traps to hold unrivalled effects of sun and shadow, and the bazaars are not as yet disfigured by

* It will be the terminus only for a month or two longer for the line has at length been continued to Aleppo.

the iron roofs that have done so much to destroy the character of those at Damascus and at Ḥomṣ. The big mosque in the centre of the town was once a Byzantine church. The doors and windows of the earlier building are easily traceable in the walls of the mosque; the lower part of the western minaret was probably the foundation of an older tower; the court is full of Byzantine shafts and capitals, and the beautiful little Ḳubbeh is supported by eight Corinthian columns. On one of these I noticed the Byzantine motive of the blown acanthus. When they grew weary of setting the leaves in a stereotyped uprightness, the stone-cutters laid them lightly round the capital, as though the fronds had drifted in a swirl of wind, and the effect is wonderfully graceful and fanciful. Kbēs and I climbed the citadel hill, and found the area on the top to be enormous, but all the cut stones of the fortifications have been removed and built into the town below. My impression is that the isolation of the mound is not natural, but has been effected by cutting through the headland that juts out into the valley, and so separating a part of it from the main ridge. If this be so, it must have been a great work of antiquity, for the cutting is both wide and deep.

THE ḲUBBEH IN THE MOSQUE AT ḤAMĀH

The chief interest of the day at Ḥamāh was supplied by the inhabitants. Four powerful Mohammadan families are reckoned as the aristocracy of the town, that of 'Aẓam Zādeh,

Teifūr, Killāni and Barāzi, of which last I had seen a member in Damascus. The combined income of each family is probably about £6000 a year, all derived from land and villages, there being little trade in Ḥamāh. Before the Ottoman government was established as firmly as it is now, these four families were the lords of Ḥamāh and the surrounding districts; they are still of considerable weight in the administration of the town, and the officials of the Sultan let them go pretty much their own way, which is often devious. An ancient evil tale of the 'Aẓam Zādeh is often told, and not denied, so far as I could learn, by the family. There was an 'Aẓam in past years who, like King Ahab, desired his neighbour's vineyard, but the owner of it refused to sell. Thereupon the great man laid a plot. He caused one of his slaves to be slaughtered and had him cut into small pieces and buried, not too deep, in a corner of the coveted property, and after waiting a suitable time he sent a message to the landlord saying, "You have frequently invited me to drink coffee with you in your garden; I will come. Make ready." The man was gratified by this condescension and prepared a feast The day came and with it the 'Aẓam prince. The meal was spread under an arbour, but when the guest saw it he declared that the spot selected did not suit him, and led the way to the exact place where his slave had been buried. The host protested, saying that it was a mean corner close to the refuse heaps, but the 'Aẓam replied that he was satisfied, and the entertainment began. Presently the guest raised his head and said, "I perceive a curious smell." "My lord," said the host, "it is from the refuse heaps." "No," said the other, "there is something more;" and summoning his servants he bade them dig in the ground whereon they sat. The quartered body of the slave was revealed and recognised, and on an accusation of murder the lord of the garden was seized and bound, and his possessions taken from him by way of compensation.

Nor, said Kbēs, have such summary methods of injustice ceased. Quite recently a quantity of onions were stolen from a shop belonging to 'Abd ul Ḳādir el 'Aẓam in the quarter immediately below my camp. The servants of 'Abd ul

THE TEKKIYAH KILLĀNIYYEH, HAMAH

Ḳādir came to the house of the sheikh of the quarter and demanded from him their master's property, and since he knew nothing of the matter and could not indicate who the thief might have been, they seized him and his son, wounding the son in the hand with a bullet, dragged them to the river bank, stripped them, beat them almost to death, and left them to get home as best they might. The incident was known all over Ḥamāh, but the government took no steps to punish 'Abd ul Ḳādir. I went to the house of Khālid Beg 'Aẓam, which is the most beautiful in the city, as beautiful as the famous 'Aẓam house in Damascus. Khālid took me into rooms every inch of which was covered with an endless variety of Persian patterns in gesso duro and woodwork and mosaic. They opened upon a courtyard set round with an arcade of the best Arab workmanship, with a fountain in the centre and pots of flowering ranunculus and narcissus in the corners. The women of the house of 'Aẓam have even a greater reputation than the sumptuous walls that hold them; they are said to be the loveliest women in all Ḥamāh.

The Killāni I visited also in their charming house by the Orontes, the Tekyah Killāniyyeh. It contains a mausoleum, where three of their ancestors are buried, and rooms looking over the river, filled with the pleasant grumbling of a Persian wheel. From thence I went to the Muteserrif, who is an old man bent almost double, and acquainted with no tongue but Turkish. I was considerably relieved to find that he bore no malice for my unruly conduct in the matter of the guard. As we walked home to lunch we met an aged Afghan clad in white. Dervīsh Effendi was his name. He stopped the station-master to inquire who I was, and having learnt that I was English he approached me with a grin and a salute and said in Persian, "The English and the Afghans are close friends." He was in fact as well informed as the British public—possibly better informed—of the interchange of visits and civilities between Kabul and Calcutta; and the moral of the episode (which developed into a long and tiresome, but most cordial, visit from Dervīsh Effendi) is that the report of what happens in the remotest corner of Asia is known almost immediately to the furthest end, and that it is scarcely an exaggeration to say that if an English regiment is cut up on the borders of Afghanistan the English tourist will be mocked at in the streets of Damascus. Islām is the bond that unites the western and central parts of the continent, as it is the electric current by which the transmission of sentiment is effected, and its potency is increased by the fact that there is little or no sense of territorial nationality to counterbalance it. A Turk or a Persian does not think or speak of "my country" in the way that an Englishman or a Frenchman thinks and speaks; his patriotism is confined to the town of which he is a native, or at most to the district in which that town lies. If you ask him to what nationality he belongs he will reply: "I am a man of Isfahān," or "I am a man of Konia," as the case may be, just as the Syrian will reply that he is a native of Damascus or Aleppo—I have already indicated that Syria is merely a geographical term corresponding to no national sentiment in the breasts of the inhabitants. Thus to one listening to the talk of the bazaars, to the shopkeepers whose trade is intimately connected with local conditions in districts very far removed from their own counters, to the muleteers who carry so much more than their loads from city to city, all Asia seems to be linked together by fine chains of relationship, and every detail of the foreign policies of Europe, from China to where you please, to be weighed more or less accurately in the balance of public opinion. It is not the part of wanderers and hearers of gossip to draw conclusions. We can do no more than report, for any that may care to listen, what falls from the lips of those who sit round our camp fires, and who ride with us across deserts and mountains, for their words are like straws on the flood of Asiatic politics, showing which way the stream is running. Personal experience has acquainted them with the stock in trade and the vocabulary of statecraft. They are familiar with war and negotiation and compromise, and with long nurtured and carefully concealed revenge. Whether they are discussing the results of a blood feud or the consequences of an international jealousy their appreciations are often just and their guesses near the mark.

For the moment, so far as my experience goes, the name of

the English carries more weight than it has done for some time past. I noticed a very distinct difference between the general attitude towards us from that which I had observed with pain five years before, during the worst moments of the Boer War. The change of feeling is due, so far as I can judge from the conversations to which I listened, not so much to our victory in South Africa as to Lord Cromer's brilliant administration in Egypt, Lord Curzon's policy on the Persian Gulf, and the alliance with the conquering Japanese.

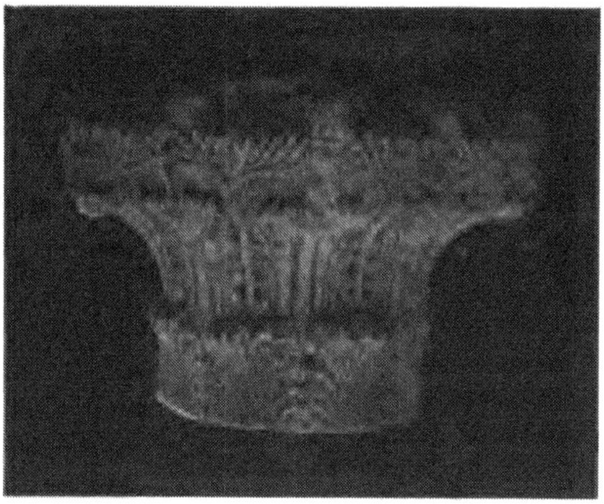

CAPITAL IN THE MOSQUE, ḤAMĀH

When I had at last got rid of the Afghan and was sitting alone on the fringe of grass that separated my tent from the city hundreds of feet below, a person of importance drove up to pay his respects. He was the Mufti, Muḥammad Effendi. He brought with him an intelligent man from Boṣrā el Ḥarīr, in the Ḥaurān, who had travelled in Cyprus and had much to say (and little good to say) of our administration there. The Mufti was a man of the same type as the Ḳāḍi of Ḥomṣ and the Sheikh Nakshibendi—the sharp-eyed and sharp-witted Asiatic, whose distinguished features are somewhat marred by an astuteness that amounts to cunning. He established himself upon the best of the camp chairs, and remarked with satisfaction:

"I asked: 'Can she speak Arabic?' and when they answered 'Yes,' verily I ordered my carriage and came."

His talk was of Yemen, whither he had been sent some years before to restore peace after the last Arab revolt. He spoke of the three days' journey over torrid desert from the coast, of the inland mountains covered with trees where there is always rain summer and winter, of the enormous grapes that hang in the vineyards, and the endless variety of fruits in the orchards, of the cities as big as Damascus, walled with great fortifications of mud a thousand years old. The Arabs, said he, were town dwellers not nomads, and they hated the Ottoman government as it is hated in few places. When the armies of the Sultan went out against them they were accustomed to flee into the mountains, where they could hold out, thought the Mufti, for an indefinite number of years. But he was wrong; a few months were enough to give victory to the Sultan's troops, what with daring generalship and the power to endure desert marches, and the rebellion failed, like many another, because the Arab tribes hate each other more vindictively than they hate the Osmanli. But, after the fashion of repressed rebellions in Turkey, it has already broken out again. The Mufti told me also that in Ḥamāh wherever they dug they found ancient foundations, even below the river level.

He was followed by my friend the Turkish telegraph clerk, who rejoiced to see me so well encamped, and then by the Muteserrif, pursuing an anxious and tottering course from his carriage through my tent ropes. The latter lent me his victoria that I might visit the parts of the town that lie on the eastern banks of the Orontes, and Kbēs and I drove off with two outriders quite exceptionally free from rags. The eastern quarter, the Hāḍir it is called, is essentially the Bedouin quarter; the city Arabic is replaced here by the rugged desert speech, and the bazaars are filled with Arabs who come in to buy coffee and tobacco and striped cloaks. It contains a beautiful little ruined mosque, said to be Seljuk, called El Ḥayyāt, the mosque of Snakes, after the twisted columns of its windows. At the northern end of the courtyard is a chamber which holds the marble sarcophagus of Abu'l Fīda, Prince of Ḥamāh, the famous geographer. He died in 1331; his tomb is carved with a fine inscription recording the date according to the era of the Hejra.

I gave a dinner party that night to the station-master, the Syrian doctor, Sallūm, and the Greek priest. We talked till late, a congenial if incongruous company. Sallūm had received his training in the American College at Beyrout, from whence come all the medical practitioners, great and small, who are scattered up and down Syria. He was a Christian, though of a different brand from the priest, and Kbēs represented yet another variety of doctrine. On the whole, said the priest, there was little anti-Christian feeling in Ḥamāh, but there was also little respect for his cloth; that very day as he walked through the town some Moslem women had thrown pebbles at him from a house-top, shouting, "Dog of a Christian priest!" Kbēs discussed the benefits conferred by the railway (a remarkably ill-managed concern I fancy) and said that without doubt Ḥamāh had profited by it. Prices had gone up in the last two years, meat that would otherwise have found no market was now sent down to Damascus and Beyrout, and he himself who, when he first came, had been able to buy a sheep for a franc, was now obliged to pay ten.

A CAPITAL, ḤAMĀH

The Muteserrif of Ḥamāh provided me with the best zaptieh that I was to have on all my travels, Ḥajj Maḥmūd, a native of Ḥamāh. He was a tall broad-shouldered man, who had been in the Sultan's own guard at Constantinople, and had made the pilgrimage three times, once as a pilgrim and twice as a soldier of the escort. He rode with me for ten days, and during that time told me more tales than would fill a volume, couched in a fine picturesque speech of which he was the master. He had travelled with a German archæologist, and knew the strange tastes of the Europeans in the matter of ruins and inscriptions.

"At Ḳal'at el Mudīk I said to him: 'If you would look upon a stone with a horse written upon it and his rider, by the

Light of God! I can show it to you!' And he wondered much thereat, and rewarded me with money. By God and Muḥammad the Prophet of God! you too, oh lady, shall gaze on it."

Now this exploit of Maḥmūd's was more remarkable than would appear at first sight, for one of the great difficulties in searching for antiquities is that the people in out-of-the-way places do not recognise a sculpture when they see it. You are not surprised that they should fail to tell the difference between an inscription and the natural cracks and weather markings of the stone; but it takes you aback when you ask whether there are stones with portraits of men and animals upon them, and your interlocutor replies: "Wāllah! we do not know what the picture of a man is like." Moreover, if you show him a bit of a relief with figures well carved upon it, as often as not he will have no idea what the carving represents.

Maḥmūd's most memorable travelling companion had been a Japanese who had been sent by his government, I afterwards learnt, to study and report on the methods of building employed in the eastern parts of the Roman empire—to such researches the Japanese had leisure to apply themselves in the thick of the war. Maḥmūd's curiosity had evidently been much excited by the little man, whose fellows were snatching victory from the dreaded Russians.

"All day he rode, and all night he wrote in his books. He eat nothing but a piece of bread and he drank tea, and when there came a matter for refusal he said (for he could talk neither Arabic nor Turkish), 'Noh! noh!' And that is French," concluded Maḥmūd.

I remarked that it was not French but English, which gave Maḥmūd food for thought, for he added presently:

"We had never heard their name before the war, but by the Face of the Truth! the English knew of them."

The Orontes makes a half circle between Ḥamāh and Ḳal'at es Seijar, and we cut across the chord of the arc, riding over the same dull cultivated plain that I had crossed on my way from Masyād. It was strewn with villages of mud-built, beehive-shaped huts; they are to be met with on the plains all the way to Aleppo, and are like no other villages save those that appear in the illustrations to Central African travel books. As a man grows rich he adds another beehive and yet another to his mansion, till he may have a dozen or more standing round a courtyard, some inhabited by himself and his family, some by his cattle, one forming his kitchen, and one his granary. We saw in the distance a village called Al Ḥerdeh, which Maḥmūd said was Christian and used to belong entirely to the Greek communion. The inhabitants lived happily together and prospered, until they had the misfortune to be discovered by a missionary, who distributed tracts and converted some sixty persons to the English Church, since when there has not been a moment's rest from brawling in Al Ḥerdeh. As we rode, Maḥmūd told tales of the Ismailis and the Noṣairis. Of the former he said that the Agha Khān's photograph was to be found in every house, but it is woman that they worship, said he. Every female child born on the 27th of Rajab is set apart and held to be an incarnation of the divinity. She is called the Rōẓah. She does not work, her hair and nails are never cut, her family share in the respect that is accorded to her, and every man in the village will wear a piece of her clothing or a hair from her body folded in his turban. She is not permitted to marry.

"But what," said I, "if she desire to marry?"

"It would be impossible," replied Maḥmūd. "No one would marry her, for is there any man that can marry God?"

The sect is known to have sacred books, but none have yet fallen into the hands of European scholars. Maḥmūd had seen and read one of them—it was all in praise of the Rōẓah, describing every part of her with eulogy. The Ismailis read the Ḳur'ān also, said he. Other strange matters he related which, like Herodotus, I do not see fit to repeat. The creed seems to spring from dim traditions of Astarte worship, or from that oldest and most universal cult of all, the veneration of the Mother Goddess; but the accusations of indecency that have been brought against it are, I gather, unfounded.*

Of the Noṣairis Maḥmūd had much to tell, for he was we

* The plural of Ismaili in the vernacular is Samawīleh. I do not know whether this is the literary form, but it is the one I have always heard.

acquainted with the hills in which they live, having been for many years employed in collecting the capitation tax among the sect. They are infidels, said he, who do not read the Ḳur'ān nor know the name of God. He related a curious tale which I will repeat for what it is worth :

"Oh lady, it happened in the winter that I was collecting the tax. Now in the month of Kānūn el Awwal (December) the Noṣairis hold a great feast that occurs at the same time as the Christian feast (Christmas), and the day before, when I was riding with two others in the hills, there fell a quantity of snow so that we could go no further, and we sought shelter at the first village in the house of the Sheikh of the village. For there is always a Sheikh of the village, oh lady, and a Sheikh of the Faith, and the people are divided into initiated and uninitiated. But the women know nothing of the secrets of the religion, for by God! a woman cannot keep a secret. The Sheikh greeted us with hospitality and lodged us, but next morning when I woke there was no man to be seen in the house, nothing but the women. And I cried: 'By God and Muḥammad the Prophet of God! what hospitality is this? and are there no men to make the coffee but only women?' And the women replied: 'We do not know what the men are doing, for they have gone to the house of the Sheikh of the Faith, and we are not allowed to enter.' Then I arose and went softly to the house and looked through the window, and, by God! the initiated were sitting in the room, and in the centre was the Sheikh of the Faith, and before him a bowl filled with wine and an empty jug. And the Sheikh put questions to the jug in a low tone, and by the Light of the Truth I heard the jug make answer in a voice that said: 'Bl. . bl. . .' And without doubt, oh lady, this was magic. And while I looked, one raised his head and saw me. And they came out of the house and seized hold of me and would have beaten me, but I cried: 'Oh Sheikh! I am your guest!' So the Sheikh of the Faith came forth and raised his hand, and on the instant all those that had hold of me released me. And he fell at my feet and kissed my hands and the hem of my coat and said: 'Oh Ḥajji! if you will not tell what you have seen I will give you ten mejīdes!' And by the Prophet of God (upon him be peace!) I have never related it, oh lady, until this day."

After four hours' ride we came to Ḳal'at es Seijar. It stands on a long hog's back broken in the middle by an artificial cutting and dropping by steep bluffs to the Orontes, which runs here in a narrow bed between walls of rock. The castle walls that crown the hill between the cutting and the river

ḲAL'AT ES SEIJAR

make a very splendid appearance from below. There is a small village of beehive huts at the bottom of the hill. The Seleucid town of Larissa must have lain on the grassy slopes to the north, judging from the number of dressed stones that are scattered there. I pitched my camp at the further end of the bridge in a grove of apricot trees, snowy with flower and a-hum with bees. The grass was set thickly with anemones and scarlet ranunculus. The castle is the property of Sheikh Aḥmed Seijari and has been held by his family for three hundred years. He and his sons live in a number of little modern houses, built out of old stones in the middle of the fortifications. He owns a considerable amount of land and about one-third of the village, the rest being unequally divided between the Killānis of Ḥamāh and the Smātiyyeh Arabs, a semi-nomadic tribe that dwells in houses during the winter. I had a letter of introduction to Sheikh Aḥmed from Muṣṭafa

Barāzi, and, though Maḥmūd was of opinion that I should not find him in the castle owing to a long-drawn trouble between the Seijari family and the Smātiyyeh, we climbed up to the gate and along a road that showed remains of vaulting, like the entrance to Ḳal'at el Ḥuṣn, and so over masses of ruin till we came to the modern village where the Seijari sheikhs live. I inquired which was the house of Aḥmed, and was directed to a big wooden door, most forbiddingly shut. I knocked and waited, and Maḥmūd knocked yet louder and we waited again. At last a very beautiful woman opened a shutter in the wall above and asked what we wanted. I said I had a letter from Muṣṭafa to Aḥmed, and wished to see him. She replied:

"He is away."

I said: "I would salute his son."

"You cannot see him," she returned. "He is in prison at Ḥamāh, charged with murder."

And so she closed the shutter, leaving me to wonder how good manners would bid me act under these delicate conditions. At that moment a girl came to the door and opened it a hand's breadth. I gave her the letter and my card written in Arabic, murmured a few words of regret, and went away. Maḥmūd now tried to explain the matter. It was one of those long stories that you hear in the East, without beginning, without end, and without any indication as to which of the protagonists is in the right, but an inherent probability that all are in the wrong. The Smātiyyeh had stolen some of the Seijari cattle, the sons of Aḥmed had gone down into the village and killed two of the Arabs—in the castle it was said that the Arabs had attacked them and that they had killed them in self-defence—the Government, always jealous of the semi-independence of ruling sheikhs, had seized the opportunity to strike down the Seijari whether they were at fault or no; soldiers had been sent from Ḥamāh, one of Aḥmed's sons had been put to death, two more were in prison, and all the cattle had been carried off. The rest of the Seijaris were ordered not to stir from the castle, nor indeed could they do so, for the Smātiyyeh were at their gates ready and anxious to kill them if they stepped beyond the walls. They appealed to Ḥamāh for protection, and a guard of some ten soldiers was posted by the river, whether to preserve the lives of the sheikhs or to keep them the more closely imprisoned it was difficult to make out. These events dated from two years back, and for that time the Seijaris had remained prisoners at Ḥamāh and in their own castle, and had been unable to superintend the cultivation of their fields, which were running in consequence to rack and ruin. Moreover, there seemed to be no prospect of improvement in the situation. Later in the afternoon a messenger arrived saying that Aḥmed's brother, 'Abd ul Ḳādir, would be pleased to receive me and would have come himself to welcome me if he could have left the castle. I went up without Maḥmūd and heard the whole story again from the point of view of the sheikhs, which helped me to no conclusion, since it was in most essentials a different story from that which I had heard from Maḥmūd. The only indisputable point (and it was probably not so irrelevant as it seems) was that the Seijari women were wonderfully beautiful. They wore dark blue Bedouin dress, but the blue cloths hanging from their heads were fastened with heavy gold ornaments, like the plaques of the Mycenæan treasure, one behind either temple. Agreeable though their company proved to be I was obliged to cut my visit short by reason of the number of fleas that shared the captivity of the family. Two of the younger women walked down with me through the ruins of the castle, but when we reached the great outer gate they stopped and looked at me standing on the threshold.

ḲAL'AT ES SEIJAR, THE CUTTING THROUGH THE RIDGE

"Allah!" said one, "you go forth to travel through the whole world, and we have never been to Ḥamāh!"

I saw them in the gateway when I turned again to wave them a farewell. Tall and straight they were, and full of supple grace, clothed in narrow blue robes, their brows bound with gold, their eyes following the road they might not tread. For whatever may happen to the sheikhs, nothing is more certain than that women as lovely as those two will remain imprisoned by their lords in Ḳal'at es Seijar.

We rode next day by cultivated plains to Ḳal'at el Mudīk, a short stage of under four hours. Although there were several traces of ruined towns—one in particular I remember at a hamlet called Sheikh Ḥadīd, where there was a mound that looked as if it might have been an acropolis—the journey would have been uninteresting but for Maḥmūd's stories. His talk ran through the characteristics of the many races that make up the Turkish empire, with most of which he was familiar, and when he came to the Circassians it appeared that he shared my aversion to them.

"Oh lady," said he, "they do not know what it is to make return for kindness. The father sells his children, and the children would kill their own father if he had gold in his belt. It happened once that I was riding from Tripoli to Ḥomṣ, and near the khān—you know the place—I met a Circassian walking alone. I said: 'Peace be upon you! Why do you walk?' for the Circassians never go afoot. He said: 'My horse has been stolen from me, and I walk in fear upon this road.' I said: 'Come with me and you shall go in safety to Ḥomṣ.' But I made him walk before my horse, for he was armed with a sword, and who knows what a Circassian will do if you cannot watch him? And after a little we passed an old man working in the fields, and the Circassian ran out to him and spoke with him, and drew his sword as though to kill him. And I called out: 'What has this old man done to you?' And he replied: 'By God! I am hungry, and I asked him for food, and he said "I have none!" wherefore I shall kill him.' Then I said: 'Let him be. I will give you food.' And I gave him the half of all I had, bread and sweetmeats and oranges. So we journeyed until we came to a stream, and I was thirsty, and I got off my mare and holding her by the bridle I stooped to drink. And I looked up suddenly and saw the

Circassian with his foot in my stirrup on the other side of the mare, for he designed to mount her and ride away. And, by God! I had been a father and a mother to him, therefore I struck him with my sword so that he fell to the ground. And I bound him and drove him to Ḥomṣ and delivered him to the Government. This is the manner of the Circassians, may God curse them!"

I asked him of the road to Mecca and of the hardships that the pilgrims endure upon the way.

"By the Face of God! they suffer," said he. "Ten marches from Ma'ān to Medā'in Ṣāleḥ, ten from there to Medīna, and ten from Medīna to Mecca, and the last ten are the worst, for the Sherīf of Mecca and the Arab tribes plot together, and the Arabs rob the pilgrims and share the booty with the Sherīf. Nor are the marches like the marches of gentlefolk when they travel, for sometimes there are fifteen hours between water and water, and sometimes twenty, and the last march into Mecca is thirty hours. Now the Government pays the tribes to let the pilgrims through in peace, and when they know that the Ḥajj is approaching they assemble upon the hills beside the road and cry out to the Amīr ul Ḥajj: 'Give us our dues, 'Abd ur Raḥmān Pasha!' And to each man he gives according to his rights, to one money, and to another a pipe and tobacco, to a third a kerchief, and to a fourth a cloak. Yet it is not the pilgrims that suffer most, but those who keep the forts that guard the water tanks along the road, and every fort is like a prison. It happened once that I was sent with the military escort, and my horse fell sick and could not move, and they left me at one of the forts between Medā'in Ṣāleḥ and Medīna till they should return. Six weeks or more I lived with the keeper of the fort, and we saw no one, and we eat and slept in the sun, and eat again, and slept, for we could not ride out for fear of the Ḥoweiṭāt and the Beni 'Atiyyeh who were at war together. And the man had lived there ten years and never gone a quarter of an hour from that spot, for he watched over the stores that feed the Ḥajj when it passes. By the Prophet of God!" said Maḥmūd, with a sweeping gesture of the hand from earth to sky, "for ten years he had seen nothing but the earth and God! Now he had a little son, and the boy was deaf and dumb, but his eyes saw further than any man's, and he watched all day from the top of the tower. And one day he came running to his father and pointed with his hands, and the father knew he had seen a raiding party far off, and we hastened within and shut the doors. And the horsemen drew near, five hundred of the Beni 'Atiyyeh, and they watered their mares and demanded food, and we threw down bread to them, for we dared not open the doors. And while they eat there came across the plain the raiders of the Ḥoweiṭaṭ, and they began to fight together by the castle wall, and they fought until the evening prayer, and those who lived rode away, leaving their dead to the number of thirty. And we remained all night with locked doors, and at dawn we went down and buried the dead. But it is better to live in a fortress by the Ḥajj road," he continued, "than to serve as a soldier in Yemen, for there the soldiers receive no pay and of food not enough on which to live, and the sun burns like a fire. In Yemen if a man stood in the shade and saw a purse of gold lying in the sun, by God! he would not go out to pick it up, for the heat is like the fire of hell. Oh lady, is it true that in Egypt the soldiers get their pay week by week and month by month?"

I replied that I believed it to be the case, such being the custom in the English army.

"As for us," said Maḥmūd, "our pay is always due to us for half a year, and often out of twelve months' pay we receive but six months'. Wāllah! I have never touched more than eight months' pay for a complete year. Once," he added, "I was in Alexandria—Māsha'llah, the fine city! Houses it has as big as the palaces of kings, and all the roads have paved edges whereon the people walk. And there I saw a cabman who sued a lady for his fare, and the judge gave it to him. By the Truth! the ways of judges are different with us," observed Maḥmūd thoughtfully; and then, with an abrupt transition, he exclaimed: "Look, oh lady! there is Abu Sa'ad."

I looked, and saw Abu Sa'ad walking in the ploughed field, with his white coat as spotless as though he had not just alighted from a journey as long as one of Maḥmūd's, and his black sleeves folded neatly against his sides, and I made haste to welcome the Father of Good Luck, for in Syria the first stork is like the first swallow with us. He cannot, however, any more than the swallow make summer, and we rode that day into Ḳal'at el Mudīk, in drenching rain.

Ḳal'at el Mudīk is the Apamea of the Seleucids. It was founded by Seleucus Nicator, that great town builder who had so many cities for his god-daughters: Seleucia in Pieria, Seleucia on the Calycadnus, Seleucia in Babylonia, and more besides. Though it has been utterly destroyed by earthquakes, enough remains in ruin to prove its ancient splendour, the wide circuit of its walls, the number of its temples and the magnificence of its columned streets. You can trace the main thoroughfares from gate to gate by the heaped masses of the colonnades, and mark the stone bases of statues at the intersections of the ways. Here and there a massive portal opens into vacuity, the palace which it served having been razed to the ground, or an armed horseman decorates the funeral stele on which the living merits of his prototype are recorded. The Christians took up the story where the Seleucid kings had left it, and the ruins of a great church with a courtyard set round with columns lie on the edge of the main street. As I plunged in the soft spring rain through deep grass and flowers and clumps of asphodel, to the discomfiture of the grey owls that sat blinking on the heaps of stones, the history and architecture of the town seemed an epitome of the

A CAPITAL, ḤAMĀH

marvellous fusion between Greece and Asia that came of Alexander's conquests. Here was a Greek king whose capital lay on the Tigris, founding a city on the Orontes and calling it after his Persian wife—what builders raised the colonnades that adorned this and all the Greek-tinged towns of Syria with classic forms used in a spirit of Oriental lavishness? what citizens walked between them, holding out hands to Athens and to Babylon?

The only inhabited part of Ḳal'at el Mudīk is the castle itself, which stands on the site of the Seleucid acropolis, a hill overlooking the Orontes valley and the Noṣairiyyeh mountains. It is mainly of Arab workmanship, though many hands have taken part in its construction, and Greek and Arabic inscriptions are built pellmell into the walls. To the south of the castle there is a bit of classical building of which I have seen no explanation. It looks as if it might be part of the proscenium of the theatre, for the rising ground behind it is scooped away in the shape of an auditorium. A very little digging would be enough to show whether traces of seats lie under the grassy bank. In the valley there is a ruined mosque and a fine khān, half ruined also. The Sheikh of the castle gave me coffee, and told me yet another version of the Seijari story, irreconcilable with either of the two first, whereat I congratulated myself on having early determined not to attempt to resolve that tangled problem. From the castle top the valley of the Orontes seemed to be all under water: it was the great swamp of the 'Asī, said the Sheikh, which dries in summer when the island villages (as I saw them now) resume their places as parts of the plain. Yes, certainly they were very unhealthy, summer and winter they were fever-stricken, and most of the inhabitants died young—lo, we belong to God and unto Him do we return! In winter and spring these short-lived folk follow the calling of fishermen, but when the swamp dried they turn into husbandmen after a fashion of their own. They cut the reeds and sowed maize upon them, and set them alight, and the maize rose out of the ashes and grew—a phœnix-like method of agriculture.

At Apamea the excellent cakes I had bought in Damascus came to an end—it seemed a serious matter at the time when the bill of fare was apt to be monotonous. Lunch was the least palatable of all our meals. Hard-boiled eggs and chunks of cold meat cease to tempt the appetite after they have been indulged in for a month or two. Gradually I taught Mikhāil to vary our diet with all the resources the country offered, olives and sheep's milk cheese, salted pistachios, sugared apricots and half-a-dozen other delicacies, including the Damascus cakes. The native servant, accustomed to feeding Cook's tourists on sardines and tinned beef, thinks it beneath the dignity of a European to eat such food, and you must go hunt the bazaars with him yourself and teach him what to buy, or you may pass through the richest country and starve on cold mutton.

CHAPTER XI

THE next day's journey is branded on my mind by an incident which I can scarcely dignify with the name of an adventure—a misadventure let me call it. It was as tedious while it was happening as a real adventure (and no one but he who has been through them knows how tiresome they frequently are), and it has not left behind it that remembered spice of possible danger that enlivens fireside recollections. We left Ḳal'at el Mudīk at eight in pouring rain, and headed northwards to the Jebel Zāwiyyeh, a cluster of low hills that lies between the Orontes valley and the broad plain of Aleppo. This range contains a number of ruined towns, dating mainly from the fifth and sixth centuries, partially re-inhabited by Syrian fellaḥīn, and described in detail by de Vogüé and Butler. The rain stopped as we rode up a low sweep of the hills where the red earth was all under the plough and the villages set in olive groves. The country had a wide bare beauty of its own, which was heightened by the dead towns that were strewn thickly over it. At first the ruins were little more than heaps of cut stones, but at Kefr Anbīl there were some good houses, a church, a tower and a very large necropolis of rock-cut tombs. Here the landscape changed, the cultivated land shrank into tiny patches, the red earth disappeared and was replaced by barren stretches of rock, from out of which rose the grey ruins like so many colossal boulders. There must have been more cultivation when the district supported the very large population represented by the ruined towns, but the rains of many winters have broken the artificial terracings and washed the earth down into the valleys, so that by no possibility could the former inhabitants draw from it now sufficient produce to sustain them. North-east of Kefr Anbīl, across a labyrinth of rocks, appeared the walls of a wonderful village, Khīrbet Ḥāss, which I was particularly anxious to see. I sent the mules straight to El Bārah, our halting place that night, engaged a villager as a guide over the stony waste, and set off with Mikhāil and Maḥmūd. The path wound in and out between the rocks, a narrow band of grass plentifully scattered with stones; the afternoon sun shone hot upon us, and I dismounted, took off my coat, bound

A HOUSE AT EL BARAH

it (as I thought) fast to my saddle, and walked on ahead amid the grass and flowers. That was the beginning of the misadventure. Khīrbet Ḥāss was quite deserted save for a couple of black tents. The streets of the market were empty, the walls of the shops had fallen in, the church had long been abandoned of worshippers, the splendid houses were as silent as the tombs, the palisaded gardens were untended, and no one came down to draw water from the deep cisterns. The charm and the mystery of it kept me loitering till the sun was near the horizon and a cold wind had risen to remind me of my coat, but, lo! when I returned to the horses it was gone from my saddle. Tweed coats do not grow on every bush in north Syria, and it was obvious that some effort must be made to recover mine. Maḥmūd rode back almost to Kefr Anbīl, and returned after an hour and a half empty handed. By this time it was growing dark; moreover a black storm was blowing up from the east, and we had an hour to ride through very rough country. We started at once, Mikhāil, Maḥmūd and I, picking our way along an almost invisible path. As ill luck would have it, just as the dusk closed in the storm broke upon us, the night turned pitch dark, and with the driving rain in our faces we missed that Medea-thread of a road. At this moment Mikhāil's ears were assailed by the barking of imaginary dogs, and we turned our horses' heads towards the point from which he supposed it to come. This was the second stage of the misadventure, and I at least ought to have remembered that Mikhāil was always the worst guide, even when he knew the direction of the place towards which he was going. We stumbled on; a watery moon came out to show us that our way led nowhere, and being assured of this we stopped and fired off a couple of pistol shots, thinking that if the village were close at hand the muleteers would hear us and make some answering signal. None came, however, and we found our way back to the point where the rain had blinded us, only to be deluded again by that phantom barking and to set off again on our wild dog chase. This time we went still further afield, and Heaven knows where we should ultimately have arrived if I had not demonstrated by the misty moon that we were riding steadily south, whereas El Bārah lay to the north. At this we turned heavily in our tracks, and when we had ridden some way back we dismounted and sat down upon a ruined wall to discuss the advisability of lodging for the night in an empty tomb, and to eat a mouthful of bread and cheese out of Maḥmūd's saddle-bags. The hungry horses came nosing up to us; mine had half my share of bread, for after all he was doing more than half the share of work. The food gave us enterprise; we rode on and found ourselves in the twinkling of an eye at the original branching off place. From it we struck a third path, and in five minutes came to the village of El Bārah, round which we had been circling for three hours. The muleteers were fast asleep in the tents; we woke them somewhat rudely, and asked whether they had not heard our

MOULDING AT EL BĀRAH AND LINTEL AT KHIRBET HĀSS

signals. Oh yes, they replied cheerfully, but concluding that it was a robber taking advantage of the stormy night to kill some one, they had paid small attention. This is the whole tale of the misadventure; it does credit to none of the persons concerned, and I blush to relate it. It has, however, taught me not to doubt the truth of similar occurrences in the lives of other travellers whom I have now every reason to believe entirely veracious.

TOMB, SERJILLA

Intolerable though El Bārah may be by night, by day it is most marvellous and most beautiful. It is like the dream city which children create for themselves to dwell in between bedtime and sleep-time, building palace after palace down the shining ways of the imagination, and no words can give the charm of it nor the magic of the Syrian spring. The generations of the dead walk with you down the streets, you see them flitting across their balconies, gazing out of windows wreathed with white clematis, wandering in palisaded gardens that are still planted with olive and with vine and carpeted with iris, hyacinth and anemone. Yet you may search the chronicles for them in vain; they played no part in history, but were content to live in peace and to build themselves great houses in which to dwell and fine tombs to lie in after they were dead. That they became Christian the hundreds of ruined churches and the cross carved over the doors and windows of their dwellings, would be enough to show; that they were artists their decorations prove; that they were wealthy their spacious mansions their summer houses and stables and out-houses testify. They borrowed from Greece such measure of cultivation and of the arts as they required, and fused with them the spirit of Oriental magnificence which never breathed without effect on the imagination of the West; they lived in comfort and security such as few of their contemporaries can have known, and the Mahommadan invasion swept them off the face of the earth.

I spent two days at El Bārah and visited five or six of the villages round about, the Sheikh of El Bārah and his son serving me as guides. The Sheikh was a sprightly old man called Yūnis, who had guided all the distinguished archaeologists of his day, remembered them, and spoke of them by name—or rather by names of his own, very far removed from the originals. I contrived to make out those of de Vogüé and Waddington, and another that was quite unintelligible was probably intended for Sachau. At Serjilla, a town with a sober and solid air of respectability that would be hard to match, though it is roofless and quite deserted, he presented me with a palace and its adjacent tomb that I might live and die in his neighbourhood, and when I left he rode with me as far as Deir Sanbīl to put me on my way. He was much exercised that day by a disturbance that had arisen in a village near at hand. A man had been waylaid by two others of a neighbouring village who desired to rob him. Fortunately a fellow townsman had come to his assistance and together they had succeeded in beating off the attack, but in the contest the friend had lost his life. His relations had raided the robbers' village and carried off all the cattle. Maḥmūd was of opinion that they should not have taken the law into their own hands.

"By God!" said he, "they should have laid the case before the Government."

But Yūnis replied, with unanswerable logic:

"Of what use was it to go to the Government? They wanted their rights."

In the course of conversation I asked Yūnis whether he ever went to Aleppo.

"By God!" said he. "And then I sit in the bazaars and watch the consuls walking, each with a man in front clothed in a coat worth two hundred piastres, and the ladies with as it were flowers upon their heads." (The fashionable European hat, I imagine.) "I always go to Aleppo when my sons are in prison there," he explained. "Sometimes the gaoler is soft-hearted and a little money will get them out."

SHEIKH YŪNIS

I edged away from what seemed to be delicate ground by asking how many sons he had.

"Eight, praise be to God! Each of my wives bore me four sons and two daughters."

"Praise be to God!" said I.

"May God prolong your life!" said Yūnis. "My second wife cost me a great deal of money," he added.

"Yes?" said I.

"May God make it Yes upon you, oh lady! I took her from her husband, and by God (may His name be praised and exalted!) I had to pay two thousand piastres to the husband and three thousand to the judge."

HOUSE AT SERJILLA

This was too much for Ḥajj Maḥmūd's sense of the proprieties.

"You took her from her husband?" said he. "Wāllah! that was the deed of a Noṣairi or an Ismaili. Does a Moslem take away a man's wife? It is forbidden."

"He was my enemy," explained Yūnis. "By God and the Prophet of God, there was enmity between us even unto death."

"Had she children?" inquired Maḥmūd.

"Ey wāllah!" assented the Sheikh, a little put about by Maḥmūd's disapproval. "But I paid two thousand piastres to the husband and three thousand——"

"By the Face of God!" exclaimed Maḥmūd, still more outraged, "it was the deed of an infidel."

And here I put an end to further discussion of the merits of the case by asking whether the woman had liked being carried off.

"Without doubt," said Yūnis. "It was her wish."

We may conclude, therefore, that ethics did not have much to do with the matter, though he indemnified so amply both the husband and the judge.

This episode led us to discuss the usual price paid for a wife.

TOMB OF BIZZOS

"For such as we," said Yūnis, with an indescribable air of social pre-eminence, "the girl will not be less than four thousand piastres, but a poor man who has no money will give the father a cow or a few sheep, and he will be content."

After he left us I rode round by Ruweiḥā that I might see the famous church by which stands the domed tomb of Bizzos. This church is the most beautiful in the Jebel Zāwiyyeh, with its splendid narthex and carved doorways, its stilted arches and the wide-spanned arcades of its nave—how just was the confidence in his own mastery over his material which encouraged the builder to throw those great arches from pier to pier is proved by the fact that one of them stands to this day. The little tomb of Bizzos is almost as perfect as it was when it was first built. By the doorway an inscription is cut in Greek:

"Bizzos son of Pardos. I lived well, I die well and well I rest. Pray for me." The strangest features in all the architecture of North Syria are the half-remembered classical motives that find their way into mouldings that are almost Gothic in their freedom, and the themes of a classical entablature that grace church window or architrave. The scheme of Syrian decoration was primarily a row of circles or wreaths filled with whorls or with the Christian monogram; but as the stonecutters grew more skilful they ran their circles together into a hundred exquisite and fanciful shapes of acanthus and palm and laurel, making a flowing pattern round church or tomb as varied as the imagination could contrive. The grass beneath their feet, the leaves on the boughs above their heads, inspired them with a wealth of decorative design much as they inspired William Morris twelve hundred years later.

There is another church at Ruweiḥā scarcely less perfect than the Bizzos church, but not so splendid in design. It is remarkable for a monument standing close to the south wall, which has been explained as a bell tower, or a tomb, or a pulpit, or not explained at all. It is constructed of two stories, the lower one consisting of six columns supporting a platform, from the low wall of which rise four corner piers to carry the dome or canopy. The resemblance to some of the North Italian tombs, as, for instance, to the monument of Rolandino, in Bologna, is so striking that the beholder instinctively assigns a similar purpose to the graceful building at Ruweiḥā.

We camped that night at Dāna, a village that boasts a pyramid tomb with a porch of four Corinthian columns, as perfect in execution and in balanced proportion as anything you could wish to see. On our way from Ruweiḥā we passed a mansion which I would take as a type of the domestic architecture of the sixth century. It stood apart, separated by a mile or two of rolling country from any village, with open balconies facing towards the west and a delightful gabled porch to the north, such a porch as might adorn any English country house of to-day. You could fancy the sixth-century owner sitting on the stone bench within and watching for his friends—he can have feared no enemies, or he would not have built his dwelling far out in the country and guarded it only with a garden palisade.

At Ḳasr el Banāt, the Maidens' Fortress as the Syrians call it, I was impressed more than at any other place with the high level that social order had reached in the Jebel Zāwiyyeh, for here were security and wealth openly displayed, and leisure wherein to cultivate the arts; and as I rode away I fell to wondering whether civilisation is indeed, as we think it in Europe, a resistless power sweeping forward and carrying upon its crest

CHURCH AND TOMB, RUWEIḤĀ

those who are apt to profit by its advance; or whether it is not rather a tide that ebbs and flows, and in its ceaseless turn and return touches ever at the flood the self-same place upon the shore.

Late at night one of Sheikh Yūnis's sons rode in to ask us whether his father were still with us. On leaving us that enterprising old party had not, it seemed, returned to the bosom of his anxious family, and I have a suspicion that his friendly eagerness to set us on our way was but part of a deep-laid plot by means of which he hoped to be able to take a hand in those local disturbances that had preoccupied him during the morning. At any rate he had made off as soon as we were out of sight, and the presumption was that he had hastened to join in the fray. What happened to him I never heard, but I am prepared to wager that whoever bit the dust at the village of El Mughāra it was not Sheikh Yūnis.

Three rather tedious days lay between us and Aleppo. We might have made the journey in two, but I had determined to strike a little to the east in order to avoid the carriage road, which was well known, and to traverse country which, though it might not be more interesting, was at least less familiar. Five hours' ride from Dāna across open rolling uplands brought us to Ṭarutīn. We passed several ancient sites, re-occupied by half-settled Arabs of the Muwāli tribes, though the old buildings were completely ruined. All along the western edges of the desert the Bedouin are beginning to cultivate the soil, and are therefore forced to establish themselves in some fixed spot near their crops. "We are become fellaḥīn," said the Sheikh of Ṭarutīn. In some distant age, when all the world is ploughed and harvested, there will be no nomads left in Arabia. In the initial stages these new-made farmers continue to live in tents, but the tents are stationary, the accompanying dirt cumulative, and the settlement unpleasing to any of the senses. The few families at Ṭarutīn had not yet forgotten their desert manners, and we found them agreeable people, notwithstanding the accuracy with which the above remarks applied to their village of hair.

I had not been in camp an hour before there was a great commotion among my men, and Mikhāil came to my tent shouting, "The Americans! the Americans!" It was not a raid, but the Princeton archæological expedition, which, travelling from Damascus by other ways than ours, was now making for the Jebel Zāwiyyeh; and a fortunate encounter my camp thought it, for each one of us found acquaintances among the masters or among the muleteers, and had time to talk, as people will talk who meet by chance upon an empty road. Moreover, the day I spent at Ṭarutīn provided me with an admirable object lesson in archæology. As the members of the expedition planned the ruins and deciphered the inscriptions, the whole fifth-century town rose from its ashes and stood before us—churches, houses, forts, rock-hewn tombs with the names and dates of death of the occupants carved over the door. Next day we had a march of ten hours. We went north, passing a small mud-village called Ḥelbān, and another called Mughāra Merzeh, where there were the remains of a church and rock-cut tombs of a very simple kind. (None of

ḲASR EL BĀNAT

R

these places are marked on Kiepert's map.) Then we turned to the east and reached Tulūl, where we came upon an immense expanse of flood water, stretching south at least twelve miles from the Maṭkh, the swamp in which the River Kuwēk rises. At Tulūl some Arab women were mourning over a new-made grave. For three days after the dead are buried they weep thus at the grave side; only at Mecca and at Medīna, said Maḥmūd, there is no mourning for those who are gone. There when breath leaves the body the women give three cries, to make known to the world that the soul has fled; but beyond these cries there is no lamentation, for it is forbidden that tears should fall upon the head of the corpse. The Lord has given and He has taken away. So we went south along the edge of the high ground to a little hill called Tell Selma, where we turned east again and rounded the flood water and rode along its margin to a big village, Moyemāt, half tents and half beehive huts built of mud. There is no other material but mud in which to build; from the moment we left the rocky ground on which Ṭarutīn stands we never saw a stone—never a stone and never a tree, but an endless unbroken cornfield, with the first scarlet tulips coming into bloom among the young wheat. It was heavy going, though it was soft to the horses' feet. If there were a little more earth upon the hills of Syria and a few more stones upon the plain, travelling would be easier in that country; but He, than whom there is none other, has ordered differently. From Moyemāt we rode north-east until we came

TOMB, DĀNA

to a village called Hober, at the foot of a spur of the Jebel el Ḥâṣṣ, and here we tried to camp, but could get neither oats nor barley, nor even a handful of chopped straw; and so we went on to Kefr 'Abīd, which is marked on the map, and pitched tents at six o'clock. The villages unknown to Kiepert are probably of recent construction, indeed many of them are still half camp. They are exceedingly numerous; about Hober I counted five within a radius of a mile or two. The Arabs who inhabit them retain their nomad habits of feud. Each village has its allies and its blood enemies, and political relations are as delicate as they are in the desert. My diary contains the following note at the end of the day: "Periwinkles, white irises of the kind that were blue at El Bārah, red and yellow ranunculus, storks, larks." These were all that broke the monotony of the long ride.

About half an hour to the north of Kefr 'Abīd there is a little beehive village which contains a very perfect mosaic of geometrical patterns. The fragments of other mosaics are to be found scattered through the village, some in the houses, and some in the courtyards, and the whole district needs careful exploration while the new settlers are turning up the ground and before they destroy what they may find. We reached Aleppo at midday, approaching it by an open drain. Whether it were because of the evil smell or because of the heavy sky and dust-laden wind I do not know, but the first impression of Aleppo was disappointing. The name, in its charming Europeanised form, should belong to a more attractive city, and attractive Aleppo certainly is not, for it is set in a barren, treeless, featureless world, the beginning of the great Mesopotamian flats. The site of the town is like a cup and saucer, the houses lie in the saucer and the castle stands on the upturned cup, its minaret visible several hours away while no vestige of the city appears until the last mile of the road. I stayed two days, during which time it rained almost ceaselessly, therefore I do not know Aleppo—an Oriental city will not admit you into the circle of its intimates unless you spend months within its walls, and not even then if you will not take pains to please—but I did not leave without having perceived dimly that there was something to be known. It has been a splendid Arab city; as you walk down the narrow streets you pass minarets and gateways of the finest period of Arab architecture; some of the mosques and baths and khāns (especially those half ruined and closed) are in the same style, and the castle is the best example of twelfth-century Arab workmanship in all Syria, with iron doors of the same period—they are dated,—and beautiful bits of decoration. There must be some native vitality still that corresponds to these signs of past greatness,

A BEEHIVE VILLAGE

but the town has fallen on evil days. It has been caught between the jealousies of European concession hunters, and it suffers more than most Syrian towns from the strangling grasp of the Ottoman Government. It is slowly dying for want of an outlet to the sea, and neither the French nor the German railway will supply its need. Hitherto the two companies have been busily engaged in thwarting one another. The original concession to the Rayak-Ḥamāh railway extended to Aleppo and north to Birijik—I was told that the tickets to Birijik were printed off when the first rails were laid at Rayak. Then came Germany, with her great scheme of a railway to Baghdad. She secured a concession for a branch line from Killiz to Aleppo, and did what she could to prevent the French from advancing beyond Ḥamāh, on the plea that the French railway would detract from the value of the German concession—my information, it may be well imagined, is not from the Imperial Chancery, but from native sources in Aleppo itself. Since I left, the French have taken up their interrupted work on the Rayak-Ḥamāh line, though it is to be carried forward, I believe, not to Birijik, but only as far as Aleppo.* It will be of no benefit to the town. Aleppo merchants do not wish to send their goods a three days' journey to Beyrout; they want a handy seaport of their own, which will enable them to pocket all the profits of the trade, and that port should be Alexandretta. Neither does the Baghdad railway, if it be continued, offer any prospect of advantage. By a branch line already existing (it was built by English and French capitalists, but has recently passed under German control) the railway will touch the sea at Mersina, but Mersina is as far from Aleppo as is Beyrout. That a line should be laid direct from Aleppo to Alexandretta is extremely improbable, since the Sultan fears above all things to connect the inland caravan routes with the coast, lest the troops of the foreigner, and particularly of England, should find it perilously easy to land from their warships and march up country. Aleppo should be still, as it was in times past, the great distributing centre for the merchandise of the interior, but traffic is throttled by the fatal frequency with which the Government commandeers the baggage camels. Last year, with the Yemen war on hand and the consequent necessity of transporting men and military stores to the coast that they might be shipped to the Red Sea, this grievance had become acute. For over a month trade had been stagnant and goods bound for the coast had lain piled in the bazaar —a little more and they would cease to come at all, the camel owners from the East not daring to enter the zone of danger to their beasts. Here, as in all other Turkish towns, I heard the cry of official bankruptcy. The Government had no funds wherewith to undertake the most necessary works, the treasuries were completely empty.

Though my stay was short I was not without acquaintances, among whom the most important was the Vāli. Kiāzim Pasha is a man of very different stamp from the Vāli of Damascus. To the extent that the latter is, according to his lights, a real statesman, in so far is Kiāzim nothing but a *farceur*.

* The line is now completed as far as Aleppo.

THE CASTLE, ALEPPO

He received me in his harem, for which I was grateful when I saw his wife, who is one of the most beautiful women that it is possible to behold. She is tall and stately, with a small dark head, set on magnificent shoulders, a small straight nose, a pointed chin and brows arching over eyes that are like dark pools—I could not take mine from her face while she sat with us. Both she and her husband are Circassians, a fact that had put me on my guard before the Vāli opened his lips. They both spoke French, and he spoke it very well. He received me in an offhand manner, and his first remark was:

"Je suis le jeune pasha qui a fait la paix entre les églises."

I knew enough of his history to realise that he had been Muteserrif of Jerusalem at a time when the rivalries between the Christian sects had ended in more murders than are customary, and that some kind of uneasy compromise had been reached, whether through his ingenuity or the necessities of the case I had not heard.

"How old do you think I am?" said the pasha.

I replied tactfully that I should give him thirty-five years.

"Thirty-six!" he said triumphantly. "But the consuls listened to me. Mon Dieu! that was a better post than this, though I am Vāli now. Here I have no occasion to hold conferences with the consuls, and a man like me needs the society of educated Europeans."

(Mistrust the second: an Oriental official, who declares that he prefers the company of Europeans.)

"I am very Anglophil," said he.

I expressed the gratitude of my country in suitable terms.

"But what are you doing in Yemen?" he added quickly.

"Excellency," said I, "we English are a maritime people, and there are but two places that concern us in all Arabia."

"I know," he interpolated. "Mecca and Medīna."

"No," said I. "Aden and Kweit."

"And you hold them both," he returned angrily—yes, I am bound to confess that the tones of his voice were not those of an Anglo-maniac.

Presently he began to tell me that he alone among pashas had grasped modern necessities. He meant to build a fine metalled road to Alexandretta—not that it will be of much use, thought I, if there are no camels to walk in it—like the road he had built from Samaria to Jerusalem. That was a road like none other in Turkey—did I know it? I had but lately travelled over it, and seized the opportunity of congratulating the maker of it; but I did not think it necessary to mention that it breaks off at the bottom of the only serious ascent and does not begin again till the summit of the Judæan plateau is reached.

This is all that need be said of Kiāzim Pasha's methods.

A far more sympathetic acquaintance was the Greek Catholic Archbishop, a Damascene educated in Paris and for some time curé of the Greek Catholic congregation in that city, though he is still comparatively young. I had been given a letter to him, on the presentation of which he received me with great affability in his own house. We sat in a room filled with books, the windows opening on to the silent courtyard of his palace, and talked of the paths into which thought had wandered in Europe; but I found to my pleasure that for all his learning and his long sojourn in the West, the Archbishop had remained an Oriental at heart.

"I rejoiced," said he, "when I was ordered to return from Paris to my own land. There is much knowledge, but little faith in France; while in Syria, though there is much ignorance, religion rests upon a sure foundation of belief."

The conclusion that may be drawn from this statement is not flattering to the Church, but I refrained from comment.

He appeared in the afternoon to return my call—from the Vāli downwards all must conform to this social obligation—wearing his gold cross and carrying his archiepiscopal staff in his hand. From his tall brimless hat a black veil fell down his back, his black robes were edged with purple, and an obsequious chaplain walked behind him. He found another visitor sitting with me in the inn parlour, Nicola Ḥomṣi, a rich banker of his own congregation. Ḥomṣi belongs to an important Christian family settled in Aleppo, and his banking house has representatives in Marseilles and in London. He and the Archbishop between them were fairly representative of the most enterprising and the best educated classes in Syria. It is they who suffer at the hands of the Turk,—the ecclesiastic, because of a blind and meaningless official opposition that meets the Christian at every turn; the banker, because his interests call aloud for progress, and progress is what the Turk will never understand. I therefore asked them what they thought would be the future of the country. They looked at one another, and the Archbishop answered:

"I do not know. I have thought deeply on the subject, and I can see no future for Syria, whichever way I turn."

That is the only credible answer I have heard to any part of the Turkish question.

The air of Aleppo is judged by the Sultan to be particularly suitable for pashas who have fallen under his displeasure at Constantinople. The town is so full of exiles that even the most casual visitor can scarcely help making acquaintance with a few of them. One was lodged in my hotel, a mild-mannered dyspeptic, whom no one would have suspected of revolutionary sympathies. Probably he was indeed without them, and owed his banishment merely to some chance word, reported and magnified by an enemy or a spy. I was to see many of these exiles scattered up and down Asia Minor, and none that I encountered could tell me for what cause they had suffered banishment. Some, no doubt, must have had a suspicion, and some were perfectly well aware of their offence, but most of them were as innocently ignorant as they professed to be. Now this has a wider bearing on the subject of Turkish patriotic feeling than may at first appear; for the truth is that these exiled pashas are very rarely patriots paying the price of devotion to a national ideal, but rather men whom an unlucky turn of events has alienated from the existing order. If there is any chance that they may be taken back into favour you will find them nervously anxious, even in exile, to refrain from action that would tend to increase official suspicion; and it is only when they have determined that there is no hope for them as long as the present Sultan lives, that they are willing to associate freely with Europeans or to speak openly of their grievances. There is, so far as I can see, no organised body of liberal opinion in Turkey, but merely individual discontents, founded on personal misfortune. It seems improbable that when the exiles return to Constantinople on the death of the Sultan they will provide any scheme of reform or show any desire to alter a system under which, by the natural revolution of affairs, they will again find themselves persons of consideration.

There is another form of exile to be met with in Turkey, the honourable banishment of a distant appointment. To this class, I fancy, belongs Nāzim Pasha himself, and so does my friend Muḥammad 'Ali Pasha of Aleppo. The latter is an agreeable man of about thirty, married to an English wife. He accompanied me to the Vāli's house, obtained permission that I should see the citadel, and in many ways contrived to make himself useful. His wife was a pleasant little lady from Brixton; he had met her in Constantinople and there married her, which may, for ought I know, have been partly the reason of his fall from favour, the English nation not being a *gens grata* at Yildiz Kiosk. Muḥammad 'Ali Pasha is a gentleman in the full sense of the word, and he seems to have made his wife happy; but it must be clearly understood that I could not as a general rule recommend Turkish pashas as husbands to the maidens of Brixton. Though she played tennis at the Tennis Club, and went to the sewing parties of the European colony, she was obliged to conform to some extent to the habits of Moslem women. She never went into the streets without being veiled; "because people would talk if a pasha's wife were to show her face," said she.

We reached the citadel in the one hour of sunlight that shone on Aleppo during my stay, and were taken round by polite officers, splendid in uniforms and clanking swords and spurs, who were particularly anxious that I should not miss the small mosque in the middle of the fortress, erected on the very spot where Abraham milked his cow. The very name of Aleppo, said they, is due to this historic occurrence, and there can be no doubt that its Arabic form, Ḥaleb, is composed of the same root letters as those that form the verb to milk. In spite of the deep significance of the mosque, I was more interested in the view from the top of the minaret. The Mesopotamian plain lay outspread before us, as flat as a board—Euphrates stream is visible from that tower on a clear day, and indeed you might see Baghdad but for the tiresome way in which the round earth curves, for there is no barrier to the eye in all that great level. Below us, were the clustered roofs of bazaar and khān, with here and there a bird's-eye glimpse of marble courtyards, and here and there the fine spire of a minaret. Trees and water were lacking in the landscape, and water is the main difficulty in Aleppo itself. The sluggish stream that flows out of the Maṭkh dries up in the summer, and the wells are brackish all the year round. Good drinking water must be brought from a great distance and costs every household at least a piastre a day, a serious addition to the cost of living. But the climate is good, sharply cold in winter and not over hot for more than a month or two in the summer. Such is Aleppo, the great city with the high-sounding name and the traces of a splendid past.

A WATER-CARRIER

CHAPTER XII

All my leisure moments during the two days in Aleppo were occupied in changing muleteers. It seemed a necessary, if a regrettable measure. At Antioch we should reach the limits of the Arabic-speaking population. Ḥabib and his father had no word of Turkish, Mikhāil owned to a few substantives such as egg, milk and piastre, while I was scarcely more accomplished. I shrank from plunging with my small party into lands where we should be unable to do more than proclaim our most pressing needs or ask the way. The remarkable aptitude of north Syrian muleteers had been much vaunted to me—the title of muleteer is really a misnomer, for as a fact the beast of burden in these parts is a sorry nag, kadīsh, as it is called in Arabic; from Alexandretta to Konia I doubt if we ever saw a mule, certainly we never saw a caravan of mules. I had heard, then, that I should not begin to know what it was to travel in comfort, without worry or responsibility, and with punctuality and speed, until I had reorganised my service, and that when I reached Konia I should be able to break up my caravan if I pleased, and as I pleased, and the Aleppo men would find their way home with another load. So I said good-bye to my Beyroutīs—and to peace.

The system on which the journey was henceforth conducted was the sweating system. The sweater was a toothless old wretch, Fāris by name, who shared with his brother one of the largest teams of baggage animals in Aleppo. Owing to his lack of teeth he spoke Arabic and Turkish equally incomprehensibly; he supplied me with four baggage-horses and rode himself on a fifth, for his own convenience and at his own expense, though he tried vainly to make me pay for his mount when we reached Konia; he hired two boys, at a starvation wage, to do all the work of the camp and the march, and fed them on starvation fare. This unhappy couple went on foot (the independent men of the Lebanon had provided themselves with donkeys), and it was a part of their contract with Fāris that he should give them shoes, but he refused to do so until I interfered and threatened to dock his wages of the price of the shoes and buy them myself. I was obliged also to look into the commissariat and see that the pair had at least enough food to keep them in working condition; but in spite of all my efforts the hired boys deserted at every stage, and I suffered continual annoyance from the delays caused by the difficulty of finding others, and, still more, from the necessity of teaching each new couple the details of their work—where the tent pegs were to be placed, how the loads were to be divided, and a hundred other small but important matters. I had also to goad Fāris, who was furnished with a greater number of excuses for shirking labour than any man in Aleppo, into doing some share of his duty, and to superintend night and morning the feeding of my horses, which would otherwise have escaped starvation as narrowly as the hired boys. Finally, when we came to Konia, I found that Fāris had turned the last of his slaves on to the street, and had refused categorically to take them back to their home at Adana, saying that when he escaped from my eye he could get cheaper men than they; and since I would not abandon two boys who had, according to their stupid best, done what they could to serve me, I was obliged to help them to return to their native place. To sum up the evidence, I should say that those who recommend the muleteers of Aleppo and their abominable system can never have directed a well-trained and well-organised camp, where the work goes as regularly as Big Ben, and the men have cheerful faces and willing hands, nor can they have experience of real business-like travel, for that is possible only with servants who show courage in difficulties, enterprise and resource. I admit that my experience is small, and I confidently assert that it will never be larger, for I would bring muleteers from Baghdad rather than engage Fāris or his like a second time.

It was just when the difficulties of the journey multiplied

that Mikhāil's virtue collapsed. Two days spent in drinking the health of his departing companions, with whom he was on excellent terms, as the members of a good camp should be, were enough to shatter the effects of two months' sobriety. From that time forward the 'arak bottle bulked large in his saddle-bags, and though an 'arak bottle can be searched for and found in saddle-bags and broken on a stone, no amount of vigilance could keep Mikhāil out of the wine shop when we reached a town. Adversity teaches many lessons; I look back with mingled feelings upon the uneasy four weeks between our departure from Aleppo and the time when Providence sent me another and a better man and I hardened my heart to dismiss Mikhāil, but I do not regret the schooling that was forced on me.

Ḥajj Maḥmūd reached at Aleppo the term of his commission, and from him also I took a most reluctant farewell. The Vāli provided me with a zaptieh whose name was Ḥajj Najīb, a Kurd of unprepossessing appearance, who proved on acquaintance a useful and obliging man, familiar with the district through which we travelled together, and with the people inhabiting it. We were late in starting, Mikhāil being sodden with 'arak and the muleteers unhandy with the loads. The day (it was March 30) was cloudless, and for the first time the sun was unpleasantly hot. When we rode away at ten o'clock it was already blazing fiercely upon us, and the whole day long there was not a scrap of shade in all the barren track. We followed for a mile or so the Alexandretta high road, passing a café with a few trees about it, soon after which we struck away to the left and entered a path that led us into the bare rocky hills, and speedily became as rocky as they. Our course was east with a touch of north. At half-past twelve we stopped to lunch, and waited a full hour for the baggage, during which time I had leisure to reflect upon the relative marching speed of the new servants and the old, and on the burning heat of the sun that had not been so noticeable when we were riding. Half an hour further we passed a hovel, Yaḳit 'Ades, where Najīb suggested that we might camp. But I decided that it was too early, and after we had given strict injunctions to Fāris concerning the route he was to follow and the exact spot where we should camp, the zaptieh and I bettered our pace, and without going beyond a walk were soon out of sight of the others. We rode along the bottom of a bare winding valley, past several places that were marked on the map though they were no more than the smallest heaps of ruins, and at four o'clock turned up the northern slope of the valley and reached a hamlet, unknown to Kiepert, which Najīb informed me to be Kbeshīn. Here amid a few old walls and many modern refuse-heaps we found a Kurdish camp, one of the spring-time camps in which half nomadic people dwell with their flocks at the season of fresh grass. The walls of the tents, if tents they may be called, were roughly built of stone to a height of about five feet, but the roofs were of goats' hair cloth, raised in the centre by tent poles. The Kurdish shepherds crowded round us and conversed with Najīb in their own tongue, which sounded vaguely familiar on account of its likeness to Persian. They spoke Arabic also, a queer jargon full of Turkish words. We sat for some time on the rubbish-heap watching for the baggage animals till I became convinced, in spite of Najīb's assurances, that some hitch must have occurred and that we might watch for ever in vain. At this point the Kurdish sheikh announced that it was dinner time, and invited us to share the meal. One of the advantages of out-door life on short commons being that there is no moment of the day when you are not willing and ready to eat, we fell in joyfully with the suggestion.

The Kurd has not been given a good name in the annals of travel. Report would have him both sulky and quarrelsome, but for my part I have found him to be endowed with most of the qualities that make for agreeable social intercourse. We were ushered into the largest of the houses; it was light and cool, airy and clean, its peculiar construction giving it the advantages of house and of tent. The food consisted of new bread and sour curds and of an excellent pillaf, in which cracked wheat was substituted for rice. It was spread upon a mat, and we sat round upon rugs while the women served us. By the time we had finished it was six o'clock but no caravan had appeared. Najīb was much perplexed, and our hosts sympathised deeply with our case, while declaring that they were more than willing to keep us for the night. Our hesitation was cut short by a small boy who came running in with the news that a caravan had been seen to pass by the village of Fāfertīn on the opposite side of the valley, and that it was then heading for Ḳal'at Sim'ān, our ultimate destination. There was no time to be lost, the sun had set, and I had a vivid recollection of our wanderings in the night about El Bārah in a

ḲAL'AT SIM'ĀN

country not dissimilar from that which lay in front of us, but before we started I took Najīb aside and asked him whether I might give money in return for my entertainment. He replied that on no account was it to be thought of, Kurds do not expect to be paid by their guests. All that was left me was to summon the children and distribute a handful of metalīks among them, an inexpensive form of generosity, and one that could not outrage the most susceptible feelings. We set off, Najīb leading the way and riding so quickly along the stony path that I had the greatest difficulty in keeping up with him. I knew that the great church of St. Simon Stylites stood upon a hill and must be visible from afar, though the famous column of the saint, round which the church was built, had fallen centuries ago. After an hour's stumbling ride Najīb pointed silently to the dim hills, and I could just make out a mass of something that looked like a fortress breaking the line of the summit. We hurried on for another half hour and reached the walls at 7.30 in complete darkness. As we rode through the huge church we heard to our relief a tinkle of caravan bells that assured us of the arrival of the tents—we heard also the shouts and objurgations of Mikhāil, who, under the influence of potations of 'arak, was raging like a wild beast and refusing to

ḲAL'AT SIM'ĀN

give the new muleteers any hint as to the way in which to deal with my English tent. Since I was the only sane person who knew how the poles were to be fitted together, the pegs driven in and the furniture opened out, I was obliged to do the greater part of the work myself by the light of two candles, and when that was over to search the canteen for bread and semen for the muleteers, an order to my rebellious cook that he should prepare the customary evening meal of rice having been greeted with derisive howls mingled with curses on all and sundry. It is ill arguing with a drunken man, but with what feelings I kept silence I hope that the recording angel may have omitted to note.

At last, when all was ready, I wandered away into the sweet Spring night, through the stately and peaceful church below the walls of which we were lying, and presently found myself in a circular court, open to the sky, from whence the four arms of the church reach out to the four points of the compass. The court had been set round with a matchless colonnade, of which many of the arches are still standing, and in the centre rose in former days the column whereon St. Simon lived and died. I scrambled over the heaps of ruin till I came to the rock-hewn base of that very column, a broad block of splintered stone with a depression in the middle, like a little bowl, filled with clear rain water in which I washed my hands and face. There was no moon; the piers and arches stood in ruined and shadowy splendour, the soft air lay still as an unruffled pool, weariness and vexation dropped from the spirit, and left it bare to Heaven and the Spring. I sat and thought how perverse a trick Fortune had played that night on the grim saint. She had given for a night his throne of bitter dreams to one whose dreams were rosy with a deep content that he would have been the first to condemn. So musing I caught the eye of a great star that had climbed up above the broken line of the arcade, and we agreed together that it was better to journey over earth and sky than to sit upon a column all your days.

The members of the American survey have mapped and thoroughly explored the northern mountains as far as Ḳal'at Sim'ān, but neither they nor any other travellers have published an account of the hilly region to the north-east of the shrine.* I, who rode through it, and visited almost all the ruined villages, found that it was generally known to the inhabitants as the Jebel Sim'ān, by which title I shall speak of it. The Mountains of Simon, with the Jebel Bārisha, to the south-west, and the Jebel el 'Ala still further to the west, belong to the same architectural system as the Jebel Zāwiyyeh, through which we had passed on our way to Aleppo. It would be possible to draw distinctions of style between the northern group and the southern; the American architect, Mr. Butler, with his wide experience of the two districts, has been

* Since writing this chapter I have learnt that Mr. Butler and his party extended their explorations to the north of Ḳal'at Sim'ān after my departure, and I look forward to a full description of the district in their future publications.

able to do so, but to the hasty observer the differences appear to depend chiefly on natural conditions and on the fact that the northern district fell more directly under the influence of Antioch, the city which was one of the main sources of artistic inspiration (not for Syria alone) in the early centuries of the Christian era. The settlements in the Jebel Sim'ān are smaller and the individual houses less spacious, possibly because the northern mountains were much more rugged and unable to support so large and wealthy a population; they would seem to have begun earlier and to have reached the highest point of their prosperity a little later, nor did they suffer the period of decline which is evident in the South during the century preceding the Arab invasion.* The finest sixth-century churches in the north show an almost florid luxuriance of decoration unapproached in the latest of the Southern churches, all of which are to be dated a century earlier, except the Bizzos church at Ruweiḥā. It is interesting to observe that the Ruweiḥā church, though it is a little later than Ḳal'at Sim'ān,

ḲAL'AT SIM'ĀN, THE WEST DOOR

* I would suggest that this decline was due in part to the excessive burden of taxation laid by Justinian on the eastern provinces of his empire during his efforts to recover the western. Readers of Diehl's great work on Justinian will remember how the social and political organisation of his dominions collapsed under the strain of his wars in Italy and North Africa. The eastern parts of the empire were the richest and suffered the most.

is far more severe in detail, and to this it may be added that even small houses in the north present not infrequently a greater variety and lavishness of decoration than is customary in the South.* When the traveller reads the inscriptions on church and dwelling, and finds the dates reckoned in the north always by the era of Antioch, he may be pardoned for sur-

ḲAL'AT SIM'ĀN, THE CIRCULAR COURT

mising that it was the magnificent hand of Antioch that touched here architrave and capital, moulding and string-course. The church of St. Simon was raised not by local effort only but as a tribute to the famous saint from the whole Christian world, and probably it was not executed by local workmen but by the builders and stone-cutters of Antioch; if that be so it is difficult not to attribute the lovely church of Ḳalb Lozeh to the same creative forces, and a dozen smaller examples, such as the east church at Bākirḥa, must be due to similar influences.

I spent the morning examining the church of St. Simon and the village at the foot of the hill, which contains some very perfect basilicas and the ruins of a great hostelry for pilgrims.

* This was noticed by Mr. Butler, "Architecture and other Arts."

At lunch time there appeared upon the scene a Kurd, so engaging and intelligent that I immediately selected him to be my guide during the next few days, the district I proposed to visit being blank on the map, stony and roadless. Mūsa was the name of my new friend, and as we rode together in the afternoon he confided to my private ear that he was by creed

ḲAL'AT SIM'ÂN, THE CIRCULAR COURT

a Yezīdi, whom the Mohammedans call Devil Worshippers, though I fancy they are a harmless and well-meaning people. The upper parts of Mesopotamia are their home, and from thence Mūsa's family had originally migrated. We talked of beliefs as we went, guardedly, since our acquaintance was as yet young, and Mūsa admitted that the Yezīdis worshipped the sun. "A very proper object of adoration," said I, and thinking to please him went on to mention that the Ismāilis worshipped both sun and moon, but he could scarcely control his disgust at the thought of such idolatry. This led me to consider within myself whether the world had grown much wiser since the days when St. Simon sat on his column, and the conclusion that I reached was not flattering.

The rain interrupted our wanderings among the villages at the foot of Jebel Sheikh Barakāt, the high peak to the south-east of Ḳal'at Sim'ān, and drove us home, but the clouds lifted again towards evening, and I, watching from the marvellous west door, saw the hills turn the colour of red copper and the grey walls of the church to gold. Mikhāil, depressed and

ḲAL'AT SIM'ĀN, THE APSE

repentant, served me with an excellent dinner, in spite of which I should have dismissed him if St. Simon could have supplied me with another cook. Indeed, I was half inclined to send back to Aleppo for a new man, but the doubt whether I should secure a good servant by proxy, combined with the clemency of indolence, led me to a course of inaction which I attempted to justify by the hope that Mikhāil's repentance would be of a lasting nature. Thus for a month we lived on a volcano with occasional eruptions, and were blown up at the end. But enough of this painful subject.

Next day I set off with Mūsa to explore the villages in the Jebel Sim'ān to the east and north-east of the church of St. Simon. We rode almost due east for rather less than an hour to Burjkeh, which exhibited all the characteristics of these villages of the extreme north. It had the tall square tower, which is nearly universal. All the stone work was massive, the blocks frequently laid not in courses, or if so laid, the courses showed great variety of depth. The church had a square apse, built out beyond the walls of the nave, and a running moulding hooded each window, passed along the level of the sill from one

ḲAL'AT SIM'ĀN, THE WEST DOOR

window to another, and ended beyond the last in a spiral, as though it had been a bit of ribbon festooned over the openings with the surplus rolled up. This moulding is peculiar to sixth-century decoration in North Syria. The houses of Burjkeh were very simple square cottages, built of polygonal masonry. Mūsa got wind of a newly opened tomb near the church. I contrived with some difficulty to crawl down into it, and was rewarded by finding on one of the loculi the date 292 of the era of Antioch, which corresponds to 243 A.D. Below the date were three lines of Greek inscription, much defaced. We rode on for half an hour to Surkanyā, a deserted village, charmingly situated at the head of a shallow rocky valley in which there were even a few trees. The houses were exceptionally massive in construction, with heavy stone balconies forming a porch over the door. One was dated, and the year was 406 A.D. The church was almost exactly similar to that at Burjkeh. Another three quarters of an hour to the north and we reached Fāfertīn, where it began to rain. We took shelter under an apse, which was all that remained of a church larger than any we had yet seen, but rude in workmanship.* The village was inhabited by a few families of Yezīdi Kurds. In the streaming rain we rode for an hour north-east to Khirāb esh Shems, but could do nothing there owing to the weather, and so north by Kalōteh to Burj el Kās, where I found my tents pitched on a damp sward. Mūsa was much distressed by the heavy rain, and said that the wet spring had been disastrous to his fields, washing down the soil from the high ground into the valleys. The work of denudation, which has so greatly diminished the fertility of North Syria, is still going forward.

A FUNERAL MONUMENT, ḲĀṬURĀ

At Burj el Kās there was a square tower on the top of the hill and some old houses that had been repaired and re-inhabited by the Kurds. On one lintel I saw the date 406 A.D., on another an inscription difficult to decipher. The end of this stone was hidden by the angle of a rebuilt house, but peering along it I

* Butler in his report states that this church is dated 372 A.D., which gives it the distinction of being the earliest dated church in Syria, if not the earliest dated church in the world.

KHIRAB ESH SHEMS

could just make out that there was a small carving at the extreme point. The owner of the house announced that it represented without doubt the Lady Mary. This would have been a curious addition to the meagre collection of sculpture in North Syria, as well as a theological innovation, and I expressed my regret that I could not see it better. Thereupon my friend fetched a pickaxe and chipped off a corner

KHIRĀB ESH SHEMS, CARVING IN A TOMB

of his house, and the figure of the Virgin proved to be a Roman eagle.

With Najīb and Mūsa I returned to the villages that I had passed in the rain the previous day. We left Najīb with the horses at Kalōteh, and ourselves walked to Khirāb esh Shems, the path being so rocky that I wished to spare my beasts a second journey over it. Khirāb esh Shems contained a fine church, twenty-one paces long from the west door to the chord of the apse. The outer walls to north and south had fallen, leaving only the five arches on either side of the nave with a clerestory pierced by ten small round-headed windows, a charming fragment like a detached loggia. Further up the hill stood a massive chapel, destitute of aisles, with an apse built out and roofed with a semi-dome of square slabs, resembling the fifth century baptistery at Dār Kīta.* In the hill side we found a number of rock-hewn tombs, in one of which I had the satisfaction to discover some curious reliefs. On the loculus to the left of the door were four roughly carved figures, their arms raised in the attitude of prayer, and on the rock wall in a dark corner a single figure clothed in a shirt and a pointed cap, holding a curious object, like a basket, in the right hand. Returning to Kalōteh we visited an isolated church on some high ground to the west of the village. On the wall by the south door there was a long inscription in Greek. The nave was separated from the aisles by four columns on either side, some of which (to judge by the fragments) had been fluted and some plain. The arcade ended against the corner of the apse with engaged fluted columns carrying beautiful Corinthian capitals. The apse, prothesis and diaconicum were all contained within the outer wall of the church. The west door showed a stilted relieving arch above a broken lintel, the lintel decorated with a row of dentils. To the south of the church there was a detached baptistery, some 9 ft. square inside, the walls still carrying the first course of the stone vault. The church must have been roofed with tiles, for I saw a number of fragments lying in the nave. A massive enclosing wall surrounded both church and baptistery. The village below contained two churches, that to the west measuring 38 ft. by 68 ft., the other 48 ft. by 70 ft. The mouldings round the doors in both churches indicate that they cannot have been earlier than

CAPITAL, UPPER CHURCH AT KALŌTEH

* Butler, "Architecture and other Arts," p. 139.

the sixth century. There were also some houses with stone verandahs.

An hour and a half to the north-west of Kalōteh lies Barād, the largest and most interesting of the villages in the Jebel Sim'ān. It is partly re-inhabited by Kurds. I found my camp pitched in an open space opposite a very lovely funeral monument consisting of a canopy carried by four piers set on a

BARĀD, CANOPY TOMB

high podium. Near it stood a large rock-cut sarcophagus and a number of other tombs, partly rock-cut and partly built. I examined two churches in the centre of the town. In one the nave, 68 ft. 6 in. long, was divided from the aisles by four great piers, 6 ft. deep from east to west, with an intercolumniation of 18 ft. The nave was 23 ft. wide and the apse 12 ft. deep. The wide intercolumniation is a proof of a comparatively late date, sixth century or thereabouts. The second church was still larger, 118 ft. 6 in. by 73 ft. 6 in., but completely ruined except for the west wall and part of the apse. To the north of it there was a small chapel, with an apse perfectly preserved; near it lay a sarcophagus which suggested that the chapel may have been a mausoleum. The eastern end of the town contained a complex of buildings of polygonal masonry, including a square enclosure with a square chamber in the centre of it, resting on a vault that was possibly a tomb. To the extreme west of the town stood a fine tower with some large and well preserved houses near it. A small church lay between it and the main body of the town. Near my camp was a curious building with two apses irregularly placed in the east wall. I take it to have been pre-Christian. The walls stood up to the vault, which was perfectly preserved. While Mūsa and I measured and planned this building we were watched by two persons in long white robes and turbans, who exhibited the greatest interest in our movements. They were, said Mūsa, Government officials, sent into the Jebel Sim'ān to take a census of the population with a view to levying the capitation tax.

The next day was one of the most disagreeable that I remember. A band of thick cloud stretched across the sky immediately above the Jebel Sim'ān, keeping us in a cold grey shadow, while to north and south we saw the mountains and the plain bathed in sunshine. We rode north for about an hour to Keifār, a large village near the extreme edge of the Jebel Sim'ān. Beyond the valley of the Afrīn, which bounds the hills to the north-west, rose the first great buttresses of the Giour Dāgh Mūsa observed that in the valley and the further hills there were no more ruined villages; they end abruptly at the limits of the Jebel Sim'ān, and Syrian civilisation seems to have penetrated no further to the north, for what reason it is impossible to say. At Keifār there were three churches much ruined, but showing traces of decoration exquisitely treated, a few good houses, and a canopy tomb something like the one at Barād. There was a large population of Kurds. We rode back to Barād and so south-east to Kefr Nebu, about an hour and a half away through bitter wind and rain. There was a Syriac inscription here on a lintel, one or two Kufic tombstones, and a very splendid house partially restored, but I was a great deal too cold to give them the attention they deserved. Chilled to the bone and profoundly discouraged by attempts at taking time exposures in a high wind, I made straight for my tents at Bāsufān, an hour's ride from Kefr Nebu, leaving unexplored a couple of ruined sites to the south.

BARĀD, TOWER TO THE WEST OF THE TOWN

Mūsa's home is at Bāsufān; we met his father in the cornfields as we came up, and:

"God strengthen your body!" cried Mūsa, giving the salutation proper to one working in the fields.

"And your body!" he answered, lifting his dim eyes to us.

"He is old," explained Mūsa as we rode on, "and trouble has

MŪSA AND HIS FAMILY

fallen on him, but once he was the finest man in the Jebel Sim'ān, and the best shot."

"What trouble?" said I.

"My brother was slain by a blood enemy a few months ago," he answered. "We do not know who it was that killed him, but perhaps it was one of his bride's family, for he took her without their consent."

"And what has happened to the bride?" I asked.

"She has gone back to her own family," said he. "But she wept bitterly."

Bāsufān is used as a *Sommerfrische* by certain Jews and Christians of Aleppo, who come out and live in the houses of the Kurds during the hot months, the owners being at that season in tents. There are a few big trees to the south of the village sheltering a large graveyard, which is occupied mostly by Moslem dead, brought to this spot from many miles round. The valley below boasts a famous spring, a spring that never runs dry even in rainless years when all its sister fountains are exhausted.

The Kurds used to grow tobacco on the neighbouring slopes, and the quality of the leaf was much esteemed, so that the crop found a ready sale, till the Government régie was established and paid the Kurds such miserable prices that they were unable to make a profit. As there was no other market, the industry ceased altogether, and the fields have passed out of cultivation except for the raising of a little corn: "and now we are all poor," said Mūsa in conclusion.

I had not been an hour in camp before the rain stopped and the sun came out, bringing back our energy with it. There was a large church at Bāsufān, which had been converted at some period into a fort by the addition of three towers. What remained of the original building was of excellent work. The engaged columns by the apse were adorned with spiral flutings—the first example I had seen—and the Corinthian capitals were deep and careful in cutting. Mūsa showed me a Syriac inscription in the south wall, which I copied with great labour and small success: the devil take all Syriac inscriptions, or endow all travellers with better wits! When this was done there still remained a couple of hours of afternoon light, and I determined to walk over the hills to Burj Ḥeida and Kefr Lāb, which I had omitted in the morning owing to the rain and the cold. Mūsa accompanied me, and took with him his "partner"—so he was introduced to me, but in what enterprise he shared I do not know. Burj Ḥeida was well worth the visit. It contained a square tower and three churches, one exceedingly well preserved, with an interesting building annexed to it, perhaps a lodging for the clergy. But the expedition was chiefly memorable on account of the conversation of my two companions. With Mūsa I had contracted, during the three days we had passed together, a firm friendship, based on my side on gratitude for the services he had rendered me, coupled with a warm appreciation of the beaming smile that accompanied them. We had reached a point of familiarity where I thought I might fairly expect him to enlighten me on the Yezīdi doctrines, for, whatever may be the custom in Europe, in Asia it is not polite to ask a man what he believes unless he regards you as an intimate. Nor is it expedient; it awakens suspicion without evoking a satisfactory answer. I began delicately as we sat in the doorway of the little church at Kefr Lāb by asking whether the Yezīdis possessed mosque or church.

"No," replied Mūsa. "We worship under the open sky. Every day at dawn we worship the sun."

"Have you," said I, "an imām who leads the prayer?"

"On feast days," said he, "the sheikh leads the prayer, but on other days every man worships for himself. We count some days lucky and some unlucky. Wednesday, Friday and Sunday are our lucky days, but Thursday is unlucky."

"Why is that?" said I.

"I do not know," said Mūsa. "It is so."

"Are you," I asked, "friends with the Mohammadans or are you foes?"

He answered: "Here in the country round Aleppo, where we are few, they do not fear us, and we live at peace with them; but every year there comes to us from Mosul a very learned sheikh who collects tribute among us, and he wonders to see us like brothers with the Muslimīn, for in Mosul, where the Yezīdis are many, there is bitter feud. In Mosul our people will not serve in the army, but here we serve like any other—I myself have been a soldier."

"Have you holy books?" said I.

"Without doubt," said he, "and I will tell you what our books teach us. When the end of the world is near Hadūdmadūd will appear on earth. And before his time the race of men will have shrunk in stature so that they are smaller than a blade of grass,—but Hadūdmadūd is a mighty giant. And in seven days, or seven months, or seven years, he will drink all the seas and all the rivers, and the earth will be drained dry."

"And then," said the partner, who had followed Mūsa's explanation eagerly, "out of the dust will spring a great worm, and he will devour Hadūdmadūd."

"And when he has eaten him," continued Mūsa, "there will

be a flood which will last seven days, or seven months, or seven years."

"And the earth will be washed clean," chimed in the partner.

"And then will come the Mahdi," said Mūsa, "and he will summon the four sects, Yezīdis, Christians, Moslems and Jews, and he will appoint the prophet of each sect to collect his followers together. And Yezīd will assemble the Yezīdis, and Jesus the Christians, and Muḥammad the Moslems, and Moses the Jews. But those that while they lived changed from one faith to another, they shall be tried by fire, to see what creed they profess in their hearts. So shall each prophet know his own. This is the end of the world."

"Do you," said I, "consider all the four faiths to be equal?"

Mūsa replied (diplomatically perhaps): "The Christians and the Jews we think equal to us."

"And the Moslems?" I inquired.

"We think them to be swine," said Mūsa.

These are the tenets of Mūsa's faith, and what they signify I will not pretend to say, but Hadūdmadūd is probably Gogmagog, if that throws any light on the matter.

The sun was setting when we rose from the church step and began to clamber homeward over the ruins of Kefr Lāb. There was some broken ground beyond the village, and I noticed large cavities under the rocks at the top of the hill. Before them Mūsa's partner paused, and said:

"In this manner of place we look for treasure."

"And do you find it?" said I.

He replied: "I have never found any, but there are many tales. Once, they say, there was a shepherd boy who lost his goat and searched for it over the hills, and at last he came upon it in a cave full of gold coins. Therefore he closed the mouth of the cave and hastened home to fetch an ass whereon he might load the gold, and in his haste he left the goat in the cave. But when he returned there was neither cave, nor goat, nor gold, search as he would."

"And another time," said Mūsa, "a boy was sleeping in the ruins of Kefr Lāb and he dreamt that he had discovered a great treasure in the earth and that he had dug for it with his hands.

and when he woke his hands were covered with the dust of gold but no memory remained to him of the place wherein he had dug."

Neither of these stories offer sufficient data, however, to warrant the despatch of a treasure-hunting expedition to the Jebel Sim'ān.

As we reached Bāsufān Mūsa asked whether his sister Wardeh (the Rose) might honour herself by paying her respects to me. "And will you," he added, "persuade her to marry?"

"To marry?" said I. "Whom should she marry?"

"Any one," said Mūsa imperturbably. "She has declared that marriage is hateful to her, and that she will remain in our father's house, and we cannot move her. Yet she is a young maid and fair."

BĀSŪFĀN, A KURDISH GIRL

She looked very fair, and modest besides, as she stood at the door of my tent in the pretty dress of the Kurdish women, with a bowl of kaimak in her hands, a propitiatory gift to me; and I confess I did not insist upon the marriage question, thinking that she could best manage her own affairs. She brought me new bread for breakfast next morning, and begged me to come and visit her father's house before I left. This I did, and found the whole family, sons and daughters-in-law and grandchildren, assembled to welcome me; and though I had but recently breakfasted, the old father insisted on setting bread and bowls of cream before me, "that the bond of hospitality may be between us." Fine, well-built people were they all, with beautiful faces, illumined by the smile that was Mūsa's chief attraction. For their sake the Kurdish race shall hold hereafter a large place in my esteem.

CHAPTER XIII

We started from Bāsufān at eight o'clock on the morning of April 4, and rode south by incredibly stony tracks, leaving Ḳal'at Sim'ān to the west and skirting round the eastern flanks of the Jebel Sheikh Barakāt. Mūsa declared that he must accompany us on the first part of our way, and came with us to Deiret 'Azzeh, a large Mohammadan village of from three hundred to four hundred houses. Here he left us, and we went down into the fertile plain of Sermeda, ringed round with the slopes of the Jebel Ḥalaḳah. At mid-day we reached the large village of Dāna, and lunched by the famous third-century tomb that de Vogüé published, to my mind the loveliest of the smaller monuments of North Syria and worthy in its delicate simplicity to stand by the Choragic Monument of Lysicrates at Athens. There was nothing else to detain us at Dāna, and having waited for the baggage animals to come up I sent them on with Mikhāil and a local guide, bidding them meet Najīb and me at the ruins of Deḥes. After some consultation Najīb and the local man decided on the spot, known to me only from the accounts of travellers, and it was not till we had reached it that I discovered that we were at Meḥes instead of Deḥes. It was all one, however, since we had met and found the place to be a convenient camping-ground. From Dāna, Najīb took me north along the Roman road by a Roman triumphal arch, the Bāb el Hawa, finely situated at the entrance of a rocky valley. We rode along this valley for a mile or two, passing a ruined church, and struck up the hills to the west by a gorge that brought us out on to a wide plateau close to the deserted village of Ksejba.* We went on to the village of Bābiska, through country which was scattered with flowers and with groups of

* The ancient towns in the Jebel Bārisha have been visited and described by the American Expedition.

ruined houses and churches: the heart leapt at the sight of such lonely and unravished beauty. On these hilltops it was difficult to say where stood Bāḳirḥa, the town I wished to visit, but near Bābiska we found a couple of shepherd tents, and from one of the inhabitants inquired the way. The shepherd was a phlegmatic man; he said there was no road to Bāḳirḥa, and that the afternoon had grown too late for such an enterprise, moreover he himself was starting off in another direction with a basket of eggs and could not help us. I, however, had not ridden so many miles in order to be defeated at the last, and with some bullying and a good deal of persuasion we induced the shepherd to show us the way to the foot of the hill on which Bāḳirḥa stands. He walked with us for an hour or so, then pointed towards the summit of the Jebel Bārisha and saying, "There is Bāḳirḥa," he left us abruptly and returned to his basket of eggs.

High up on the mountain side we saw the ruins bathed in the afternoon sun, and having looked in vain for a path we pushed our horses straight in among the boulders and brakes of flowering thorn. But there is a limit to the endurance even of Syrian horses, and ours had almost reached it after a long day spent in clambering over stones. We had still to get into camp, Heaven alone knew how far away; yet I could not abandon the shining walls that were now so close to us upon the hill, and I told the reluctant Najīb to wait below with the horses while I climbed up alone. The day was closing in, and I climbed in haste; but for all my haste the scramble over those steep rocks, half-buried in flowers and warm with the level sun, is a memory that will not easily fade. In half an hour I stood at the entrance of the town, below a splendid basilica rich in varied beauty of decoration and design. Beyond it the ruined streets, empty of all inhabitants, lay along the mountain side, houses with carved balconies and deep-porched doorways, columned market-places, and the golden sunlight over all. But I was bent upon another pilgrimage. A broad and winding road led up above the town until it reached the boundary of the flowered slopes, and nothing except a short rocky face of hill lay between the open ground where the path ended and the summit of the range. The mountain was cleft this way and that by precipitous gorges, enclosing

TOMB AT DĀNA

between their escarpments prospects of sunlit fertile plain, and at the head of the gorges on a narrow shelf of ground stood a small and exquisite temple. I sat down by the gate through which the worshippers had passed into the temple court. Below me lay the northern slopes of the Jebel Bārisha and broad fair valleys and the snow-clad ranks of the Giour Dāgh veiled

THE BĀB EL HAWA

in a warm haze. Temple and town and hillside were alike deserted save that far away upon a rocky spur a shepherd boy piped a wild sweet melody to his scattered flocks. The breath of the reed is the very voice of solitude; shrill and clear and passionless it rose to the temple gate, borne on deep waves of mountain air that were perfumed with flowers and coloured with the rays of the low sun. Men had come and gone, life had surged up the flanks of the hills and retreated again, leaving the old gods to resume their sway over rock and flowering thorn, in peace and loneliness and beauty.

So at the gate of the sanctuary I offered praise, and having given thanks went on my way rejoicing.

Najīb welcomed me back with expressions of relief.

"By God!" said he, "I have not smoked a single cigarette

since I lost sight of your Excellency, but all this hour I have said: 'Please God she will not meet with a robber among the rocks.'"

Therewith, to make up for lost opportunity, he lighted the cigarette that his anxiety had not prevented him from rolling during my absence, and though I will not undertake to affirm that it was indeed the only one, the sentiment was gratifying. I thought at the time (but next day's march proved me to be wrong) that we rode down to the plain of Sermeda by the roughest track in the world. When we got to the foot of the hill we turned up a valley to the south, a narrow ribbon of cultivation winding between stony ranges. Presently it widened, and we passed a large modern village, where we received the welcome news that our camp had been seen ahead; at a quarter past six we struggled into Meḥes or Deḥes, whichever it may have been, feeling that our horses would have been put to it if they had been asked to walk another mile. An enchanting camp was Meḥes. It was not often that I could pitch tents far from all habitation. The muleteers pined for the sour curds and other luxuries of civilisation, and indeed I missed the curds too, but the charm of a solitary camp went far to console me. The night was still and clear, we were lodged in the ruined nave of a church, and we slept the sleep of the blessed after our long ride.

There was one more ruin that I was determined to visit before I left the hills. It was the church of Ḳalb Lōzeh, which from descriptions seemed to be (as indeed it is) the finest building after Ḳal'at Sim'ān in all North Syria. I sent the baggage animals round by the valleys, with strict, but useless, injunctions to Fāris that he was not to dawdle, and set out with Mikhāil and Najīb to traverse on horseback two mountain ranges, the Jebel Bārisha and the Jebel el 'Ala. It is best to do rock climbing on foot; but if any one would know the full extent of the gymnastic powers of a horse, he should ride up the Jebel el 'Ala to Ḳalb Lōzeh. I had thought myself tolerably well versed in the subject, but I found that the expedition widened my experience not a little. We rode straight up an intolerably stony hill to the west of Meḥes, and so reached the summit of the Jebel Bārisha. The ground here was much

THE TEMPLE GATE, BĀKIRḤA

broken by rocks, but between them were tiny olive groves and vineyards and tiny, scattered cornfields. Every ledge and hollow was a garden of wild flowers; tall blue irises unfurled their slender buds under sweet-smelling thickets of bay, and the air was scented with the purple daphne. This paradise was inhabited by a surly peasant, the least obliging and the most taciturn of men. After much unsuccessful bargaining (the price he set on any service he might render us was preposterous, but we were in his hands and he obliged us to give way) he agreed to guide us to Ḳalb Lōzeh, and conducted us forthwith down the Jebel Bārisha by a precipitous path cut out of the living rock. It was so steep and narrow that when we met a party of women coming up from the lower slopes with bundles of brushwood —brushwood! it was flowering daphne and bay—we had great difficulty in edging past them. At the bottom of this breakneck descent there was a deep valley with a lake at one end of it, and in front of us rose the Jebel el 'Ala, to the best of my judgment a wall of rock, quite impossible for horses to climb. The monosyllabic peasant who directed us—I am glad I do not remember his name—indicated that our path lay up it, and Najīb seeming to acquiesce, I followed with a sinking heart. It was indescribable. We jumped and tumbled over the rock faces and our animals jumped and tumbled after us, scrambling along the edge of little precipices, where, if they had fallen they must have broken every bone. Providence watched over us and we got up unhurt into a country as lovely as that which we had left on top of the Jebel Bārisha. At the entrance of an olive grove our guide turned back, and in a few moments we reached Ḳalb Lōzeh.

Whether there was ever much of a settlement round the great church I do not know; there are now but few remains of houses, and it stands almost alone. It stands too very nearly unrivalled among the monuments of Syrian art. The towered narthex, the wide bays of the nave, the apse adorned with engaged columns, the matchless beauty of the decoration and the justice of proportion preserved in every part, are the features that first strike the beholder; but as he gazes he becomes aware that this is not only the last word in the history of Syrian architecture, spoken at the end of many centuries of endeavour, but that it is also the beginning of a new chapter in the architecture of the world. The fine and simple beauty of Romanesque was born in North Syria. It is curious to consider to what developments the genius of these architects might have led if they had not been checked by the Arab invasion. Certain it is that we should have had an independent school of great builders, strongly influenced perhaps by classical tradition and yet more strongly by the East, but everywhere asserting an unmistakable personality as bold as it was imaginative and delicate. There is little consolation in the reflection that the creative vigour that is evident at Ḳalb Lōzeh never had time to pass into decadence.

I had heard or read that in the mountains near Ḳalb Lōzeh were to be found a few Druze villages, inhabited by emigrants from the Lebanon, but as I had not yet come upon them I had almost forgotten their existence. Near the church stood half a dozen hovels, the inhabitants of which came out to watch me as I photographed. Almost unconsciously I was struck by some well-known look in the koḥl-blackened eyes and certain peculiarities of manner that are difficult to specify but that combine to form an impression of easy and friendly familiarity with perhaps a touch of patronage in it. When the women joined the little crowd my eye was caught by the silver chains and buckles that they wore, which I remembered vaguely to have remarked elsewhere. As we were about to leave, an oldish man came forward and offered to walk with us for an hour, saying that the way down to Ḥārim was difficult to find, and we had not walked fifty yards together before I realised the meaning of my subconscious recognition.

"Māsha'llah!" said I, "you are Druzes."

The man looked round anxiously at Najīb and Mikhāil, following close on our heels, bent his head and walked on without speaking.

"You need not fear," said I. "The soldier and my servant are discreet men."

He took heart at this and said:

"There are few of us in the mountains, and we dread the Mohammadans and hide from them that we are Druzes, lest they should drive us out. We are not more than two hundred houses in all."

ḲALB LŌZEH

"I have been hoping to find you," said I, "for I know the sheikhs in the Ḥaurān, and they have shown me much kindness. Therefore I desire to salute all Druzes wherever I may meet with them."

"Allah!" said he. "Do you know the Ṭurshān?"

"By God!" said I.

"Shibly and Yaḥya his brother?"

"Yaḥya I know, but Shibly is dead."

"Dead!" he exclaimed. "Oh Merciful! Shibly dead!" And with that he drew from me all the news of the Mountain and listened with rapt attention to tales for which I had not thought to find a willing ear so far from Ṣalkhad. Suddenly his questions stopped and he swerved off the path towards a vineyard in which a young man was pruning the vines.

THE APSE, ḲALB LŌZEH

"Oh my son!" he cried. "Shibly el Aṭrash is dead! Lend me thy shoes, that I may walk with the lady towards Ḥārim, for mine are worn."

The young man approached, kicking off his red leather slippers as he came.

"We belong to God!" said he. "I saw Shibly but a year ago." And the news had to be repeated to him in detail

We journeyed on along the stony mountain tops, brushing through purple daphne that grew in wonderful profusion, and talking as we went as though we had been old friends long parted. When we came to the lip of the Jebel el 'Ala we saw Ḥārim below us, and I insisted that my companion should spare himself the labour of walking further. He agreed, with great reluctance, to turn back, and stood pouring out blessings on me for full five minutes before he would bid me farewell, and then returned to us again that he might be sure we had understood the way.

"And next time you come into the Jebel el 'Ala," said he, "you must bring your camp to Ḳalb Lōzeh and stay at least a month, and we will give you all you need and show you all the ruins. And now may you go in peace and safety, please God; and in peace and in health return next year."

"May God prolong your life," said I, "and give you peace!"

So we separated, and my heart was warm with an affection for his people which it is never difficult to rekindle. Cruel in battle they may be—the evidence against them is overwhelming; some have pronounced them treacherous, others have found them grasping; but when I meet a Druze I do not hesitate to greet a friend, nor shall I until my confidence has been proved to have been misplaced.

Ḥārim castle stands on a mound at the entrance of one of the few gorges that give access to the Jebel el 'Ala. Beyond it lies the great Orontes plain that was a granary in old days to the city of Antioch. Much of the northern part of the plain was under water, the swampy lake which the Syrians call El Baḥra having been extended by the recent rains to its fullest limit. We turned south from Ḥārim and rode along the foot of the slopes of the Jebel el 'Ala to Salḳīn, a memorable ride by reason of the exceeding beauty of the land through which we passed. I have seen no such abundant fertility in all Syria. Groves of olive and almond shared the fat ground with barley and oats; tangled thickets of gorse and broom, daphne and blackberry, edged the road, and every sunny spot was blue with iris stylosa. Salḳīn itself lay in a wooded valley amid countless numbers of olive-trees that stretched almost to the Orontes, several miles away. We dismounted before we reached the town in an open spot between olive-gardens. It was five o'clock, but Fāris had not arrived, and we disposed ourselves comfortably under the trees to wait for him. Our advent caused some excitement among the people who were sitting on the grass enjoying the evening calm; before long one, who was evidently a person of consideration, strolled up to us, accompanied by a servant, and invited me to come and rest in his house. He was a portly man, though he had barely touched middle age, and his countenance was pleasant; I accepted his invitation, thinking I might as well see what Salḳīn had to offer. Opportunities of enlarging the circle of your acquaintance should always be grasped, especially in foreign parts.

ḤĀRIM

I soon found that I had fallen into the hands of the wealthiest inhabitant of the town. Muḥammad 'Ali Agha is son to Rustum Agha, who is by birth a Circassian and was servant in the great Circassian family of Kakhya Zādeh of Hamadān—that is their Arabic name, the Persians call them Kat Khuda Zādeh. The Kakhya Zādehs migrated to Aleppo two centuries back; by such transactions as are familiar to Circassians, they grew exceedingly rich and are now one of the most powerful families in Aleppo. Their servants shared in their prosperity, and Rustum Agha, being a careful man, laid by enough money to buy land at Salḳīn near his master's large estate in the Orontes valley. Fortune favoured him so well that the hand of a daughter of the Kakhya house was accorded to his son. I did not learn all these details at once, and was astonished while I sat in Muḥammad 'Ali's harem to observe the deference with which he treated his wife, wondering why the sharp-featured, bright-eyed little lady who had borne him no sons should be addressed by her husband with such respect, for I did not then know that she was sister to Reshīd Agha Kakhya Zādeh. Muḥammad 'Ali's only child, a girl of six years old, what though she were of so useless a sex, was evidently the apple of her father's eye. He talked to me long of her education and prospects, while I ate the superlatively good olives and cherry jam that his maid servants set before me. The Khānum was so gracious as to prepare the coffee with her own hands, and to express admiration of the battered felt hat that lay, partly concealed by its purple and silver kerchief, on the divan beside me.

"Oh, the beautiful European hat!" said she. "Why do you wear a mendīl over it when it is so pretty?"

And with that she stripped it of the silk scarf and camel's hair rope, and placing it in all its naked disreputableness on her daughter's black curls, she declared that it was the most becoming head-dress in the world.

At six o'clock news was brought that my baggage animals had arrived, but before I could be allowed to return to my tents Rustum Agha had to be visited. He was lying on a couch heaped with wadded silken coverlets in an upper chamber overlooking the beautiful rushing stream and the two great cypresses that add much to the picturesqueness of Salḳīn. These trees stand like tall black sentinels before the gate of the house, which is the first and the largest in the winding village street. Rustum Agha was very old and very sick. His face lay like the face of a corpse upon the pale primrose silk of the bedclothes. He seemed to be gratified by my visit, though when he opened his lips to greet me he was seized with such an intolerable fit of coughing that his soul was almost shaken out of his body. As soon as he recovered he asked for the latest tidings of Russia and Japan, and I marvelled that he, who seemed so near his end, had the patience to ask anything of us, but whether we could see the lagging garnerer with the scythe hobbling up between the cypresses at the door.

As I sat down to dinner in my tent two of Muḥammad 'Ali's servants staggered into camp bearing a large jar of olives grown in the gardens of Salḳīn and preserved in their own oil. They brought too a request from their master that he might come and spend an hour with me, and I sent back a message praying that he would honour me. He appeared later, with one or two people in attendance to carry his hubble-bubble, and settled himself for a comfortable chat to the gurgling accompaniment of the water pipe, a soothing and an amicable sound conducive to conversation. He told me that Salḳīn was one of the many Seleucias, and that it had been founded by Seleucus I.

SALḲIN

himself as a summer resort for the inhabitants of Antioch. The spot on which I was camped, said he, and the graveyard beyond it, formed the site of the Seleucid town, "and whenever we dig a grave we turn up carved stones and sometimes writing." It seems not unnatural that the fertile foothills should have been selected by the people of Antioch for their country houses, but I have no further evidence to support the statement. He said also that his brother-in-law, Reshīd Agha, was staying with him, and he expressed a hope that I would call on him before I left next day.

If Reshīd Agha Kakhya Zādeh is the chief magnate of the district he is also the chief villain. I found him sitting in the early morning under the cypresses by the foaming stream, and a more evil face in a sweeter setting and lighted by a fairer sun it would have been hard to picture. He was a tall man with an overbearing manner; his narrow forehead sheltered a world of vicious thoughts, his eyes squinted horribly, his thick sensuous lips spluttered as they enunciated the vain boastings and the harsh commands that formed the staple of his conversation. He was wrapped in a pale silk robe, and he smoked a hubble-bubble with a jewelled mouthpiece. By his side lay a bunch of Spring flowers, which he lifted and smelt at as he talked, finally offering the best of them to me. It is one of the privileges of the irresponsible traveller that he is not called upon to eschew the company of rogues, and when I found that my friend Muḥammad 'Ali was about to accompany Reshīd Agha to the latter's house at Alāni and that this lay upon my path, I agreed to their suggestion that we should start together. The animals were brought out, we mounted under the cypresses and trotted off through olive-groves towards the Orontes valley. Reshīd Agha rode a splendid Arab mare; her black livery shone with the grooming she had received, she was lightly bitted, her headstall was a silver chain, her bridle was studded with silver ornaments, her every movement was a pleasure to behold. Her master appealed repeatedly to Muḥammad 'Ali, who jogged along by his side on a fine mule, for admiration of his mount, and when the latter had replied obsequiously with the required praise, his words were taken up and reinforced by an old fat man who rode with us upon a lean pony. He was jester and flatterer in ordinary to the Kakhya Zādeh, and, if his countenance spoke truly, panderer to his employer's vices and conniver at his crimes—among such strange company I had fallen that April morning. Ḥājj Najīb trotted along contentedly enough behind us; but Mikhāil, whose sense of the proprieties was strong, could barely conceal his disapproval, and answered in monosyllables when the jester or Reshīd Agha addressed him, though he unbent to Muḥammad 'Ali, whom he judged (and rightly) to be of another clay. We rode for an hour over soft springy ground, Reshīd pointing out the beauties of his property as we went.

"All these olive-gardens are mine," said he, "by God and the Prophet of God! there are no such olives in the land. Every year I come out from Aleppo and see to the olive harvest with my own eyes lest the knaves who work for me should cheat me, God curse them! And therefore I have built myself a house at Alāni—God knows a man should make himself comfortable and live decently. But you shall see it, for you must eat with me; my table is spread for all comers. And around the house I have planted fields of mulberry-trees; ten thousand stripling trees I have set in the last five years. I shall raise silkworks,

TRAVELLERS

please God! in great number. Oh Yūsef! show her the boxes of eggs that came from the land of France."

The jester drew out of his breast a little cardboard box marked with the brand of a French firm; but before I could express my respect for the Agha's industry his attention had been distracted by some peasants who were pruning the olives not to his liking, and he spurred his mare up to the trees and poured out volleys of oaths and execrations upon the unfortunate men, after which he returned to my side and resumed the tale of his own prowess.

The house was large and new, and furnished throughout with plush and gilt-framed mirrors. Nothing would satisfy the Agha but that I should see and admire every corner, and the jester gave me the lead in praise and congratulation. From him I gathered that I was chiefly called upon to exalt the merits of the iron stoves that were prominent in each of the rooms—no doubt they added to the comfort if not to the picturesqueness of the establishment. This over we sat down on a divan to wait till lunch was ready. The Agha employed the time in relating to me with an over-emphasised indignation his struggles against the corrupt and oppressive government under which he lived, but he omitted to mention that what he suffered at the hands of those above him he passed on with interest to those below.

"By God!" he spluttered, "you have seen how I labour among my olive-trees, how I plant mulberries and send for the silkworm eggs from afar, that I may make a new trade at Alāni. Is the Vāli grateful? No, by the Prophet! He sends his men and they say: 'Stop! till we see how much more we can tax you!' And when I would have set up a mill by the river for the grinding of my corn, they said: 'Stop! it is not lawful.' Then they sent for me in the middle of the harvest, and I rode hastily to Aleppo, and day by day and week by week they kept me waiting, and forbade me to leave the city. And by God!" shouted the Agha, thumping on a little inlaid table with his fist, "I baffled them! I went to the Ḳāḍi, and said: 'From whom is the order?' He said: 'From the Vāli.' Then I went to the Vāli and said: 'From whom is the order?' And he answered: 'I know not; perchance from the Ḳāḍi.' And I bade them put it in writing, but they dared not, and so they let me go."

In the middle of these tales three visitors were announced. They took a deferential seat on the opposite divan, and expended themselves in salutations and compliments. The Agha received them as an emperor might receive his subjects, and one of them presently seized the opportunity of saying to me in a stage whisper audible to all:

"You have seen what manner of man is the Agha? He is like a king in this country." Whereat the Agha grew yet more regally gracious.

We sat down at last to a board loaded with every variety of Syrian delicacy, and few cuisines can beat the Syrian at its best. The Agha talked and ate with equal eagerness, and pressed one dish after another upon his guests. When the feast was in full swing a servant came to him and said that there was a certain fellāḥ who wished to speak with him.

"Let him come!" said the Agha indifferently A ragged peasant figure appeared in the doorway and gazed with eyes half sullen, half frightened at the company, and the profusion of delicate meats.

"Peace be upon you, oh Agha!" he began.

But as soon as he saw the suppliant the Agha started to his feet in a very fury of passion. His face became purple, his squinting eyes started from his head, and he thumped the table with his clenched fist while he cried:

"Begone! and may God curse you and your offspring, and destroy your father's house! Begone, I tell you, and bring the money, or I will send you to prison with your wife and your family, and you shall starve there till you die."

"Oh Agha!" said the man, with a certain dignity that faced the other's rage, "a little time. Grant me a little time."

"Not a day! not an hour!" yelled the Agha. "Away! go! and to-night you shall bring me the money."

The peasant vanished from the doorway without another word, the Agha sat down and continued his interrupted conversation and his interrupted meal; the other guests ate on as if nothing had happened, but I felt a little ashamed of my place at Reshīd's right hand, and I was not sorry to bid him farewell.

The Agha sent us down to the Orontes and caused us to be conveyed across the stream in his own ferry-boat. When we reached the other side Mikhāil ostentatiously took a crust from his pocket and began to eat it.

"Have you not eaten at Alāni?" said I.

"I do not eat with such as he," replied Mikhāil stiffly.

At this Najīb, whom no such scruple had withheld from enjoying the unwonted luxury of an ample meal, nodded his head and said:

"The Agha is an evil man, may God reward him according to his deeds! He squeezes their last metalīk from the poor, he seizes their land, and turns them out of their houses to starve."

"And worse than that," said Mikhāil darkly.

"By God!" said Najīb. "Every man who has a fair wife or a fair daughter stands in fear of him, for he will never rest until the woman is in his hands. By God and Muḥammad the Prophet of God! many a man has he killed that he might take his wife into his own harem, and no one is hated more than he."

"Cannot the law prevent him?" said I.

ANTIOCH

"Who shall prevent him?" said Najīb. "He is rich—may God destroy his dwelling!"

"Oh Mikhāil!" said I as we picked our way across the muddy fields. "I have travelled much in your country and I have seen and known many people, and seldom have I met a poor man whom I would not choose for a friend nor a rich man whom I would not shun. Now how is this? Does wealth change the very heart in Syria? For, look you, in my country not all the powerful are virtuous, but neither are they all rogues. And you and the Druze of Ḳalb Lōzeh and Mūsa the Kurd, would you too, if you had means, become like Reshīd Agha?"

"Oh lady," said Mikhāil, "the heart is the same, but in

your country the government is just and strong and every one of the English must obey it, even the rich; whereas with us there is no justice, but the big man eats the little, and the little man eats the less, and the government eats all alike. And we all suffer after our kind and cry out to God to help us since we cannot help ourselves. But at least I did not eat the

ANTIOCH

bread of Reshīd Agha," concluded Mikhāil rather sententiously; and at this Najīb and I hung our heads.

Then followed five hours of the worst travelling. It may have been a judgment upon Najīb and me for sitting at the table of the wicked, but, like most of the judgments of Providence, it fell impartially on the just and the unjust, for Mikhāil endured as much as we. All that we had suffered the day before from the rocks we now suffered at the opposite end of the scale from the mud. The torture was a thousand times more acute. For five hours we crossed hills of earth on which there was never a stone, but the sticky slime of the slopes alternated with deep sloughs, where our horses sank up to their girths, and when at last we emerged from this morass into the Orontes valley man and beast were exhausted. The rising ground, which we had left, now rose into rocky ridges and peaks, the broad valley lay on our right hand, half full of flood water, and beyond it stood a splendid range of mountains. It was not long before we caught sight of the Byzantine towers

ON THE BANK OF THE ORONTES, ANTIOCH

and walls crowning the ridges to the left, and between hedges of flowering bay we stumbled along the broken pavement of the Roman road that led to Antioch. The road was further occupied by a tributary of the Orontes, which flowed merrily over the pavement. It was with some excitement that I gazed on the city of Antioch, which was for so many centuries a cradle of the arts and the seat of one of the most gorgeous civilisations that the world has known. Modern Antioch is like the pantaloon whose clothes are far too wide for his lean shanks; the castle walls go climbing over rock and hill, enclosing an area from which the town has shrunk away. But it is still one of the loveliest of places, with its great ragged hill behind it, crowned with walls, and its clustered red roofs stretching down to the wide and fertile valley of the Orontes. Earthquakes and the changing floods of the stream have overturned and covered with silt the palaces of the Greek and of the Roman city, yet as I stood at sunset on the sloping sward of the Noṣairiyyeh graveyard below Mount Silpius, where my camp was pitched, and saw the red roofs under a crescent moon, I recognised that beauty is the inalienable heritage of Antioch.

CHAPTER XIV

A FURTHER acquaintance with Antioch did not destroy the impressions of the first evening. The more I wandered through the narrow paved streets the more delightful did they appear. Except the main thoroughfare, which is the bazaar, they were almost empty; my footsteps on the cobble-stones broke through years of silence. The shallow gables covered with red tiles gave a charming and very distinctive note to the whole city, and shuttered balconies jutted out from house to house. Of the past there is scarcely a vestige. Two fine sarcophagi, adorned with putti and garlands and with the familiar and, I fancy, typically Asiatic motive of lions devouring bulls, stand in the Serāya, and one similar to these, but less elaborate, by the edge of the Daphne road. I saw, too, a fragment of a classical entablature in the courtyard of a Turkish house, and a scrap of wall in the main street that may certainly be dated earlier than the Mohammadan invasion—its courses of alternate brick and stone resembled the work on the Acropolis. For the rest the Antioch of Seleucus Nicator is a city of the imagination only. The island on which it was built has disappeared owing to the changing of the river bed, but tradition places it above the modern town. The banks of the Orontes must have been lined with splendid villas; I was told that the foundations of them were brought to light whenever a man dug deep enough through the silt, and that small objects of value, such as coins and bronzes, were often unearthed. Many such were brought to me for sale, but I judged them to be forgeries of an unskilful kind, and I was confirmed in my opinion by a Turkish pasha, Rifa't Agha, who has occupied his leisure in making a collection of antiquities. He possesses a fine series of Seleucid coins, the earlier nearly as good as the best Sicilian, the later nearly as bad as the worst Byzantine, and a few bronze lamps, one of which, in the shape of a curly-haired Eros head, is a beautiful example of Roman work. The Agha presented me with a

THE CORN MARKET, ANTIOCH.

small head, which I take to have been a copy of the head of Antioch with the high crown, and though it was but roughly worked, it possessed some distinction borrowed from a great original.

Forty years ago the walls and towers of the Acropolis were still almost perfect; they are now almost destroyed. The inhabitants of Antioch declare that the city is rocked to its foundations every half-century, and they are in instant expectation of another upheaval, the last having occurred in 1862; but it is prosperity not earthquake that has wrought the havoc in the fortress. The town is admirably situated in its rich valley, and connected with the port of Alexandretta by a fairly good road; it might easily become a great commercial centre, and even under Turkish rule it has grown considerably in the past fifty years, and grown at the expense of the Acropolis. To spare himself the trouble of quarrying, the Oriental will be deterred by no difficulty, and in spite of the labour of transporting the dressed stones of the fortress to the foot of the exceedingly steep hill on which it stands, all the modern houses have been built out of materials taken from it. The work of destruction continues; the stone facing is quickly disappearing from the walls, leaving only a core of a rubble and mortar which succumbs in a short time to the action of the weather. I made the whole circuit of the fortress one morning, and it took me three hours. To the west of the summit of Mount Silpius a rocky cleft seamed the hillside. It was full of rock-cut tombs, and just above my camp an ancient aqueduct spanned it. On the left hand of the cleft the line of wall dropped by precipitous rocks to the valley. Where large fragments remained it was evident that the stone facing had alternated with bands of brick, and that sometimes the stone itself had been varied by courses of smaller and larger blocks. The fortifications embraced a wide area, the upper part leading by gentle slopes, covered with brushwood and ruined foundations, to the top of the hill. In the west wall there was a narrow massive stone door, with a lintel of jointed blocks and a relieving arch above it. The south wall was broken by towers; the main citadel was at the south-east corner. From here the walls dropped down again steeply to the city and passed some distance to the east of it. They can be traced, I believe, to the Orontes. I did not follow their course, but climbed down from the citadel by a stony path into a deep gorge that cuts through the eastern end of the hill. The entrance to this gorge is guarded by a strong wall of brick and stone, which is called the Gate of Iron, and beyond it the fortifications climb the opposite side of the ravine and are continued along the hill top. I do not know how far they extend; the ground was so rough and so much overgrown with bushes that I lost heart and turned back. There was a profusion of flowers among the rocks, marigold, asphodel, cyclamen and iris.

Beyond the gorge of the Iron Gate, on the hill-side facing

ROMAN LAMP IN RIFA'T AGHA'S COLLECTION

the Orontes, there is a cave which tradition calls the cave of St. Peter. The Greek communion has erected a little chapel at its mouth. Yet further along the hill is a still more curious relic of ancient Antioch, the head of a Sphinx carved in relief upon a rock some 20 ft. high. Folded about her brow she wears a drapery that falls on either side of her face and ends where the throat touches the bare breast. Her featureless countenance is turned slightly up the valley, as though she watched for one that shall yet come out of the East. If she could speak she might tell us of great kings and gorgeous pageants, of battle and of siege, for she has seen them all from her rock on the hill side. She still remembers that the Greeks she knew marched up from Babylonia, and since even the Romans did not teach her that the living world lies westward, I could not hope to enlighten her, and so left her watching for some new thing out of the East.

There was another pilgrimage to be made from Antioch: it was to Daphne, the famous shrine that marked the spot where the nymph baffled the desire of the god, the House of the Waters it is called in Arabic. It lies to the west of the town, about an hour's ride along the foot of the hills, and in the Spring a more enchanting ride could not be found. The path led through an exquisite boscage of budding green, set thickly with flowering hawthorn and with the strange purple of the Judas tree; then it crossed a low spur and descended into a steep valley through which a stream tumbled towards the Orontes.

HEAD OF A SPHINX, ANTIOCH

No trace remains of the temples that adorned this fairest of all sanctuaries. Earthquakes and the mountain torrents have swept them down the ravine. But the beauty of the site has not diminished since the days when the citizens of the most luxurious capital in the East dallied there with the girls who served the god. The torrent does not burst noisily from the mountain side; it is born in a deep still pool that lies, swathed in a robe of maidenhair fern, in thickets "annihilating all that's made to a green thought in a green shade." From the pool issues a translucent river, unbroken of surface, narrow and profound; it runs into swirls and eddies and then into foaming cataracts and waterfalls that toss their white spray into the branches of mulberry and plane. Under the trees stand eleven water-mills; the ragged millers are the only inhabitants of Apollo's shrine. They brought us walnuts to eat by the edge of the stream, and small antique gems that had dropped from the ornaments of those who sought pleasures less innocent perhaps than ours by the banks of that same torrent.

It is impossible to travel in North Syria without acquiring a

DAPHNE

keen interest in the Seleucid kings, backed by a profound respect for their achievements in politics and in the arts; I was determined therefore to visit before I pushed north the site of Seleucia Pieria, the port of Antioch and the burial-place of Seleucus Nicator. Inland capital and seaport sprang into being at the same moment, and were both part of one great conception that turned the lower reaches of the Orontes into a rich and populous market—in those days kings could create world-famous cities with a wave of the sceptre, and the Seleucids were not backward in following the example Alexander had set them. Like Apamea, Seleucia has shrunk to the size of a hamlet, or perhaps it would be truer to say that it has split up into several hamlets covered by the name of Sweidiyyeh. (The nomenclature is confusing, as each group of farms or huts has a separate title.) The spacing of the population at the mouth of the Orontes is due to the occupation in which the inhabitants of the villages are engaged. They are raisers of silkworms, an industry that requires during about a month in the Spring such continuous attention that every man must live in the centre of his mulberry-groves, and is consequently separated by the extent of them from his neighbours. After three hours' ride through a delicious country of myrtle thickets and mulberry gardens we reached Sweidiyyeh, a military post and the most important of the scattered villages. Here for the first and only time on my journey I was stopped by an officer, the worse for 'arak, who demanded my passport. Now passport I had none; I had lost it in the Jebel Zāwiyyeh when I lost my coat, and it is a proof of how little bound by red tape the Turkish official can show himself to be that I travelled half the length of the Ottoman Empire without a paper to my name. On this occasion the zaptieh who was with me demonstrated with some heat that he would not have been permitted to accompany me if I had not been a respectable and accredited person, and after a short wrangle we were allowed to pursue our way. The reason of this meticulous exactitude was soon made clear: the villages on the coast contain large colonies of Armenians; they are surrounded by military stations, to prevent the inhabitants from escaping either inland to other parts of the empire or by sea to Cyprus, and the comings and goings of strangers are carefully watched. One of the objects that the traveller should ever set before himself is to avoid being drawn into the meshes of the Armenian question. It was the tacit conviction of the learned during the Middle Ages that no such thing as an insoluble question existed. There might be matters that presented serious difficulties, but if you could lay them before the right man—some Arab in Spain, for instance, omniscient by reason of studies into the details of which it was better not to inquire—he would give you a conclusive answer. The real trouble was only to find your man. We, however, have fallen from that faith. We have proved by experience that there are, alas! many problems insoluble to the human intelligence, and of that number the Turkish empire owns a considerable proportion.

The Armenian question is one of them, and the Macedonian question is another. In those directions madness lies.

It was with the determination not to waver in a decision that had contributed, largely, I make no doubt, to happy and prosperous journeyings, that I rode down to Chaulīk, the port of ancient Seleucia. I found my resolve the less difficult to observe because the Armenians talked little but Armenian and Turkish, at any rate the few words of Arabic that some of them possessed were not sufficient to enable them to enter into a detailed account of their wrongs. He who served me that afternoon as a guide was a man of so cheerful a disposition that he would certainly have selected by preference a different topic. His name was Ibrahīm, he was bright-eyed and intelligent, and his cheerfulness was deserving of praise, since his yearly income amounted to no more than 400 piastres, under £2 of English money. From this he proposed to save enough to bribe the Turkish officials at the port that they might wink at his escape in an open boat to Cyprus: "for," said he, "there is no industry here but the silkworms, and they give me work for two months in the year, and for the other ten I have nothing to do and no way of earning money." He also informed me that the Noṣairis who inhabited the adjoining villages were unpleasant neighbours.

"There is feud between you?" said I.

"Ey wāllah!" said he with emphatic assent, and related in illustration the long story of a recent conflict which, as far as it was comprehensible, seemed to have been due entirely to the aggressions of the Armenians.

"But you began the stealing," said I when he had concluded.

"Yes," said he. "The Noṣairis are dogs." And he added with a smile: "I was imprisoned in Aleppo for two years afterwards."

"By God! you deserved it," said I.

"Yes," said he, as cheerfully as ever.

And this, I rejoice to say, was all that Ibrahīm contributed to the store of evidence on the Armenian question.

The Bay of Seleucia is not unlike the Bay of Naples and scarcely less beautiful. A precipitous ridge of the hills, honeycombed with rock-hewn tombs and chambers, forms a background to the mulberry-gardens, and, sweeping round, encloses the bay to the north. Below it lie the walls and water-gates of the port, silted up with earth and separated from the sea by a sandy beach. The Orontes flows through sand and silt farther to the south, and the view is closed by a steep range of hills culminating at the southern point in the lovely peak of Mount Cassius, which takes the place of Vesuvius in the landscape. I pitched my camp near the northern barrier in a little cove divided from the rest of the bay by a low spur which ran out into a ruin-covered headland that commanded the whole sweep of the coast, and I pleased myself with the fancy that it was on this point that the temple and tomb of Seleucus Nicator had stood, though I do not know whether its exact stuation has ever been determined. Below it on the beach lay an isolated rock in which a columned hall had been excavated. This hall was fragrant of the sea and fresh with the salt winds that blew through it: a very temple of nymphs and tritons. Ibrahīm took me up and down the face of the precipitous cliffs by little paths and by an old chariot-road that led to the city on the summit of the plateau. He said that to walk round the enclosing wall of the upper city took six hours, but it was too hot to put his statement to the test. We climbed into an immense number of the artificial caves, in many of which there were no loculi. They may have been intended for dwellings or storehouses rather than for tombs. At this time of the year they were all occupied by the silkworm breeders, who were now at their busiest moment, the larvæ having just issued from the egg. The entrance of each cave was blocked by a screen of green boughs to keep out the sun, and the afternoon light filtered pleasantly through the budding leaves. At the southern end of the cliff there was a large necropolis, consisting of small caves set round with loculi, and of rock-hewn sarcophagi decorated, when they were decorated at all, with the garland motive that adorns the sarcophagi at Antioch. The most important group of tombs was at the northern end of the cliff. The entrance to it was by a pillared portico that led into a double cave. The larger chamber contained some thirty to forty loculi and a couple of canopied tombs, the canopies cut out of the living rock; the smaller held about half the number of

THE GARĪZ

loculi, the roof of it was supported by pillars and pilasters, and I noticed above the tombs a roughly cut design consisting of a scroll of ivy-shaped and of indented leaves.

The builders of Seleucia seem to have been much pre-occupied with the distribution of the water-supply. Ibrahîm showed me along the face of the cliff a channel some 2 ft. wide and 5 ft. high, which was cut 3 or 4 ft. behind the surface of the rock, and carried water from one end of the city to the other. We traced its course by occasional air-holes or breaches in the outer wall of rock. The most difficult problem must have been the management of the torrent that flowed down a gorge to the north of the town. A great gallery had been hewn through the spur to the south of my camp to conduct the water to the sea and prevent it from swamping the houses at the foot of the cliff. The local name for this gallery is the Garīz. It began at the mouth of a narrow ravine and was tunnelled through a mass of rock for several hundred yards, after which it continued as a deep cutting open to the air till it reached the end of the spur. At the entrance of the tunnel there was an inscription in clear-cut letters, "Divus Vespasianus" it began, but the rest was buried in the rocky ground. There were several others along the further course of the Garīz, all of them in Latin: I imagine that the work was not Seleucid, but Roman.

To one more spectacle Ibrahīm tempted me. He declared that if I would follow him through the mulberry-gardens below the cliff he would show me "a person made of stone." My curioisty was somewhat jaded by the heat and the long walk, but I toiled back wearily over stones and other obstacles to find a god, bearded and robed, sitting under the mulberry trees. He was not a very magnificent god; his attitude was stiff, his robe roughly fashioned, and the top of his head was gone, but the low sun gilded his marble shoulder and the mulberry boughs whispered his ancient titles. We sat down beside him, and Ibrahīm remarked:

"There is another buried in this field, a woman, but she is deep deep under the earth."

"Have you seen her?" said I.

"Yes," said he. "The owner of the field buried her, for he

thought she might bring him ill luck. Perhaps if you gave him money he might dig her up."

I did not rise to the suggestion; she was probably better left to the imagination.

Close to the statue I saw a long moulded cornice which was apparently *in situ*, though the wall it crowned was buried in a corn-field: so thickly does the earth cover the ruins of Seleucia. Some day there will be much to disclose here, but excavation will be exceedingly costly owing to the deep silt and to the demands of the proprietors of mulberry grove and cornfield. The site of the town is enormous, and will require years of digging if it is to be properly explored.

THE STATUE IN THE MULBERRY-GARDEN

Near my tents a sluggish stream flowed through clumps of yellow iris and formed a pool in the sand. It provided water for our animals and for the flocks of goats that Armenian shepherd boys herded morning and evening along the margin of the sea. The spot was so attractive and the weather so delightful that I spent an idle day there, the first really idle day since I had left Jerusalem, and as I could not hope to examine Seleucia exhaustively, I resolved to see no more of it than was visible from my tent door. This excellent decision gave me twenty-four hours, to which I look back with the keenest satisfaction, though there is nothing to be recorded of them except that I was not to escape so lightly from Armenian difficulties as I had hoped. I received in the morning a long visit from a woman who had walked down from Kabūseh, a village at the top of the gorge above the Garīz. She spoke English, a tongue she had acquired at the missionary schools of 'Aintāb, her home in the Kurdish mountains. Her name was Kymet. She had left 'Aintāb upon her marriage, a step she had never ceased to regret, for though her husband was a good man and an honest, he was so poor that she did not see how she was to bring up her two children. Besides, said she, the people round Kabūseh, Noṣairis and Armenians alike, were all robbers, and she begged me to help her to escape to Cyprus. She told me a curious piece of family history, which showed how painful the position of the sect must be in the heart of a Mohammadan country, if it cannot be cited as an instance of official oppression. Her father had turned Muslim when she was a child, chiefly because he wished to take a second wife. Kymet's mother had left him and supported her children as best she might, rather than submit to the indignity that he had thrust upon her, and the bitter quarrel had darkened, said Kymet, all her own youth. She sent her husband down next morning with a hen and a copy of verses written by herself in English. I paid for the hen, but the verses were beyond price. They ran thus:

Welcome, welcome, my dearest dear, we are happy by your coming!
  For your coming welcome! Your arrival welcome!
Let us sing joyfully, joyfully,
  Joyfully, my boys, joyfully!
The sun shines now with moon clearly, sweet light so bright, my dear boys,
  For your reaching welcome! By her smiling welcome!
The trees send us, my dear boys, with happiness the birds rejoice;
  Its nice smelling welcome! In their singing welcome!

I remain,
Yours truly,
GEORGE ABRAHAM.

I hasten to add, lest the poem should be considered compromising, that its author was not George Abraham, who as I found in the negotiations over the hen had no word of English; Kymet had merely used her husband's name as forming a more impressive signature than her own. Moreover the boys she alludes to were a rhetorical figure. I can offer no suggestion as to what it was that the trees sent us; the text appears to be corrupt at this point. Perhaps "us" should be taken as the accusative.

It was with real regret that I left Seleucia. Before dawn, when I went down to the sea to bathe, delicate bands of cloud were lying along the face of the hills, and as I swam out into the warm still water the first ray of the sun struck the snowy peak of Mount Cassius that closed so enchantingly the curve of the bay. We journeyed back to Antioch as we had come, and pitched tents outside the city by the high road. Two days later we set off at 6.30 for a long ride into Alexandretta. The road was abominable for the first few miles, broken by deep gulfs of mud, with here and there a scrap of pavement that afforded little better going than the mud itself. After three hours we reached the village of Kāramurt, and three quarters of an hour further we left the road and struck straight up the hills by a ruined khān that showed traces of fine Arab work. The path led up and down steep banks of earth between thickets of flowering shrubs, gorse and Judas trees, and an undergrowth of cistus. We saw to the left the picturesque castle of Baghrās, the ancient Pagræ, crowning a pointed hill: I do not believe that the complex of mountains north of Antioch has ever been explored systematically, and it may yet yield fragments of Seleucid or Roman fortifications that guarded the approach to the city. Presently we hit upon the old paved road that follows a steeper course than the present carriage road; it led us at one o'clock (we had stopped for three quarters of an hour to lunch under the shady bank of a stream) to the summit of the Pass of Bailān, where we joined the main road from Aleppo to Alexandretta. There was no trace of fortification, as far as I observed, at the Syrian Gates where Alexander turned and marched back to the Plain of Issus to meet Darius, but the pass is very narrow and must have been easy to defend against northern invaders. It is the only pass practicable for an army through the rugged Mount Amanus. The village of Bailān lay an hour further in a beautiful situation on the northern side of the mountains looking over the Bay of Alexandretta to the bold Cilician coast and the white chain of Taurus. From Bailān it is about four hours' ride to Alexandretta.

As we jogged down towards the shining sea by green and flowery slopes that were the last of Syria, Mikhāil and I fell into conversation. We reviewed, as fellow travellers will, the incidents of the way, and remembered the adventures that had befallen us by flood and field, and at the end I said:

"Oh Mikhāil, this is a pleasant world, though some have spoken ill of it, and for the most part the children of Adam are good not evil."

LOWER COURSE OF THE GARĪZ

Y

"It is as God wills," said Mikhāil.

"Without doubt," said I. "But consider, now, those whom we have met upon our journey, and think how all were glad to help us, and how well they used us. At the outset there was Najīb Fāris, who started us upon our way, and Namrūd and Ḍablān—"

"Māsha'llah!" interrupted Mikhāil. "Ḍablān was an

SARCOPHAGUS IN THE SERAYA, ANTIOCH.

excellent man. Never have I seen an Arab so little grasping, for he would scarcely eat of the food that I prepared for him."

"And Sheikh Muḥammad en Naṣṣār," I pursued, "and his nephew Fāiz, and the Ḳāimaḳām of Ḳal'at el Ḥuṣn, who lodged us for two nights and fed us all, and the Ḳāimaḳām of Drekish, who made a great reception for us, and the zaptieh Maḥmūd——" (Mikhāil gave a grunt here, for he had been at daggers drawn with Maḥmūd.) "And Sheikh Yūnis," I went on hastily, "and Mūsa the Kurd, who was the best of all."

"He was an honest man," observed Mikhāil, "and served your Excellency well."

"And even Reshīd Agha," I continued, "who was a rogue, treated us with hospitality."

"Listen, oh lady," said Mikhāil, "and I will make it clear to you. Men are short of vision, and they see but that for which they look. Some look for evil and they find evil; some look for good and it is good that they find, and moreover some are fortunate and these find always what they want. Praise be to God! to that number you belong. And, please God! you shall journey in peace and return in safety to your own land, and there you shall meet his Excellency your father, and your mother and all your brothers and sisters in health and in happiness, and all your relations and friends," added Mikhāil comprehensively, "and again many times shall you travel in Syria with peace and safety and prosperity, please God!"

"Please God!" said I.

INDEX

PRINTED IN GREAT BRITAIN BY THE WHITEFRIARS PRESS, LTD., LONDON AND TONBRIDGE.

CPSIA information can be obtained
at www.ICGtesting.com
Printed in the USA
LVHW031931271122
734109LV00012B/922

9 781142 173876